LEGENDARY LOCALS

OF

WHEELING

WEST VIRGINIA

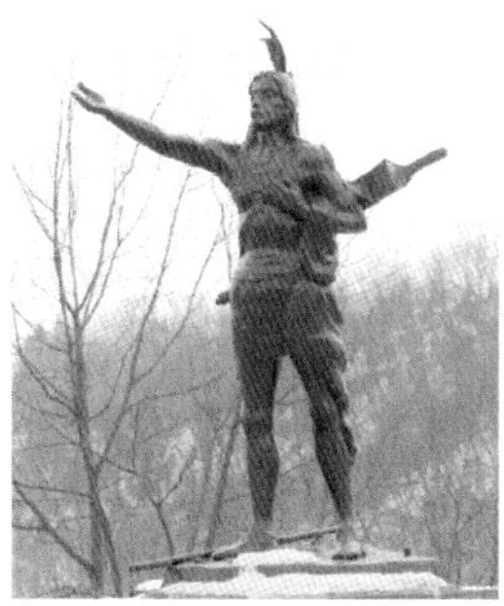

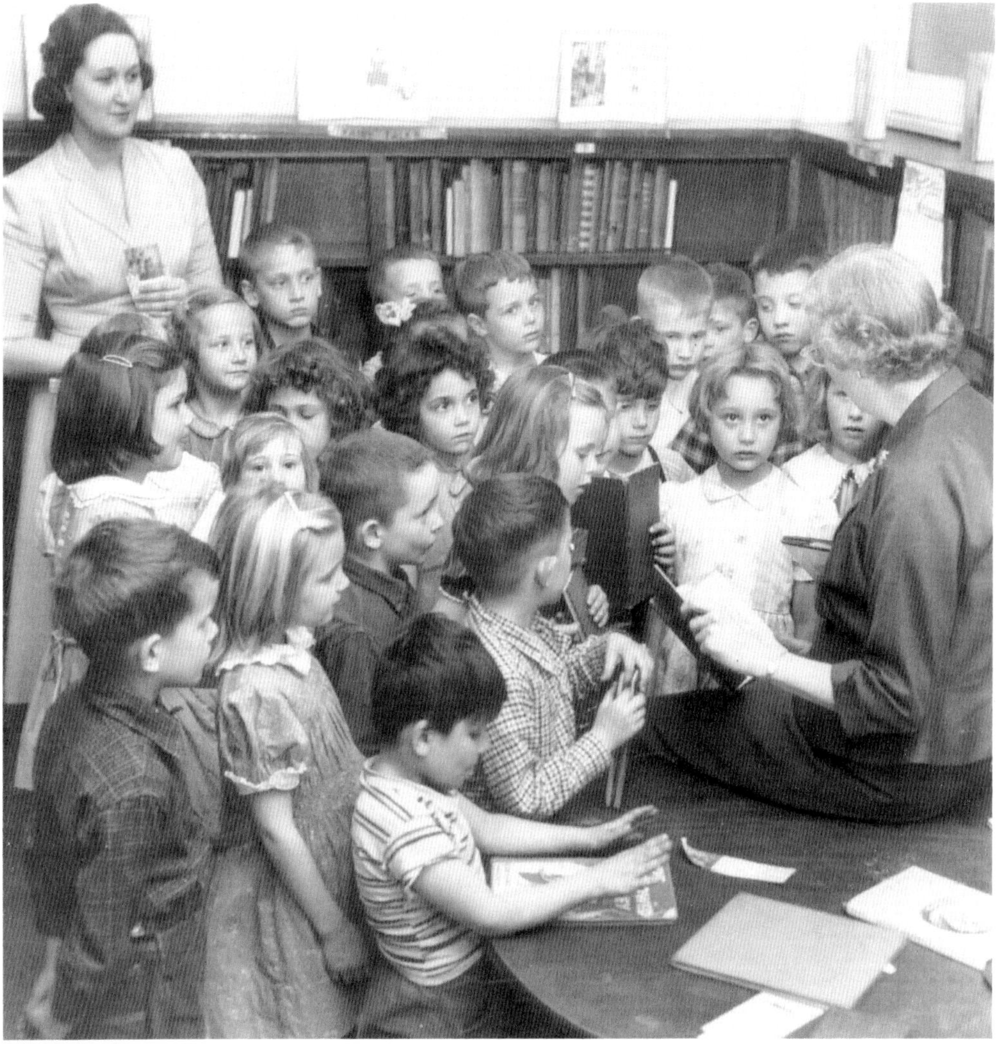

Virginia Ebeling
Virginia Ebeling (right) is pictured with a visiting class at the Ohio County Public Library in 1955. (Ohio County Public Library.)

Page 1: The Mingo
An iconic image to all who call Wheeling home, this statue's inscription reads "THE MINGO. Original Inhabitant of this Valley Extends GREETINGS and PEACE to all Wayfarers. Presented to the City of Wheeling by the Kiwanis Club and George W. Lutz. 1928." (Photograph by Seán Duffy.)

LEGENDARY LOCALS

OF

WHEELING

WEST VIRGINIA

SEÁN DUFFY AND BRENT CARNEY

LEGENDARY LOCALS

ISBN 978-1-4671-0062-5

Legendary Locals is an imprint of Arcadia Publishing
Charleston, South Carolina

Printed in the United States of America

Library of Congress Control Number: 2012950058

For all general information, please contact Arcadia Publishing:
Telephone 843-853-2070
Fax 843-853-0044
E-mail sales@arcadiapublishing.com
For customer service and orders:
Toll-Free 1-888-313-2665

Visit us on the Internet at www.arcadiapublishing.com

Dedication
For Miss Virginia Ebeling and all those who have made our public library what it is today, and for the good people of Wheeling, legendary locals all.

On the Cover: From left to right:
(TOP ROW): Augustus Pollack, stogie maker (Courtesy Ohio County Public Library, page 70); Sara Lucy Bagby Johnson, slave fugitive (Courtesy Western Reserve Historical Society, page 18); J. McHenry Jones, educator and author (Courtesy West Virginia State University Archives & Special Collections, page 25); Eleanor Steber, opera star (Courtesy Ohio County Public Library, page 32); Chuck Howley, NFL star (Courtesy Jack Schuetz and Chuck Howley, page 54).
(MIDDLE ROW): Clyde Thomas, city councilman (Courtesy Ann Thomas, page 121); Rose Gacioch, baseball player (Courtesy Center for History at the Northern Indiana Historical Society, page 47); Jesse Reno, Civil War general (Courtesy Library of Congress, page 19); Mollie O'Brien, singer-songwriter (Courtesy Mollie O'Brien, page 39); James "Doc" White, pharmacist (Courtesy Wheeling Hall of Fame, page 120).
(BOTTOM ROW): Doc Williams, country music legend (Courtesy of Doc Williams Enterprises, page 37); Chickie Williams, country music legend (Courtesy of Doc Williams Enterprises, page 37); Paul McGinnis, World War II veteran (Courtesy Paul McGinnis, page 110); Betty Zane, frontier legend (Courtesy Ohio County Public Library, page 14); Walter Reuther, labor leader (Courtesy Walter P. Reuther Library at Wayne State University, page 119).

CONTENTS

ACKNOWLEDGMENTS

This book was a true community project. While Brent and I wrote some of the captions, we mostly served as editors, photograph researchers, and organizers. The majority of the writing was done by family members, colleagues, and various members of Wheeling's heritage community. We would like to thank our contributors (initials serve to identify the captions to which they contributed): Michael Beatty (MB), Thomas Beatty (TB), John Bowman (JB), Margaret Brennan (MBr), Pat Cassidy (PC), Dominick Cerrone (DC), George Fetherling (GF), Jeanne Finstein (JF), Anne Foreman (AF), Hydie Friend (HF), Jon-Erik Gilot (JG), Susan Haddad (SH), Marc Harshman (MH), the Hazlett family (HZ), Travis Henline (TH), William Hintzen (WH), Bill Hogan (BH), Susan Hogan (SH), Mary Ann Howley (MAH), Curtis Johnson (CJ), Chuck Julian (CJu), Craig Karges (CK), Rebekah Karelis (RK), Joe Laker (JL), Keith Maillard (KM), Steve Novotney (SN), Jim O'Brien (JO), Mollie O'Brien (MO), Tim O'Brien (TO), Sean O'Leary (SO), Ed Phillips (EP), Paul Rinkes (PR), Art Rooney Jr. (AR), Joe Roxby (JR), Ted Rybeck (TR), Charlie Schlegel (CS), Scott Shalaway (SS), Phyllis Sigal (PS), Barbara Smik (BS), and Ryan Stanton (RS). Special thanks go to Kate Quinn (KQ) for taking on extra duty as a writer. Captions written by Brent and I are indicated by BC and SD.

We would also like to thank the following organizations and individuals for images or research assistance: Archives of the Diocese of Wheeling-Charleston, Ancella Radford Bickley, Jeanne Carter, Center for History at the Northern Indiana Historical Society (Kristen Madden), Linda Comins, Michelle A. Day (Woodland Cemetery Foundation of Cleveland, Ohio), Catherine Fett (Mail America), Noel Foreman, Good Shepherd Nursing Home, Barbara Gregorich, Library of Congress, John Kniesner, Martins Ferry Public Library (Yvonne Myers), Museums of Oglebay Institute (Holly McCluskey and Christin Byrum), Ohio County Public Library (OCPL), Sasha Reuther, San Diego Air & Space Museum, Tamara Saviano (John Corbett Music), Walter P. Reuther Library at Wayne State University, Western Reserve Historical Society (Vicki Catozza), West Virginia Independence Hall, West Virginia and Regional History Collection at West Virginia University (John Cuthbert), West Virginia State University Archives & Special Collections (Ellen H. Ressmeyer), and Wheeling Park High School.

Special thanks go to the Wheeling Hall of Fame (WHOF) Board, which graciously allowed us to include modified versions of the biographies and images of hall of fame members.

Regarding credits, the author of each caption is noted first, followed by the source of the photograph. If only one name is listed, that person or organization provided both.

Finally, it is important to note that all author proceeds generated by the sale of this book will be donated directly to the Ohio County Public Library.

INTRODUCTION

When some people think of Wheeling, they picture the historic monuments, such as West Virginia Independence Hall and the Wheeling Suspension Bridge. Others may recall pivotal events, such as the Battle for Fort Henry or Sen. Joseph McCarthy's infamous speech about "secret communists." However, it is Wheeling's citizens who have shaped the monuments, fought the wars, and sung the arias. Inside each of these individuals is where the truly important stories begin.

The history of Wheeling is both diverse and resonant. Beginning with the Zane brothers pioneering a trail through Wheeling, to their sister, the legendary Betty Zane, saving Fort Henry from an Indian attack by retrieving much-needed gunpowder, our history has always proved engaging. Betty's heart-pounding run inspired her great-grandnephew Zane Grey to write a novel about her, *Betty Zane*. Other Colonial characters include the controversial Indian hunter Lewis Wetzel, whose battles with the "Turkey Gobbler" mesmerized Pres. Theodore Roosevelt as a youth. Maj. Samuel McColloch's daring ride off the steep cliff of Wheeling Hill so thoroughly convinced the local Indians of his bravery that they continued to hunt him until they caught him and ate his heart in order to acquire his strength.

Wheeling's businessmen, such as the rival brewers Henry Schmulbach and Anton Reymann, competed even after death with the height of their gravestones. Tobacco titans the Bloch brothers and Mifflin Marsh used innovative advertising techniques to entice customers. More than 20,000 Mail Pouch barns still stand along America's roads and have become a cherished piece of folk Americana. Marsh Wheeling Stogies have appeared in several movies, including *Jaws*, *Missing*, *The Green Mile*, and *Fool's Parade*. Walter Reuther was named by *Time* magazine as one of the most important labor leaders of the 20th century, while James Alvan Macauley also graced the cover of *Time* as head of the Packard car company.

Wheeling can also boast an interesting assortment of artists and athletes. Opera star Eleanor Steber stunned audiences with her arias at the Metropolitan Opera, while jazz legend Leon "Chu" Berry's jam sessions with Cab Calloway inspired Charlie "Bird" Parker to name his son Chu. Writers Rebecca Harding Davis, Keith Maillard, and George Fetherling have gained international fans, and Marc Harshman is the current West Virginia poet laureate. Actor John Corbett is so proud of his hometown that he worked the city into several episodes of the television show *Northern Exposure*. Chuck Howley was the MVP of Super Bowl V, and Bob Nutting is the current chairman of the board of the Pittsburgh Pirates. Jack Glasscock and Jesse Burkett played in the big leagues during the 19th century, while Bill Mazeroski hit the winning home run in Game 7 of the 1960 World Series.

Wheeling's wild assortment of colorful characters includes "father of oral surgery" Simon Hullihen and Civil War hero Gen. Jesse Reno. Faith Daniels was coanchor of the *CBS Morning News*, and silent movie star Lina Basquette went on a date with Adolf Hitler. West Virginia legislator Jesse A. Bloch cast the decisive vote for the state's ratification of the 19th Amendment guaranteeing suffrage for women. Walter L. Fisher rose to the position of US secretary of the interior, while all 400-plus pounds of gangster "Big" Bill Lias were later mentioned in the US Senate's Kefauver Hearings on crime.

These eclectic citizens and their singular stories have combined to make Wheeling the unique city that it is today. This book is a collaboration with numerous community members to pay homage to our beloved city of Wheeling and, especially, the remarkable people it has produced. This collection is meant to be a representative, but certainly not exhaustive, sample of some of Wheeling's and the Upper Ohio Valley's best in many fields. There were many hundreds if not thousands of good people who could have been selected and who also deserve to be remembered as legendary locals. But in the interest of space and time, difficult choices had to be made. Nevertheless, we are honored to have this opportunity to illuminate the lives of some of the well-known and unsung heroes of Wheeling.

CHAPTER ONE

Legends of History

A rugged frontier outpost that grew into a transportation hub, Wheeling is a small American city with a very rich history, featuring an array of colorful characters. The violent struggles between the region's American Indian inhabitants (primarily Shawnee, Wyandot, Delaware, and Mingo, including the Mingo leader Logan) and European settlers characterized the early days, with Wheeling's Fort Henry as a focal point. The events garnered international attention, even inspiring a series of comic books created in 1962 by the Italian Hugo Pratt, titled, "Fort Wheeling." A dedicated group of living historians diligently continues to keep the memory of those days alive with Fort Henry Days, an annual community celebration featuring reenactments of the sieges of Fort Henry and events like the "Foreman Massacre," centered around a grand encampment held in early September, typically at Site 1 at Oglebay Park. Frontier researchers and writers like Joe Roxby and Alan Fitzpatrick and artists like Anne Hazlett Foreman and Cecy Rose have done their part to preserve the fascinating personalities of this era. Further confirming the city's important role during the period, the Daughters of the American Revolution selected Wheeling for a Madonna of the Trail monument (featuring a pioneer woman and her children), placed along National Road near Wheeling Park in 1928.

Wheeling also played a role in the period between the American Revolution and the Civil War. Wheeling native John Joliffe Yarnall served and was wounded aboard Commodore Oliver Hazard Perry's flagship, the *Lawrence*, during the Battle of Lake Erie in the War of 1812. Due to Yarnall's heroism, two US battleships were named in his honor.

Just after the American Civil War began and Virginia seceded from the Union in April 1861, unhappy western Virginians met in Wheeling to consider their own kind of secession. Wheeling men like Chester Hubbard, James Paxton, John McLure, Alfred Caldwell, and Johann Ludwig Stifel participated in the conventions. And on June 20, 1863, the new state of West Virginia—the only state born of the Civil War—was officially welcomed into the Union. Wheeling had served as the intellectual birthplace of a state.

Community groups like the Ohio Valley Civil War Roundtable and the Wheeling Civil War 150 Committee are working to commemorate Wheeling's vital role in the war and in statehood during the 2013 sesquicentennial observance.

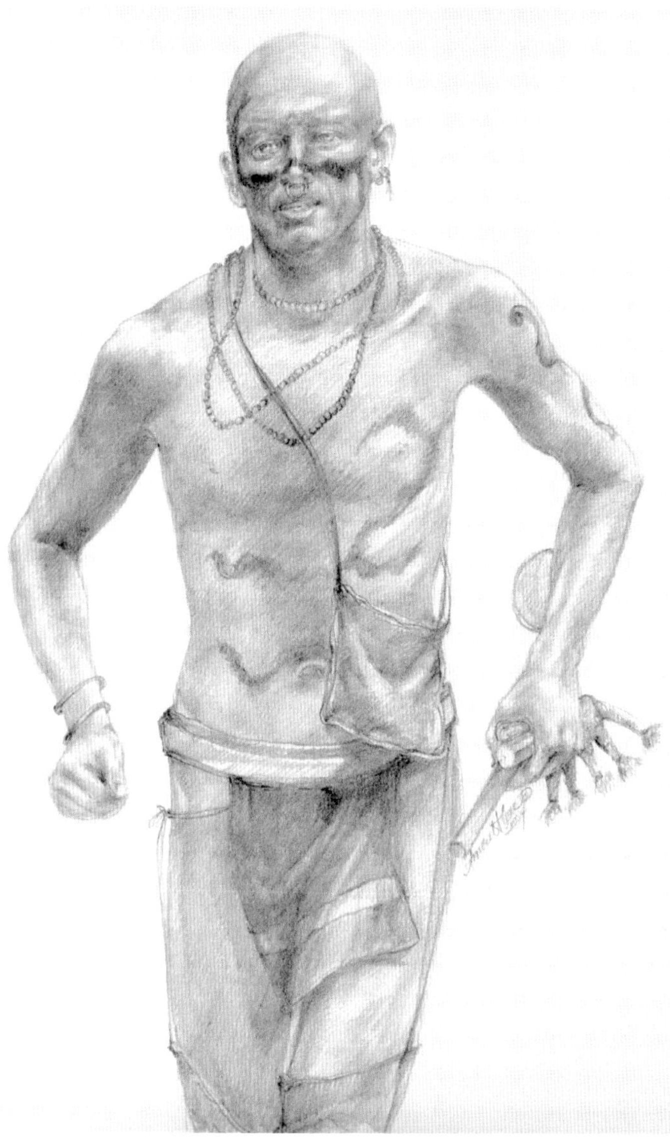

"Skull Place"

The Upper Ohio Valley was home to American Indian peoples for more than 16,000 years. Archaeological evidence suggests that there were multiple occupation sites in the Wheeling area over several millennia. When European explorers and settlers made their way into the region in the 18th century, they encountered the Shawnee, Wyandot, Delaware (Lenape), and Mingo (pictured) peoples. Indeed, "Wheeling" is derived from *wee-lunk* in the Lenape language, meaning "head place" or "skull place," a reference to a human skull that was placed on a pole near the mouth of Wheeling Creek as a deterrent to encroachment. These tribes considered the area their homeland, and when confronted with the expansion efforts of westward-pushing colonists, they vigorously defended their territory, seeking to make the Ohio River the final barrier between Indian and European. As animosities intensified during the period of the American Revolution, the tribes of the region joined forces with the British and attacked the Wheeling settlements, laying siege to Fort Henry on two occasions. After 1794, however, regional American Indians relocated farther west, and the days of border warfare concluded. (TH; image courtesy Anne Foreman.)

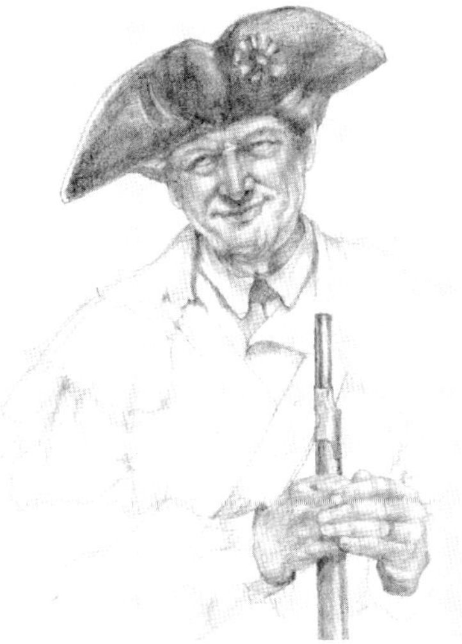

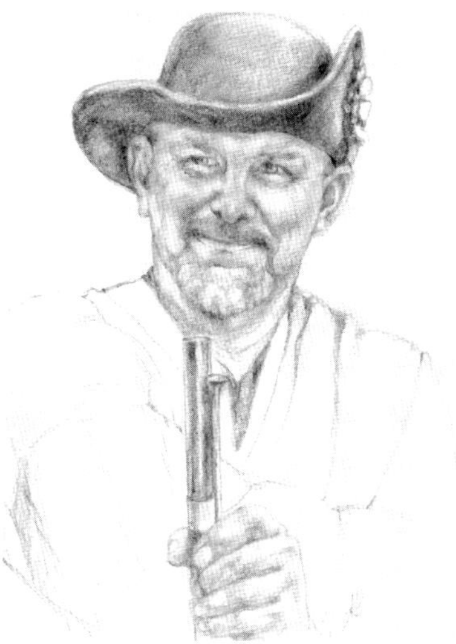

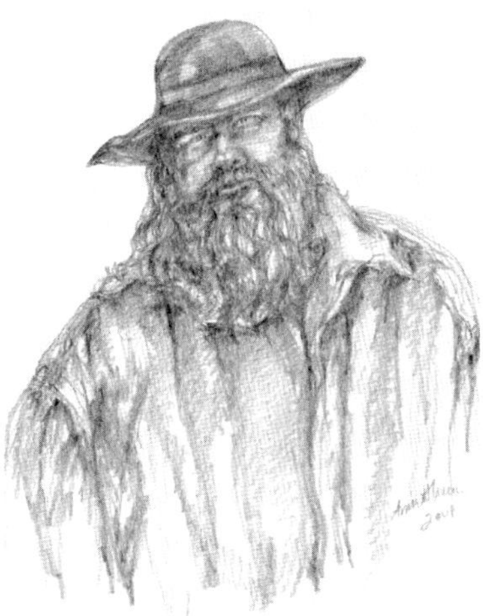

Founding Brothers

The westward movement of the American frontier to the Ohio River coincided with Wheeling's birth as a city. Wheeling was founded in 1769 with the arrival of the Zane brothers, Ebenezer (top), Jonathan (middle), and Silas (bottom). Andrew followed a couple of years later. How the Zane brothers discovered the area is not entirely clear. The Zanes had been captured and later adopted by the Wyandots during the French and Indian War. They may have discovered the area on a hunting trip with their captors, or they may have migrated north from their homestead around Moorefield, West Virginia, along the McColloch Trace and then explored west along the old Nemacolin Trail

Settlement on the frontier at this time usually followed a particular pattern. Several men of an extended family group would go west and build cabins, clear a couple of acres, and plant a corn crop for each family. In the summer, they would return home and bring the rest of the family in the fall. The first winter was hard, but at least the families would have minimal shelter and a food supply.

The Zanes' peaceful existence was shattered in 1774. Later, Ebenezer, Jonathan, and Andrew were present at the first siege of Fort Henry on September 1, 1777. Andrew would nearly duplicate McColloch's leap from Wheeling Hill a few hours earlier without the benefit of a horse. All four brothers were present at the second siege of Fort Henry, September 11–13, 1782. At the start of that storied fight, Jonathan Zane gave a fire-eating speech that was credited for steeling the resolve of the defenders in the face of overwhelming odds. Jonathan was considered an Indian fighter and scout of the same caliber as Sam Brady or Lewis Wetzel.

At the close of the Indian Wars, Ebenezer and Jonathan Zane blazed a trail through Ohio from Wheeling to Maysville, Kentucky. Ebenezer handled the business and political affairs, and Jonathan oversaw the actual road construction. This was the first road through Ohio, and it opened the state for settlement. The brothers founded a second city, Zanesville, Ohio, that bears their name. Ebenezer and Jonathan Zane would achieve one other distinction their brothers Andrew, Silas, and several other notable frontiersmen would not: they died peacefully at home. (JR; images courtesy Anne Foreman.)

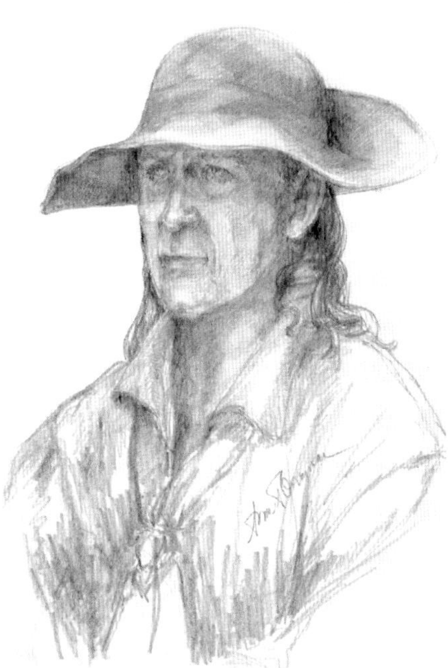

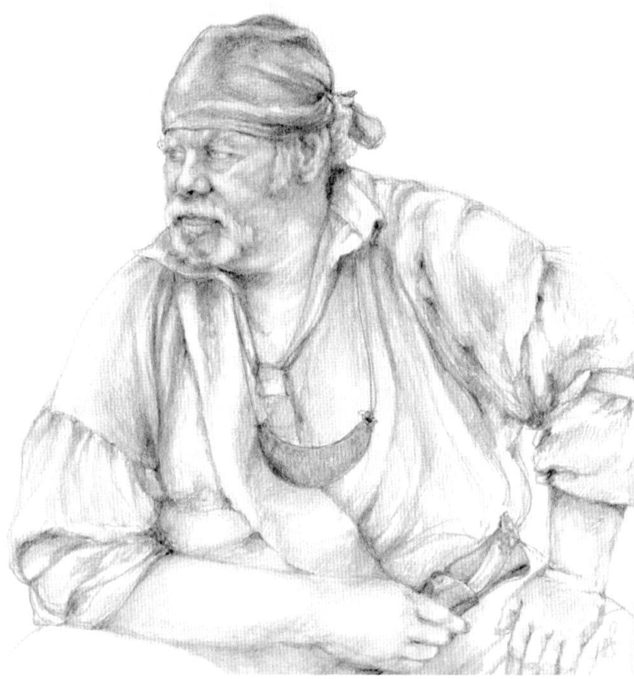

A Tale of Three Sams

Wheeling's early history during the Indian Wars (1774–1794) produced a number of legendary characters. Sam McColloch, Sam Mason, and Sam Brady were three of the most colorful.

Sam McColloch (1752–1782) was the commander of Van Meter's Fort, a member of the Virginia Legislature, and a major in the local militia. On the morning of September 1, 1777, the Indians attacked Fort Henry. McColloch (left) and two others rode to relieve the fort. He spurred his mount to the top of Wheeling Hill with his would-be captors at his heels. There, he was trapped by another raiding party coming from the other direction. Preferring a quick death or freedom to captivity or torture, Sam took his only avenue of escape and plunged his horse down a nearly vertical hillside, 300 feet to the creek below. Miraculously, the horse and rider made it to the bottom unharmed. A monument at the crest of Wheeling Hill marks "McColloch's Leap." Not to be denied, Indians finally settled accounts with McColloch about six weeks before the second major battle of Fort Henry in 1782.

If McColloch was the embodiment of civic virtue, Sam Mason (1750–1803) was one of the darker figures of the era. Prior to 1782, he was a militia captain, magistrate, and, like McColloch, a hero of the first battle of Fort Henry. Mason (right) kept a tavern in the area of the present-day Generations Club. Later, he opened another tavern at the infamous Cave-in Rock along the Ohio River. "Wilson's Liquor Vault and House of Entertainment" was a combination frontier fence, bar, and bordello. Lusty and thirsty boatmen flocked to his establishment, but only once. The crews were murdered and the cargoes continued south, manned by Mason's confederates. Fed up with his murder, mayhem, and brown-water piracy, local regulators began to make the lower Ohio Valley dangerous for Mason to operate. So he shifted his operations farther south to the Mississippi River. During that period, Mason's gang included two of the most dangerous thrill-killers ever to haunt American soil, Micajah and Wiley Harpe. The Harpe brothers proved so bloodthirsty that they were driven from Mason's murderous band. By 1803, a dead-or-alive reward was placed upon Mason, and a mysterious stranger soon appeared with Mason's head in a ball of clay. While waiting for the reward money, the stranger was discovered to be Wiley Harpe, who was promptly hanged for his own evil deeds. Wild West historian Paul Wellman called Mason "the first genius of American Outlawry." (JR; images courtesy Anne Foreman.)

A Tale of Three Sams

Sam Brady (1756–1795), the least recognized of the trio, was one of the greatest Indian fighters of his day. He was blessed with the woodsman's skills of a Lewis Wetzel and the personality of a born leader. From the early 1780s, he led a band of scouts who watched the trails and acted as an early warning system for Indian attacks. Man for man, the group was probably much superior to the far more famous Rogers Rangers that preceded them. Brady participated in some notable rescues and effected one of the two most dramatic escapes recorded during eastern Indian conflicts.

In October 1781, Brady was captured by Indians. He was taken to a village near Fremont, Ohio, and forced to run the gauntlet. As the Indians were preparing to burn him at the stake, he grabbed an infant and tossed him into the flames. During the brief pandemonium that ensued, Brady made a mad dash for freedom, bare yards ahead of an enraged mob. In the course of his escape, he made his famous leap across the Cuyahoga River and hid submerged in the body of water that now bears his name to evade capture. Naked, wounded, unarmed, and followed by the best trackers of the era, Brady was able to cross 150 miles of wilderness and get home safely. When Gen. Anthony Wayne conducted the campaign that finally ended the eastern Indian wars, he selected Sam Brady to be his chief of scouts. Like Gen. George Patton, Brady lived just long enough to end the war in which he had been so much a central figure. He died on New Year's Day 1795 at West Liberty, West Virginia, as a result of a hunting accident. (JR; image courtesy Anne Foreman.)

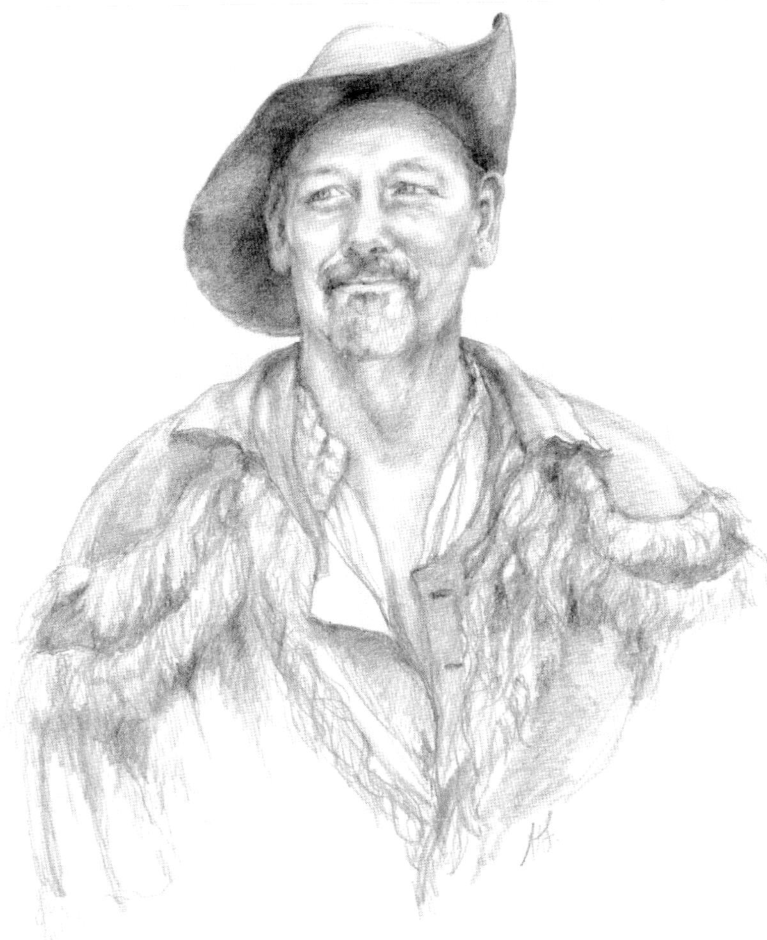

The Heroine of Fort Henry

Elizabeth "Betty" Zane was the youngest sister of the Zane brothers. While her older brothers were founding the city, Betty stayed with relatives in Philadelphia. She arrived on the frontier in 1782, when she was about 16 years old. The Indian Wars of the Upper Ohio Valley ran from 1774 to 1794. Her arrival in 1782 was not quite at the midpoint of the conflict, but on the frontier, that year was one of the deadliest.

The winter of 1781–1782 had been relatively mild. As a result, the frontier did not experience the seasonal lull from Indian raids it normally enjoyed between November and April. The Moravian Massacre, Crawford's Defeat, and several other smaller raids that spring and summer fueled enough vendettas to keep the frontier aflame in a bloody, no-quarter conflict

Locally, the war reached its bloody zenith on the afternoon of September 11, 1782. A scout spotted a force of approximately 260 Indians and 40 British rangers a couple of hours west of Fort Henry. By early that evening, they had laid a loose siege line around the fort and demanded the fort's surrender. Their demand was refused, and the battled started in earnest. The emotional high point of the battle occurred about noon of the second day, when the defenders found they were out of gunpowder. It was the firepower of the fort that kept the enemy at bay, and without it, the fort would fall. More of it was stored at Ebenezer's blockhouse a short distance away, but who would go and get it? Betty Zane stepped forward, noting that, should she fall, she would be less missed than a man. Dashing out of the south sally port, she made it to the blockhouse without a shot fired at her. As she stepped out to return, all hell broke loose as nearly every Indian and British ranger fired at her. Miraculously, she made it back unharmed with her precious load of gunpowder, and the fort was saved.

That courageous act made her a legend in her own lifetime. With the publication of the book *Betty Zane* by Zane Grey in 1903, she would rank just under Daniel Boone and Davy Crockett in the pantheon of American frontier history for many years. Betty Zane's courageous act was the defining event of Wheeling's early days. (JR; top image, courtesy OCPL; bottom image, courtesy Anne Foreman.)

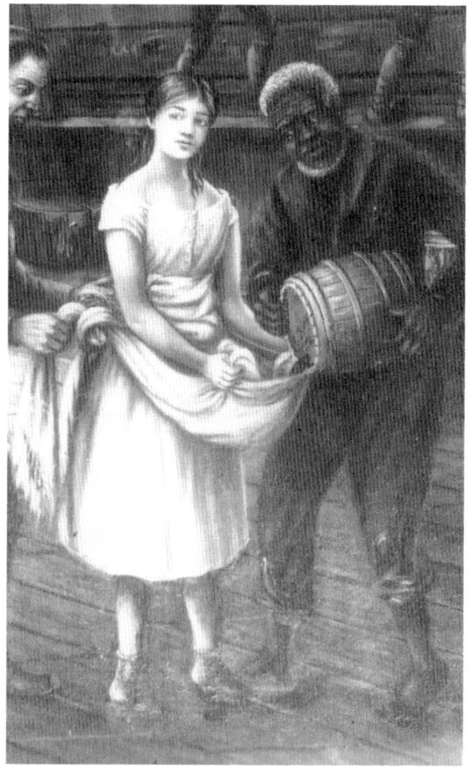

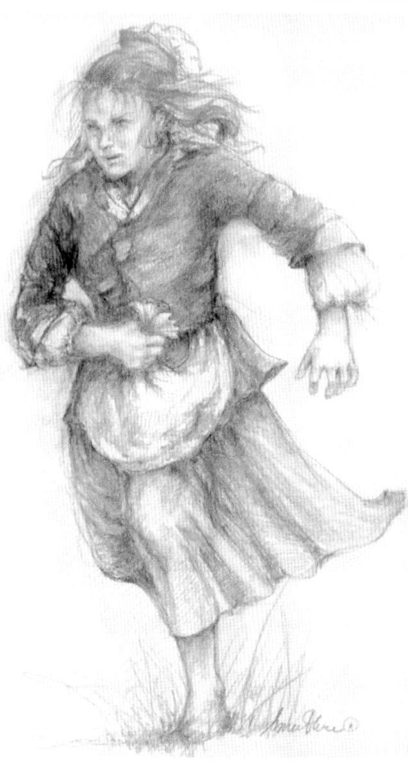

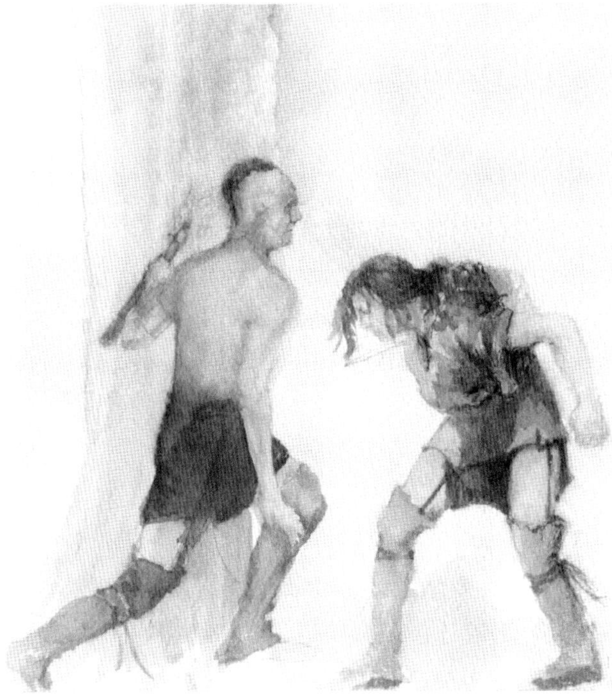

"The Death Wind"
Lewis Wetzel (1763–1808) is considered the greatest of all frontiersmen, scouts, and Indian fighters of the Border Wars of the Upper Ohio Valley. He was raised on a farm on Wheeling Creek, 14 miles from its confluence with the Ohio River.

He first gained fame at age 13, when he and younger brother Jacob were abducted from their home and taken into the Ohio country. The boys managed to escape, elude their Indian captors, and reach the settlement at Wheeling.

Along with his athletic abilities and woodcraft, Wetzel taught himself to load a rifle while running at full speed—no easy task with a flintlock. He once wagered that he could run faster than any man in a military company while at the same time reloading and firing his rifle, while his competitor ran at his top speed. Wetzel won the bet.

This skill was never more necessary than in June 1782, when he and two companions were ambushed by a large party of Indians. One of the men was killed, while Wetzel and the other escaped. Reloading as he ran, Wetzel killed three of the pursuers, and the others gave up the chase.

When Col. Benjamin Logan destroyed the Shawnee villages at Wapatomica, Ohio, in 1786, it was Lewis Wetzel who returned to Fort Harmar in Marietta to give the news of the expedition, reporting directly to General Harmar. Wetzel gained notoriety in 1789 when he shot and wounded an Indian who was employed as a runner for Harmar. Much misinformation has been written about this incident. In fact, the Indian recovered and returned to his home village, while Wetzel was released by the federal judge at Cincinnati.

After the conclusion of the Indian Wars, Wetzel earned a living as a hunter and trapper. He was also in great demand as a scout and guard on the riverboats that carried produce down the Mississippi River to New Orleans. Eventually, he settled in Mississippi, where he contracted yellow fever in the summer of 1808. In 1941, his remains were recovered and returned to Marshall County, West Virginia, where he was reinterred in 1942.

Wetzel was never a pioneer, like Daniel Boone, but was a scout and frontiersman. Time and time again, he saved frontier settlements from disaster by giving timely warning of a projected Indian assault. In his time, there was no man more highly respected by his peers. (WH; image courtesy Anne Foreman.)

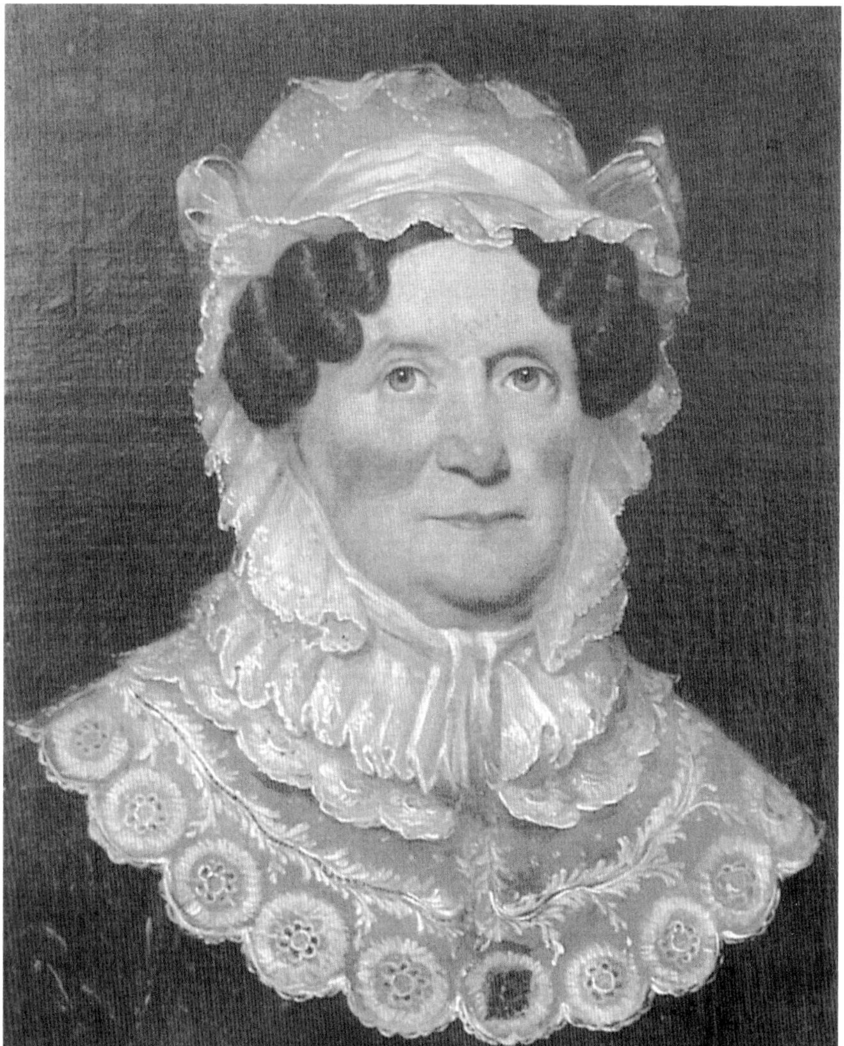

Lydia Boggs Shepherd Cruger

Lydia Boggs Shepherd Cruger (1766–1867) lived through both the American Revolution and the Civil War. She was the daughter of a militia captain. Her family lived near Wheeling during the Indian Wars, and Lydia was present at the sieges of Fort Henry. She met Moses Shepherd at the 1782 siege, and they were married shortly thereafter. As wealthy plantation owners, the couple ascended to the apex of early Wheeling society, counting many influential individuals, such as US senator Henry Clay, among their friends. At their mansion, Shepherd Hall, they hosted the elite of the age, including the Marquis de Lafayette and US presidents Andrew Jackson and James K. Polk. Senator Clay used his influence, at the request of the Shepherds, to ensure that the new National Road was constructed to pass directly by the Shepherd plantation. The construction included what is now the oldest bridge in West Virginia, a three-span elliptical stone arch crossing Wheeling Creek, built in 1817. To show their gratitude, the Shepherds commissioned a monument to Clay, to be erected on their property, which subsequently became known as Monument Place and is now home to the Osiris Shrine Temple. Moses Shepherd died in 1832. Lydia later married Daniel Cruger. She died a recluse in 1867. (SD; image courtesy Museums of Oglebay Institute.)

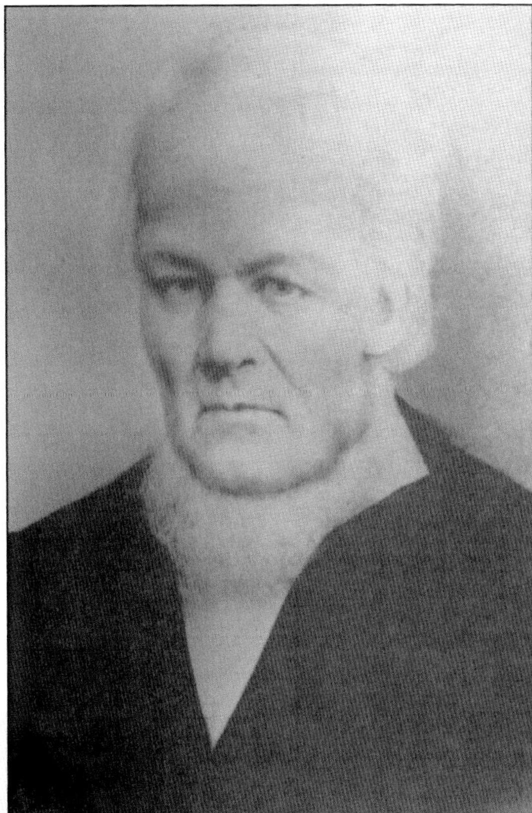

Carpenter of the Corps

Patrick Gass (1771–1870) was a carpenter with the Lewis and Clark expedition's Corps of Discovery. After learning his trade as an apprentice in Pennsylvania, Gass joined the Army. He was recruited by Meriwether Lewis in 1803 for the 1804–1806 expedition. When the corps disbanded, Gass retired to Wellsburg, Virginia, and in 1807, published his journal of the expedition. In 1812, Gass reenlisted, serving in the War of 1812. He returned to Wellsburg in 1815. (JB.)

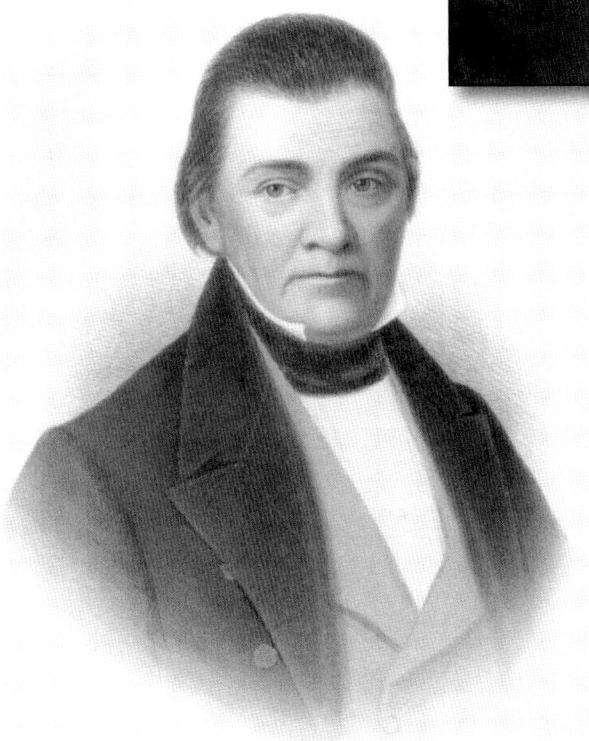

Archibald Woods

Archibald Woods (1764–1846) enlisted in the Virginia militia at age 16 and served in the Revolutionary War. In 1783, he journeyed to the Ohio Valley, where he settled in what is now the Woodsdale section of Wheeling, building a home in the midst of orchards. The road to that home still bears the name Homestead Lane, and another is named Orchard Road. Woods served in the Virginia House of Delegates and voted on the US Constitution in 1788. (JF; image courtesy OCPL.)

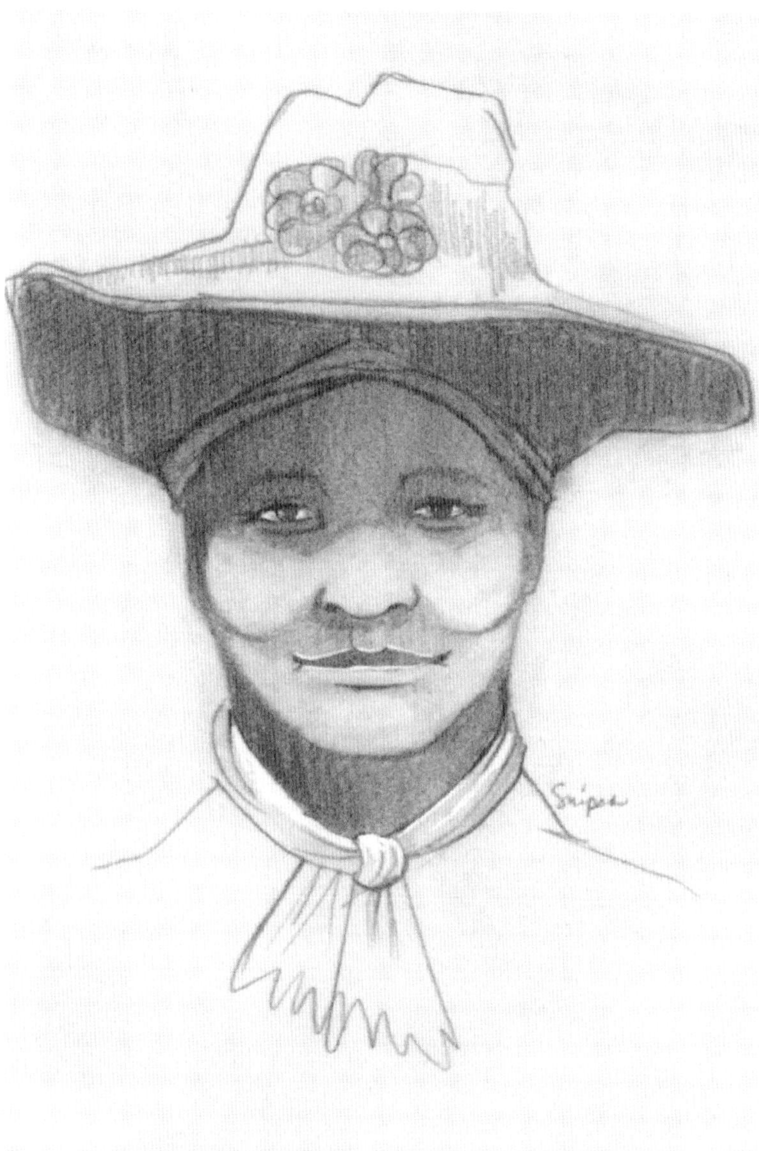

The Last Fugitive

Sara Lucy Bagby Johnson (1843–1906) was the last slave in the United States prosecuted under the Fugitive Slave Act, the federal law declaring that runaway slaves be returned to their owners. Lucy was born in Virginia in the early 1840s, and in 1852, she was purchased from a slave trader in Richmond by John Goshorn of Wheeling for $600.

In 1857, Goshorn gave her as a gift to his son William S. Goshorn. In October 1860, she escaped from Wheeling and made her way to Cleveland. Her owner pursued her there, had her arrested, declared his property, and returned to Wheeling by train in January 1861. After the Emancipation Proclamation of 1863, Lucy walked to Pittsburgh, where she married George Johnson. They relocated to Cleveland, where Lucy worked as a cook and house servant. She died on July 14, 1906, of septicemia and is buried in a recently marked grave in Cleveland's Woodland Cemetery. (MBr; image courtesy Western Reserve Historical Society.)

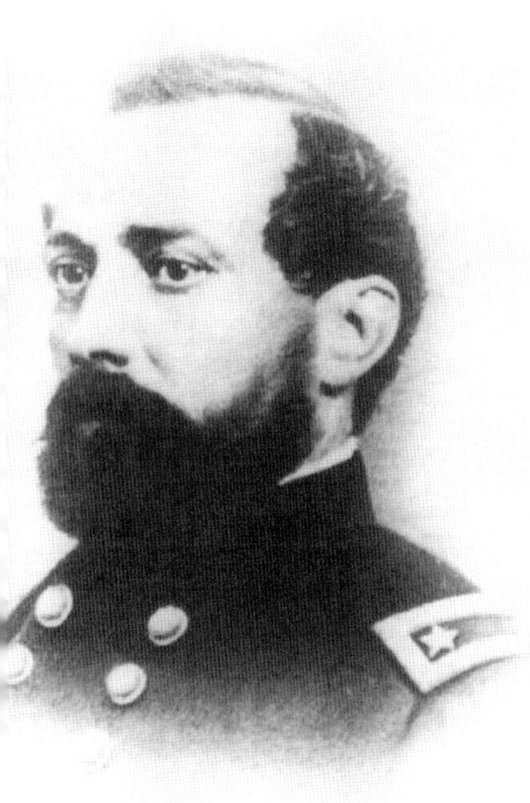

Gen. Jesse Reno

Born in Wheeling, Jesse Reno became close friends with Thomas "Stonewall" Jackson at West Point. He fought in the Mexican-American War, then taught math at West Point, where he was known as a "soldier's soldier." He was second in command to Gen. Ambrose Burnside at the Battle of South Mountain, where he rallied the men to defend the right gap from invading Confederates. He was killed by a sharpshooter. Reno, Nevada, was named in his honor. (KQ; photograph courtesy Library of Congress.)

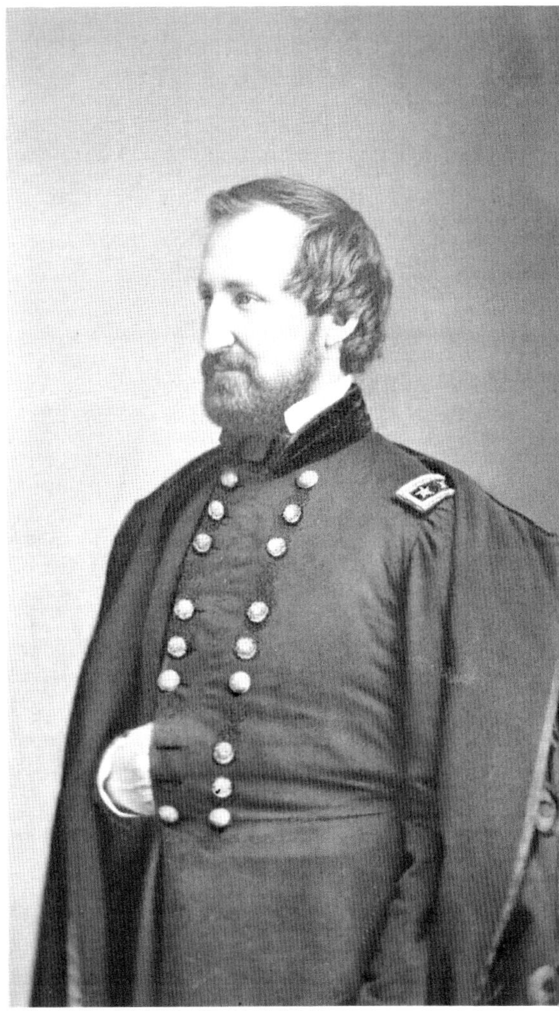

William S. Rosecrans

General Rosecrans (1819–1898) won the Civil War battles of Rich Mountain and Corrick's Ford. Given command of Western Virginia, Rosecrans was stationed in Wheeling at the Charles Wells Russell house. He designed one of the most successful battlefield ambulances used in the war. Later, while in command of Mississippi, Rosecrans won the Battle of Iuka. In Tennessee, he captured Chattanooga but was defeated at Chickamagua. Sent to Missouri, Rosecrans defeated Gen. Sterling Price. After the war, he was ambassador to Mexico. (EP; photograph courtesy Library of Congress.)

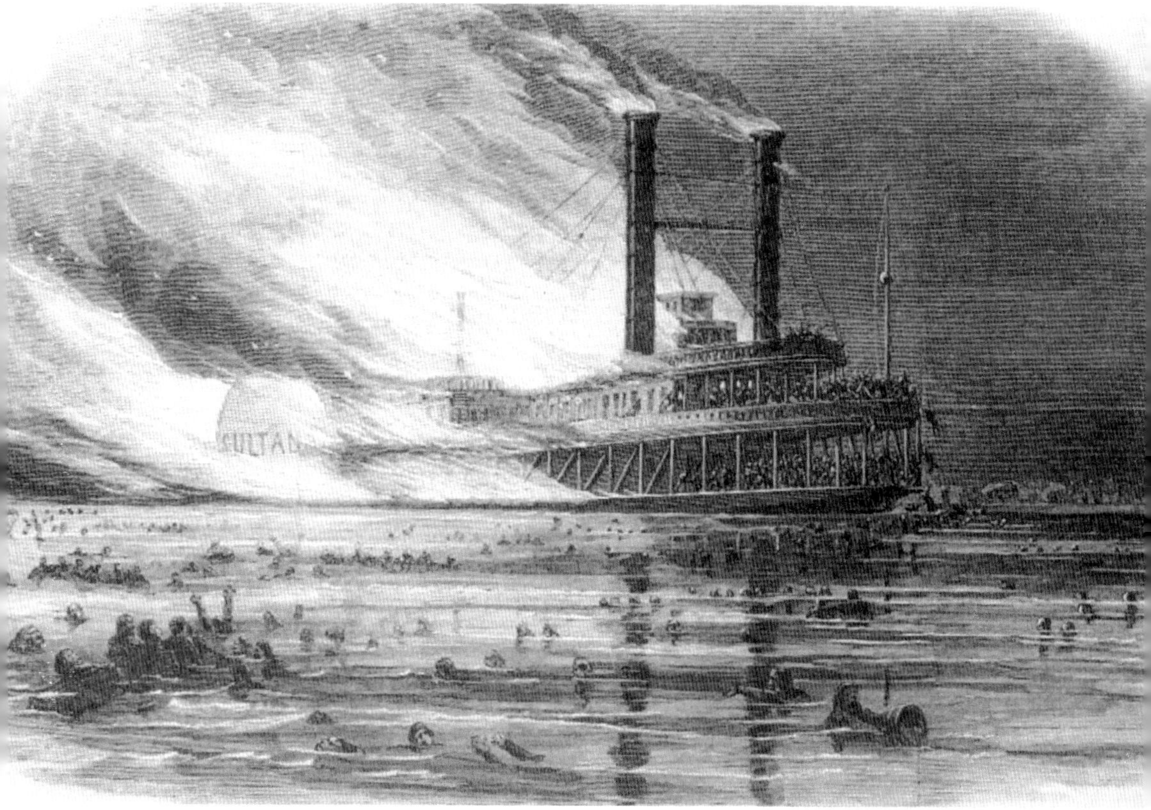

Sultana Disaster

America's worst maritime disaster occurred at the end of the Civil War on the Mississippi River. On April 27, 1865, a steamboat contracted by the federal government to return prisoners from Southern prison camps exploded, killing three-quarters of the approximately 2,300 people on board.

Among the Wheeling survivors were Henry Foster, a brick-maker who was rescued five hours after the explosion; George Loy, who served with Carlin's Battery and is buried at Mt. Wood cemetery; James McKendry, a blacksmith and toolmaker who lived until 1893; Theophilas Richardson, who spent three hours in the freezing water before being rescued; George Smith, a machinist with Hobbs, Taylor & Co., who survived five hours in the water and lived until 1912; and Zachary Taylor Woodyard, who had contracted scurvy, rheumatism, and catarrh while at Andersonville. Those from Wheeling who did not survive included William Cruddas, Alexander Manners, and Allen Stephens.

One of the heroes of Andersonville was Wheeling resident James Duncan, who was in charge of the camp's bakery and employed many soldiers from Wheeling to prevent them from starvation. He was tried in the South after the war for misappropriation of foodstuff and murder. He was convicted and jailed at Fort Pulaski but escaped with assistance from former prisoners whom he had helped at the prison camp and who knew him to be innocent of the charges. (KQ; image courtesy Library of Congress.)

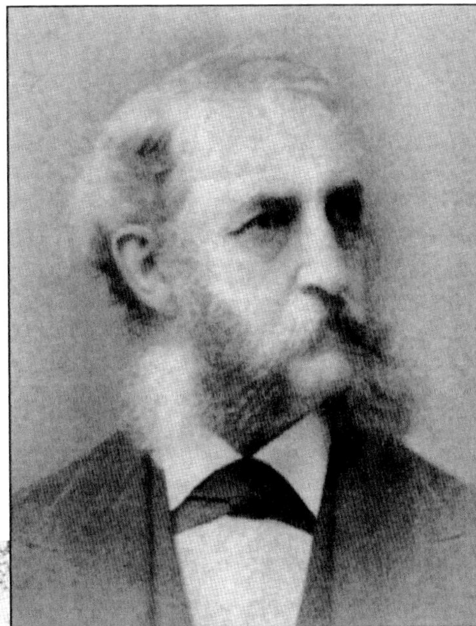

James W. Paxton
An opponent of the secession of Virginia, Paxton (1821–1896) was a member of the convention that reorganized the state government and one of the Council of Five appointed to aid and advise Gov. Francis Pierpont. Paxton helped frame the state's first constitution and was one of the commissioners who went to Washington to present it to Congress for approval. He later donated the Paxton Fountain, which stood in front of the state capitol building in Wheeling. (JF; photograph courtesy West Virginia Independence Hall.)

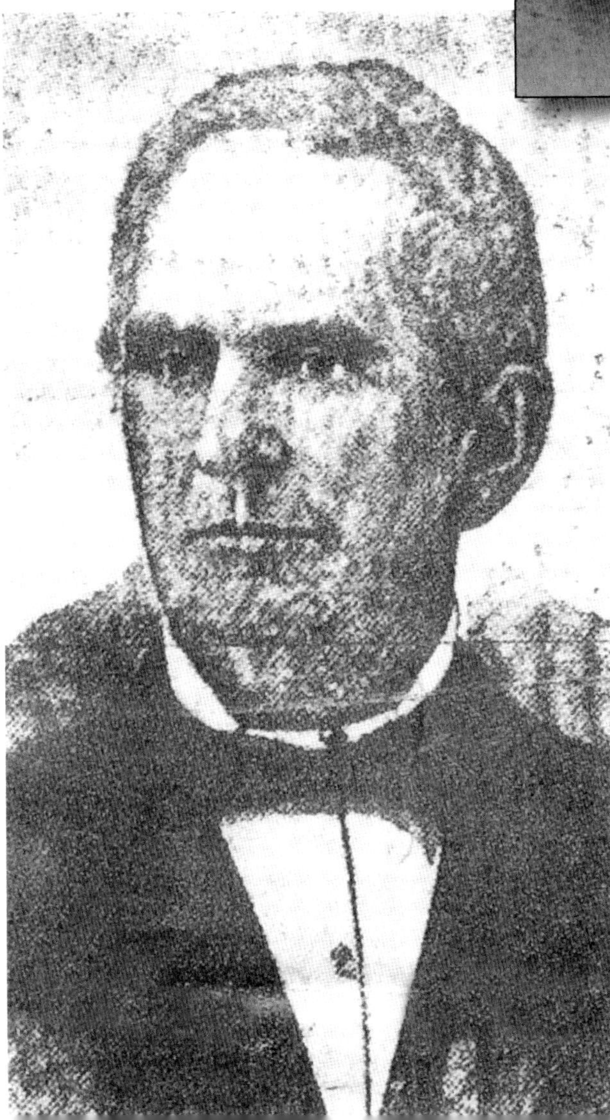

John McLure Jr.
McLure (1816–1893), who became a riverboat captain at the age of 24, was a delegate to the May 1861 statehood convention. During the war, he commanded the steamboat fleet on the Great Kanawha River and, later, a fleet of troop transport steamboats on the Mississippi River. He bought his uncle's McLure House Hotel in 1873 and, in 1875, was chairman of the Wheeling Removal Committee that returned the seat of government from Charleston to Wheeling. (JB.)

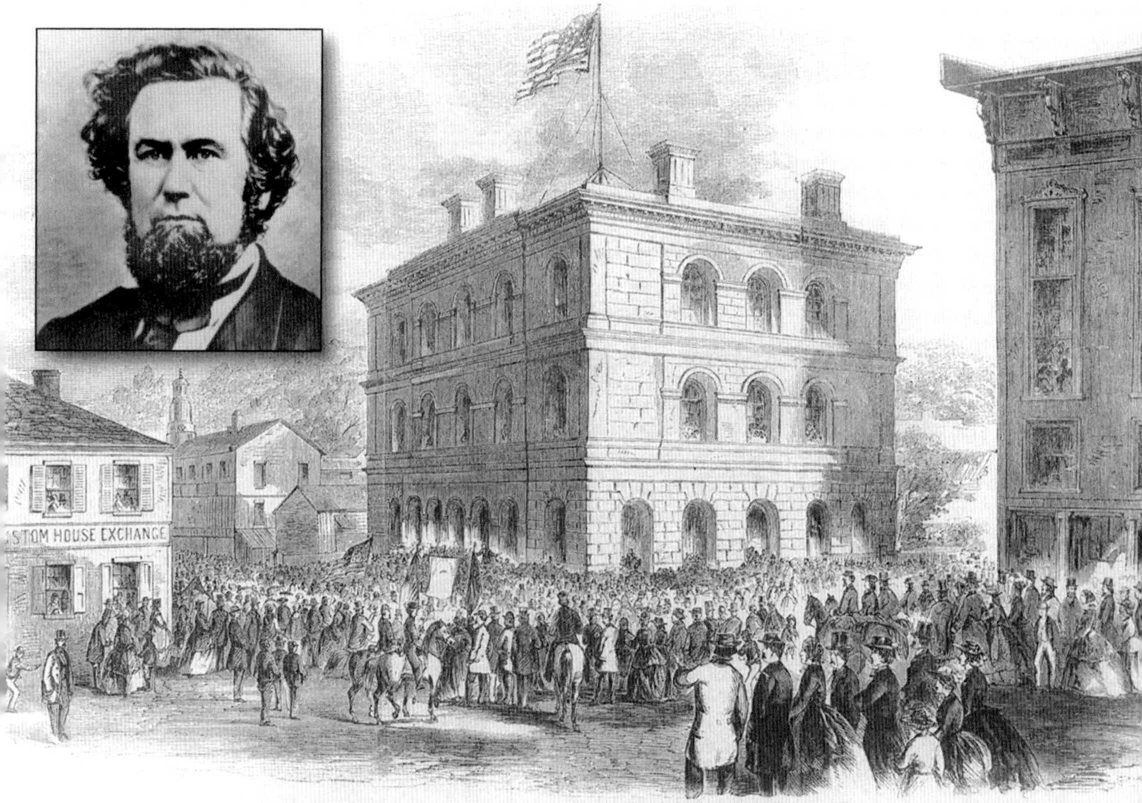

No. 195.—THE CUSTOM HOUSE AT WHEELING, VA., NOW THE SEAT OF THE NEW GOVERNMENT OF VIRGINIA

Birthplace of a State

During the spring of 1861, Virginia's legislature met in special session in the city of Richmond to debate the question of secession from the United States. That body took its final vote on the issue on April 17, with the majority of delegates voting in favor of joining the Confederacy. Most delegates from Northwestern Virginia, however, voted against leaving the union, and they returned to their districts, where mass meetings were organized to decide a course of action. Soon after, a call was made for a formal convention, and it was decided that Wheeling would be the safest, most appropriate place. Little was accomplished in the first convention of May 1861, but in June, the second convention witnessed the formation of a new government for the commonwealth, the "Restored Government of Virginia." This government used the city's US Custom House (now the site of the West Virginia Independence Hall museum) for its legislative and executive functions, and over the following two years, Wheeling served as the capital of all Virginia. The Restored Government had two principal aims: to restore law and order to the commonwealth and to create a separate and distinct state out of Virginia's western region. In November 1861, this body met in convention at the custom house to draft a constitution for the proposed new state of "Kanawha," and after vigorous discussion and debates, a framework was developed for a new state, to be called "West Virginia." After tireless efforts by the Restored Government, Pres. Abraham Lincoln decided in favor of the new state, which officially came into existence on June 20, 1863. Wheeling served as both the birthplace and the first capital of this new state.

A principal figure in these events, Francis Pierpont (inset), a lawyer from Marion County, Virginia, was unanimously elected governor of the Restored Government of Virginia. Using a borrowed office in Wheeling's custom house, Pierpont led loyal Virginia throughout the Civil War and during the first three years of Reconstruction. Considered the "Father of West Virginia," his efforts for the statehood movement were critical to its success. (Both, TH, West Virginia Independence Hall.)

CHAPTER TWO

Arts and Literature

Home to numerous theaters and frequently visited by writers, singers, actors, and other artists of national and international renown, Wheeling has always been welcoming of the arts.

The town's persistent love of music is evidenced by its early German singing societies, standout performers like jazz great Chu Berry and big band singer Nan Wynn, as well as by its present-day annual blues and jazz festivals. Thanks to the tireless and determined efforts of many of its citizens, Wheeling has been blessed with its own symphony orchestra since 1929, a rare feature for a city of its size.

Educators like Warwood High School band director J. Loran Mercer and Stefano Ceo, founder of the Wheeling Junior Symphony Orchestra, helped keep the town's musical tradition alive.

Wheeling was also the birthplace of Billy Cox, bassist for rock legend Jimi Hendrix. Musician Jamie Peck, who has worked for many years with B.E. Taylor, won an Emmy for the music he composed for the WQED series "Pittsburgh from the Air." Singer-songwriter Tom Breiding, born and raised in Warwood, honors regional blue-collar workers in his music. Now an international country music legend, Glen Dale's own Brad Douglas Paisley got his first big break playing at Jamboree USA at Wheeling's Capitol Music Hall when he was just 14.

Homegrown writers Keith Maillard and George Fetherling have taken their place alongside local Ohio Valley legends such as poet James Wright (Martins Ferry, Ohio) and novelist Davis Grubb (Moundsville). Playwright and novelist Leo Brady was born in Wheeling, and playwrights Sean O'Leary, Jeremy Richter, and Tom Stobart continue the tradition. Sean Hennen helps compose scripts for the CBS television drama *Person of Interest*. Quality community theater thrives in Wheeling, at Oglebay Institute's Towngate Theatre.

Motion pictures, such as *Whatever* (1998), *Unstoppable* (2010), and *Doughboy* (2011), have been filmed in and around the Wheeling area, often featuring local talent, like actress Emily Capehart and producer Kristin Seibert. In addition to homegrown talent such as actress Joanne Dru (and her brother Peter Marshall), television star Joyce DeWitt, 19th-century stage actress Henrietta Crosman, contemporary actress Michelle Duffy, and young Broadway star Kelsey Fowler, a number of internationally renowned celebrities hail from nearby towns, including Dean Martin (Steubenville, Ohio) and Clark Gable (Cadiz, Ohio).

Wheeling has also produced an impressive number of fine visual artists. Morgan Rhees was a standout 19th-century portrait artist, and Wesley J. Wagner was known for his landscape paintings of the Ohio Valley. Contemporary artists such as Marilyn Hughey Phillis (watercolor), Bob Villamagna (assemblage, collage, and mixed media) and Robert Sako have helped keep Wheeling artistically relevant. Wheeling has also benefited from the presence of Oglebay Institute's Stifel Fine Arts Center and the Artworks Around Town gallery.

As part of its modern renaissance, Wheeling now hosts an annual festival organized by an arts and cultural commission that is determined to make Wheeling an arts destination and to advance the quality of life and vibrancy of the city.

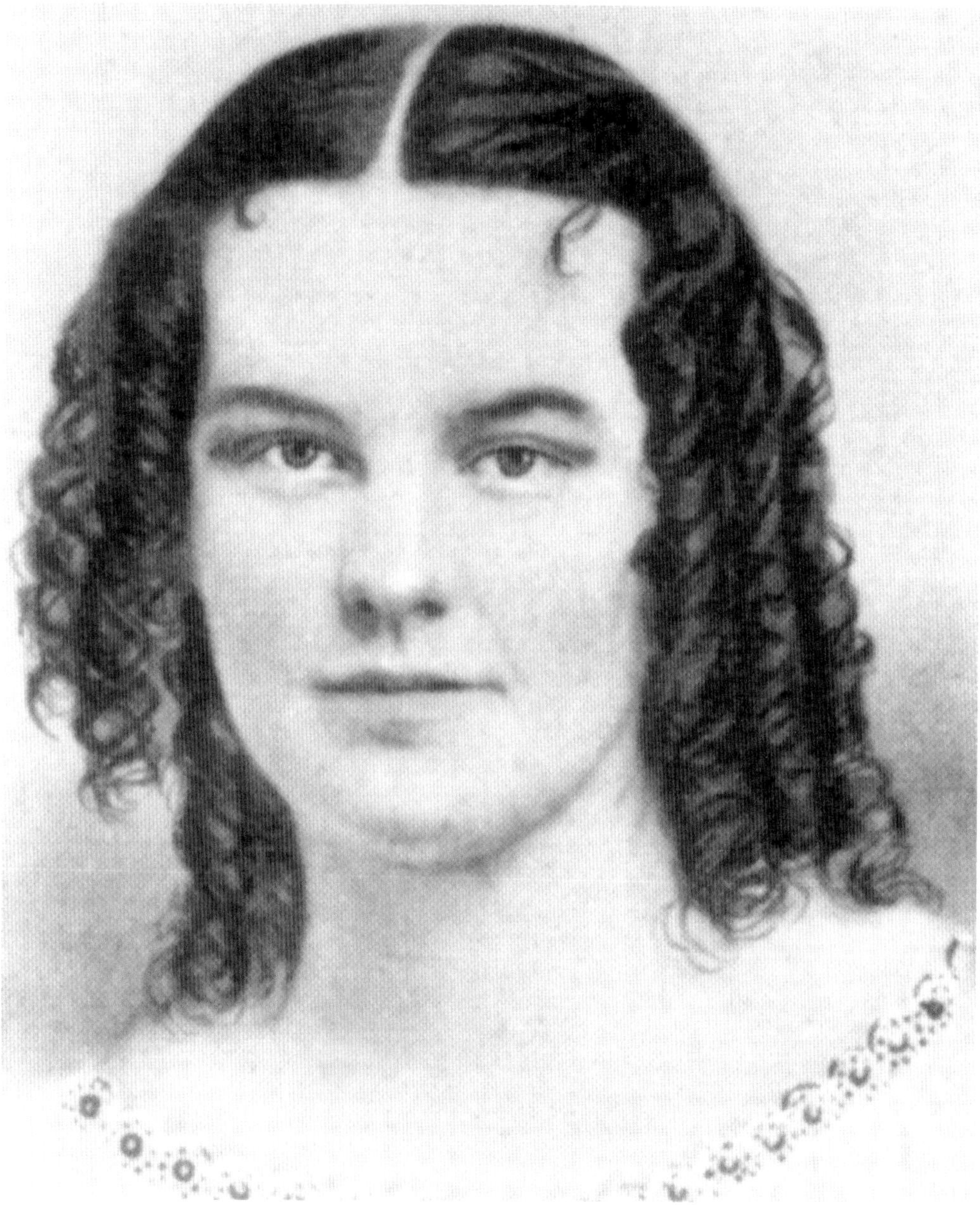

Rebecca Harding Davis

Davis was a contributor to the leading magazine in America, the *Atlantic Monthly,* and served on the editorial staff of the *New York Tribune*. Davis (1831–1910) was born in Washington, Pennsylvania, and moved to Wheeling at the age of five. Her mother was educated by Alexander Campbell, and she schooled her five children at home. Davis attended the Washington Female Seminary in Pennsylvania.

In 1861, at age 30, she published *Life in the Iron Mills*, a realistic story that brought her national acclaim. The book captured the attention of L. Clarke Davis, a Philadelphia journalist. The two married on March 4, 1863. Rebecca moved to Philadelphia and continued her literary pursuits while raising three children. She died at the Mount Kisco, New York, home of her son, author Richard Harding Davis, on September 29, 1910, and is buried in Philadelphia's Leverington Cemetery. (MBr; image courtesy OCPL.)

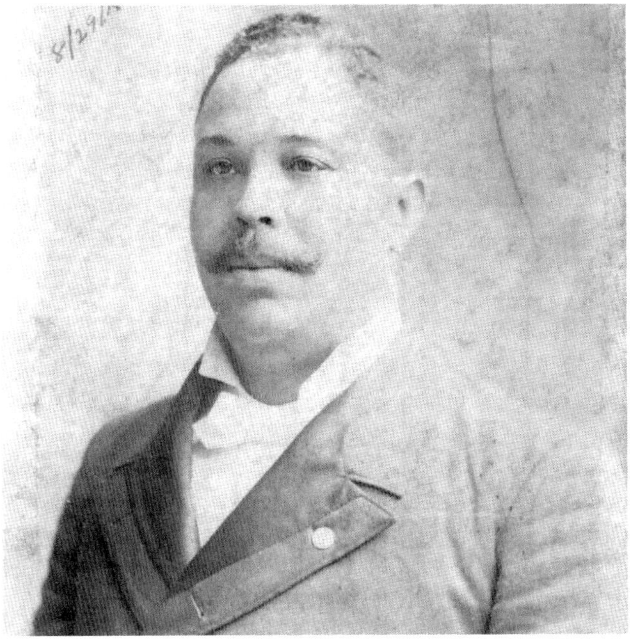

James McHenry Jones

Jones (1858–1909) was one of West Virginia's most prominent African American educators and community leaders during the half-century after the Civil War. Born in Gallipolis, Ohio, to Joseph Jones and Temperance Reed, James was the sixth of 10 children. Influenced by the Baptist preacher Thomas Jefferson Ferguson, the family aspired to middle-class status and stressed education. James asked and received permission to attend the previously all-white Pomeroy High School. Following his graduation in 1882, he became principal of Lincoln School in Wheeling. Jones married twice, both times to women he hired to teach at schools he headed.

James made his mark as an educator at Lincoln Common School in Wheeling, founded in 1866 to educate Negro children, and at the West Virginia Colored Institute, located near Charleston. During his tenure at Lincoln (1882–1898), Jones doubled the number of teachers and students, broadened the curriculum, and rebuilt the school after a fire in 1892. At the Colored Institute, he increased federal and state funding, erected classrooms, a dormitory, and shop buildings, and broadened the curriculum to include teacher and military training programs. Students spent half of their time on academic studies and the other half in the trades building, learning various manual skills.

Jones became influential through political contacts and participation in black fraternal institutions. He supported George Atkinson, a Wheeling attorney, newspaperman, and politician. When Atkinson successfully ran for governor of West Virginia in 1896, Jones seconded his nomination and founded the Atkinson Republican Club, made up of more than 100 African American voters. Jones joined the Grand United Order of Odd Fellows, a black fraternal organization, while still a young man. He held many positions within the fraternity and, in 1897, went to England as America's delegate to the British Odd Fellows annual meeting. He gave speeches to showcase the achievements of African Americans.

Jones's novel *Hearts of Gold* was published in 1896, but only eight copies survived until West Virginia University Press republished it in 2010. Among the issues facing African Americans discussed in the novel were education, the press, fraternal organizations, lynching, and convict labor. Like Booker T. Washington, Jones favored an accommodationist strategy, whereby African Americans would prove their worth. As he said to the British Odd Fellows in 1897, it would be "through the associations of class and especially middle-class values and morals, [that] African-Americans could decrease the force of racism and acquire acceptance in the social order." (JL; photograph courtesy West Virginia State University Archives & Special Collections.)

James Wright

A critic writing in the *Oxford Companion to Twentieth-Century Poetry* praised James Wright for his ability "to appeal directly to the feelings of his readers as few other American poets of his generation" could do. Wright, whose father was a die-setter at the Hazel-Atlas Glass Company in Wheeling, was born in 1927 on Union Street in Martins Ferry, Ohio. Growing up there during the Depression left an indelible mark on his writing and his view of the world.

Readers in the Upper Ohio Valley take special delight in the local references scattered throughout Wright's *Collected Poems* (which won the Pulitzer Prize in 1972). Examples include "Autumn Begins in Martins Ferry, Ohio" and "In Response to a Rumor that the Oldest Whorehouse in Wheeling, West Virginia, Has Been Condemned." The latter poem utilizes poetic license, as the establishment in question, at Twenty-third and Water Streets, was neither the oldest nor the last. But to think of Wright as a regional or folk poet is to ignore the obvious facts about him.

Wright never lived in the area again once he left for military service. Instead, he was educated at elite universities by two famous professor-poets, John Crowe Ransom and Theodore Roethke, and became an important academic himself. He was a cosmopolitan individual, living for periods in Italy and other places and frequently translating the work of important Spanish- and German-language poets. His first poetry collection, published when he was 20, was quite conservative; each subsequent collection, however, was less so. Aside from *Collected Poems*, his best-known book is *The Branch Will Not Break*. It appeared in 1963, when Wright was becoming a nationally known poetry impresario, often mentioned in the same breath as his colleague and collaborator, Robert Bly.

Whatever the changes in his style through the years, one element in Wright's work never altered: his sympathetic concern with the poor and the disenfranchised. This brought him some opprobrium, even in the Upper Ohio Valley. Paul Rieger, who spent a lifetime assembling an astonishing collection of rare books and pamphlets about the Upper Ohio Valley, now housed at Bethany College, called Wright "one of that class of poet/critics that was part of the 'Protest Generation,' who could find little good to say about society, nationally or locally—for which virtue his effete compeers laureated him."

For several years following Wright's death in 1980, the Martins Ferry Public Library sponsored an annual poetry conference in his name. (GF; photograph courtesy Martins Ferry Public Library.)

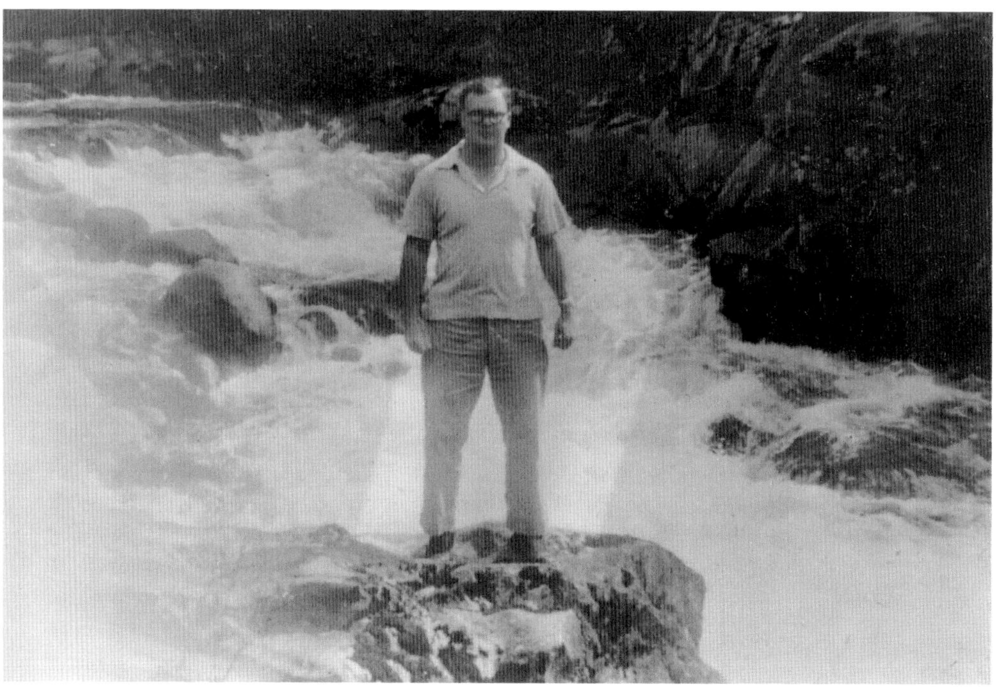

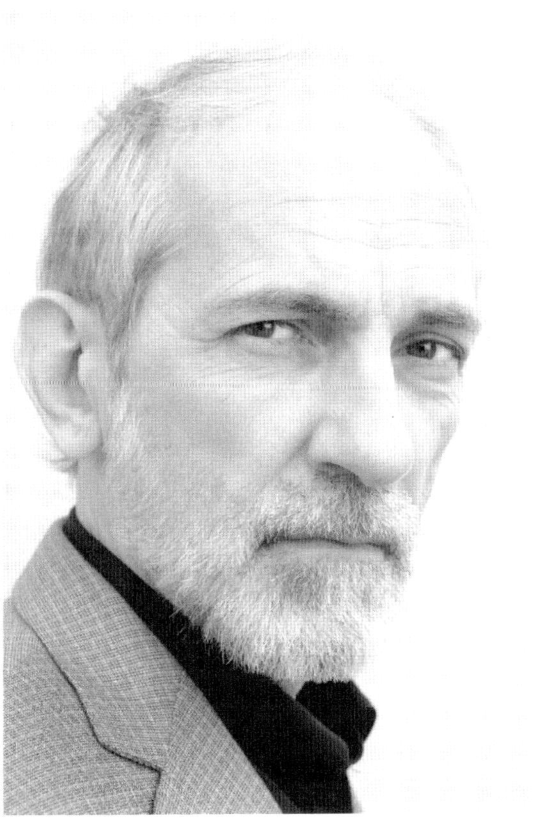

George Fetherling

Born in Wheeling in 1949, Fetherling is an international author of fiction, poetry, and cultural criticism who has lived the life of a writer in all three hubs of English-language publishing: New York, London, and Toronto. He has produced more than 50 books and has been translated into numerous languages. He is the son of another George Fetherling, who was a machinist at the Blaw-Knox plant on the peninsula. The younger Fetherling's childhood was spent mostly on Chapline Hill Road in Bethlehem, where his parents struggled to pay off a small four-room house they found shortly after World War II. But he was temperamentally a downtown kid who resided at a string of different addresses on the island and in Centre Wheeling. His first job was as a dishwasher at Louie's Famous Hotdogs on Eleventh Street (he was fired for incompetence). Later, he worked as a gofer at Paul Hankish's Academy Billiards at Fifteenth Street Place and Market Street. Hankish required several gofers, as he had lost both his legs when rival gangsters wired dynamite to the ignition of his automobile in 1964. George edged nearer his eventual profession when he worked for Ogden Nutting as a junior reporter for the *Intelligencer* before leaving for New York.

There are many references to Wheeling in Fetherling's work. In the novel *Jericho*, for example, he distills the essence of Centre Wheeling in the 1940s, disguising the neighborhood as an area called Snaketown and giving it a different geographical setting. Another of his novels, *Walt Whitman's Secret* (later adapted for the stage by his fellow Wheelingite Sean O'Leary), contains sly Wheeling references and uses slang and speech patterns that Fetherling remembers from elderly residents during his youth. *Singer, An Elegy* is a book-length poem mourning the loss of both his father and Wheeling's once-vibrant downtown. He has also written a pocket narrative of the city's past, *Wheeling: A Brief History*.

Like other Wheeling writers, from Davis Grubb to Keith Maillard, Fetherling has seen the city most clearly from a great distance. He now commutes seasonably between Toronto, Ontario, and Vancouver, British Columbia. (GF.)

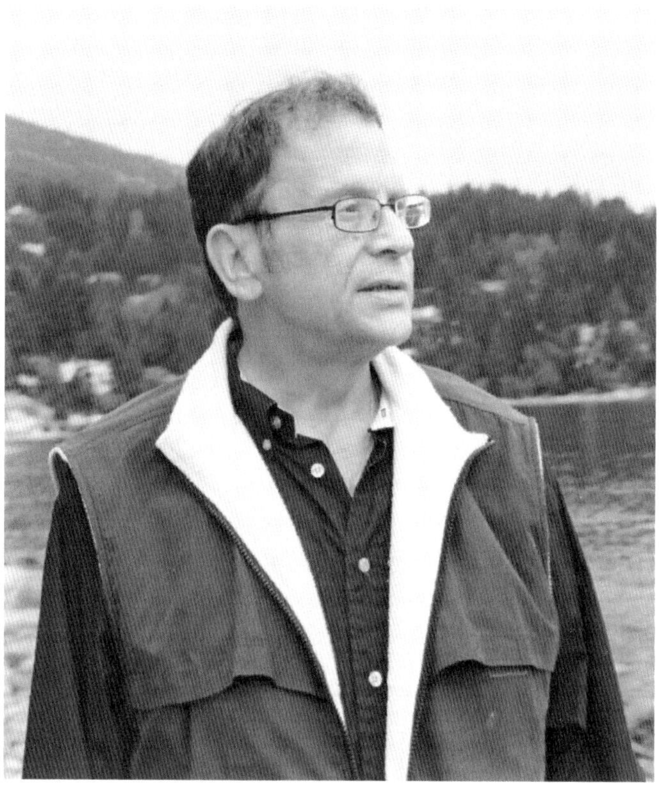

Keith Maillard

When he was little, Keith Maillard felt sorry for other kids who hadn't been lucky enough to be born in the greatest place in the world—Wheeling Island. "The Island and the river lie at the deepest parts of my psyche," Maillard explained, "a foundation for who I am." On his mother's side, his family lived in one little town or another along the Ohio River for five generations, and the stories he heard growing up inspired him to become a storyteller himself. He might have physically left Wheeling years ago, but the city—partially mythologized under the fictitious name Raysburg—is a place he visits often; it has been a setting in 11 of his novels.

Most writers cannot remember the exact moment at which they decided on their profession, but Maillard can. "I was fourteen," he recalled, "visiting a friend in Martins Ferry, and, while reading an account of the great modernist writers like Joyce and Eliot, something went click in my mind, and I decided that was the path I was going to follow." From sixth grade through high school, aided by an academic scholarship, he attended Linsly Military Institute, where he received an excellent education and plenty of positive support. He attended WVU for a while, then, in the footsteps of Jack Kerouac, wandered around America and ended up, in the late 1960s, working in the movement against the Vietnam War and writing for the "underground press." "Although I was not draft eligible," he said, "I was deeply saddened by the tragic events at Kent State in 1970 and immigrated to Canada. I am now one of the strange Janus-faced people who stand on borders and look both ways—a dual citizen of Canada and the United States."

The writing life has been good to him. He has been short-listed for both the Governor General's Award for Fiction and the Commonwealth Literary Prize. He won the Ethel Wilson fiction prize, the Gerald Lampert Award for best first book of poetry, and, for *The Clarinet Polka*, the Creative Arts Prize from the Polish American Historical Association. In 2004, he received the Literary Merit Award from the West Virginia Library Association, was placed on the West Virginia literary map, and was inducted into the Wheeling Hall of Fame—an honor that touched him deeply. He teaches at the University of British Columbia, helping younger writers learn the craft. (KM; photograph courtesy keithmaillard.com.)

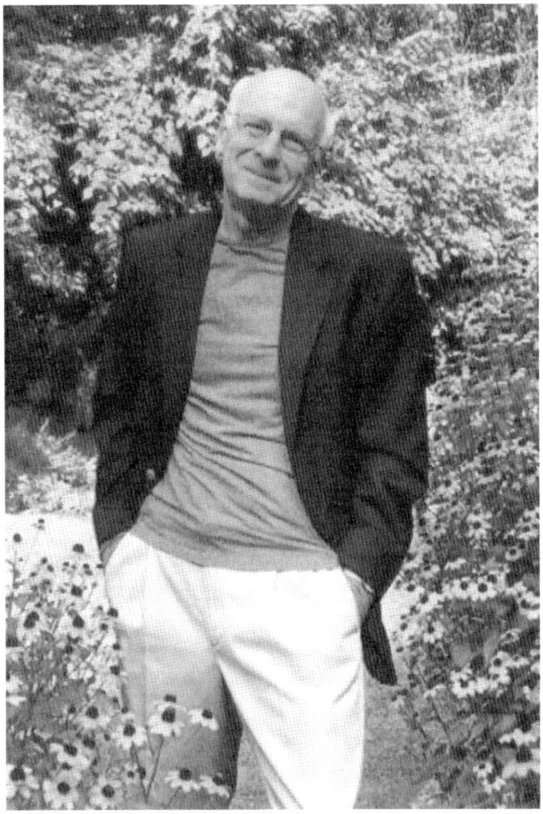

Marc Harshman
West Virginia poet laureate Marc Harshman, his wife, and daughter have lived simply among the foothills beside the Upper Ohio River Valley for nearly 40 years. Here and there goes on the kind of independence, self-reliance, neighboring, and husbandry that Harshman values and that remind him of the energetic attentiveness necessary to pursue any craft. It nurtures, in part, his own writing. To paraphrase Wendell Berry, he finds that "region," in the sense that it matters to him, is a place where "local life is aware of itself." He has nearly always lived in such places. He has known the name of the next ridge and the creeks and hollows that surround it. Living in town, he has known the streets and the name of the old bus stop at the end of the road. Harshman is aware that his current neighborhood, though forgotten by most, was once called Beech Glen. He knows the folks next door, and they know him. And they, too, thankfully, know these names. And about these aspects and much else, they can speak with a shared language and a shared knowledge of their place. This is what matters most to Marc Harshman about where he lives.

"As for the writing itself," Harshman explains, "I believe I was first formed by a love of hearing the spoken word and then coming to read it through the good example of my parents, whom I can still see sitting in the living room reading themselves and surrounded by books. I especially remember my father reading aloud the poetry of James Whitcomb Riley and the echoes of those words and how those corny rhymes fascinated me. And yet though not high art they planted an important seed that told me that words could be made to sing."

John Clare, a 19th-century English poet, once stated, "I write because when I was happy, it made me happier and when sad, it comforted me." Harsman concurs. For him, "poetry is something I must do, that I feel called to do. Regardless of distractions or mood or health, I get up every day and feel compelled to place words on paper, to work my way with words through that day and all the others to follow, to let words map for me a way forward through my life." (MH.)

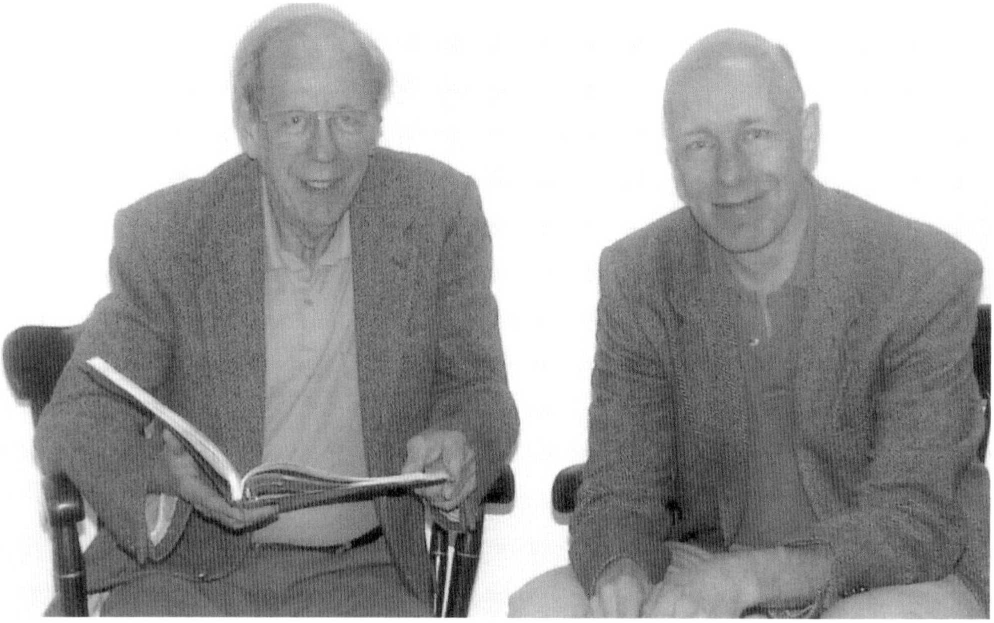

Harold and Sean O'Leary
Father and son, Harold and Sean O'Leary have made their marks in theater. Hal (left) is the founder and long-time artistic director of Oglebay Institute's Towngate Theatre, one of this country's most venerable community theaters. But, many Ohio Valley residents will remember Hal for the "Creative Dramatics" program he brought to elementary schools in the 1960s and 1970s. For many children, those occasions were their first and most memorable experiences in the creative arts. Hal retired from Towngate in 2008. He was then inducted into the Wheeling Hall of Fame and awarded an honorary doctor of humane letters degree by West Liberty University in 2010. Sean's plays have won major national awards from the National Endowment for the Arts and the state of West Virginia. In 2004, Sean was added to the Literary Map of West Virginia. (SO.)

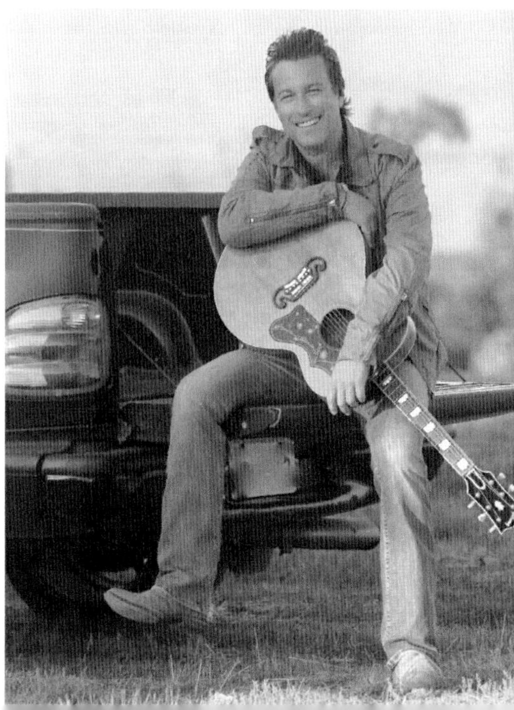

John Corbett
An international movie and television star, Corbett's acting in the television series *Northern Exposure* merited eight major honors, including Outstanding Supporting Actor in a Drama Series in 1992. Corbett took every opportunity to mention his hometown and his alma mater, Wheeling Central Catholic High School, on the show, which always delighted viewers from Wheeling. His breakthrough role on the big screen came with the lead in *My Big Fat Greek Wedding*, the most successful independent film comedy ever made to date. An accomplished musician, John's album *Leaving Nothing Behind* is the work of an artist who grew up in the shadow of Wheeling's Capitol Music Hall, just a few miles from where Brad Paisley was raised. (WHOF/John Corbett Music; photograph by Bo Derek.)

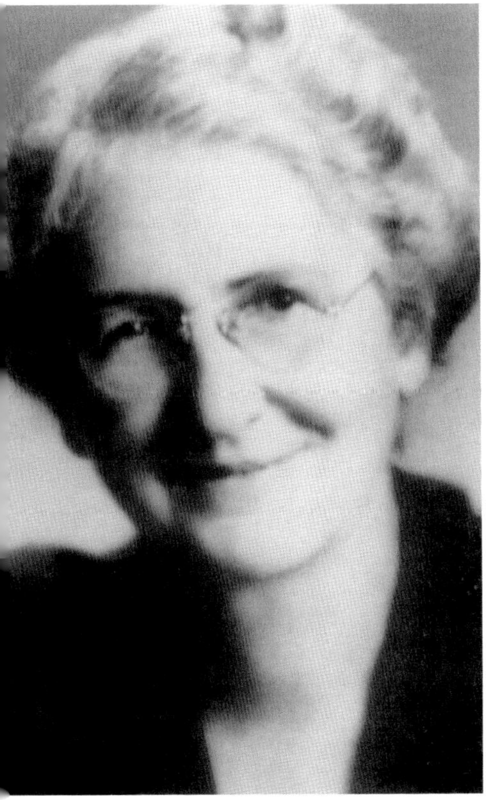

Eleanor Glass Caldwell

An accomplished musician who played piano, drums, xylophone, and cello for the Wheeling Symphony Orchestra, Caldwell (1887–1979) also served as its librarian. She founded the Wheeling Symphony Society in 1929 and, in 1952, established a trust fund to ensure its continuation. A generous patron of the arts, she was also a vigorous campaigner for women's suffrage, served on the Ohio County Public Library Board, and played an excellent game of tennis. (WHOF.)

Earl Summers Jr.

A renowned musician and orchestra leader, Summers (1916–2004) was a charter member of the Wheeling Symphony Orchestra, serving with the ensemble for 61 years, including 42 years as concertmaster. He performed with many local theater orchestras and bands, including his own. Known as Wheeling's "Mr. Music," he also served as first violin for the Columbus Symphony, Pittsburgh Opera, and the Pittsburgh Ballet orchestras. He was concertmaster for Pittsburgh's Civic Light Opera Orchestra. Summers also loved jazz and popular music. In this photograph, Summers is playing violin at the Ohio County Public Library c. 1950s. (OCPL.)

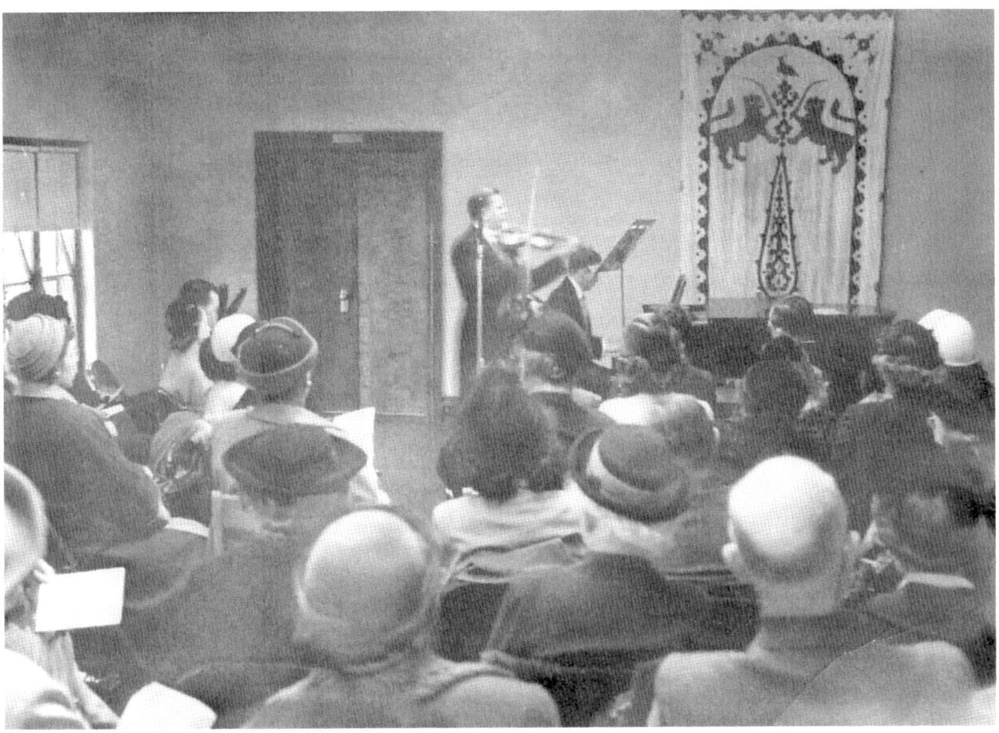

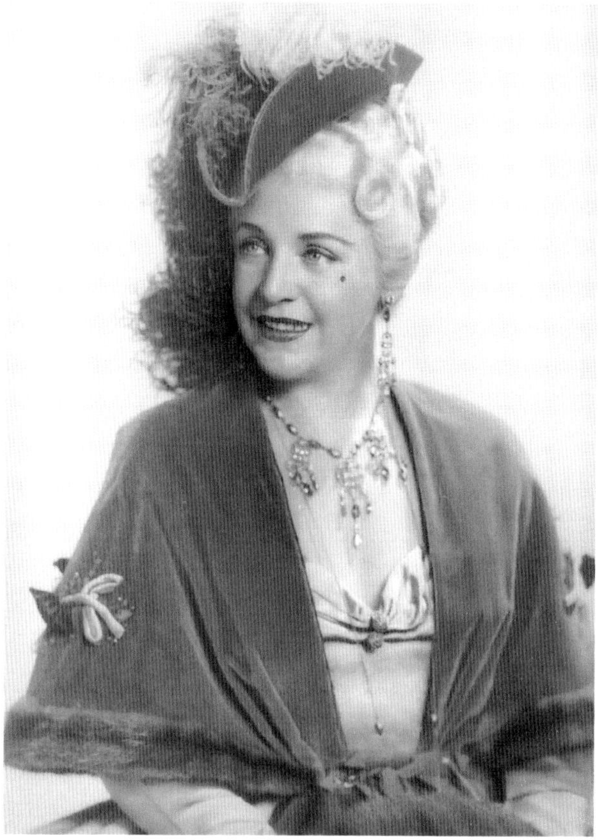

Eleanor Steber

When Eleanor Steber (1916–1990) sang for the 1940 Metropolitan Opera Auditions of the Air, a star was born. Her triumph in the auditions launched a glorious career in grand opera. She became one of the first American-trained singers to become a headliner at The Met.

The Wheeling soprano made her Metropolitan debut as Sophia in *Der Rosenkavalier* and went on to sing more than 50 leading roles at the New York opera company. In fact, she held the honor of having sung more premieres at The Met than anyone else. Before her rise to stardom, The Met had never mounted such operas as *The Abduction from the Seraglio*, *Arabella*, *Vanessa*, and *Wozzeck*.

In addition to her legions of American fans, Steber enjoyed a wide international following. She made cultural tours on behalf of the US State Department and appeared in 15 Asian countries. She was heard in Europe at such music centers as Bayreuth, Edinburg, Salzburg, Vienna, Belgrade, and Brussels. Her numerous recordings with RCA, Columbia, and Odyssey earned wide acclaim. For 10 years, Steber starred on *The Voice of Firestone* radio and television shows.

She learned piano as a child in Wheeling and studied voice with her mother, Ida Amelia Nolte Steber. After graduation from Warwood High School, she graduated from the New England Conservatory of Music in Boston. She studied under the tutelage of the late William L. Whitney. Among her accomplishments was the singing of three diverse operas—*La Traviata*, *Lohengrin*, and *The Girl of the Golden West*—on three consecutive nights. She made front-page news when she sang Desdemona in *Othello* and Fiordiligi in *Cosi Fan Tutte* in one day at The Met.

Steber was elected to the West Virginia Hall of Fame and was bestowed with honorary degrees from West Virginia University, Bethany College, Florida Southern, Ithaca, Temple, and the New England Conservatory of Music. She taught at the Juilliard School of Music at Lincoln Center. The Eleanor Steber Music Foundation was established to provide financial assistance to young singers. (WHOF, OCPL.)

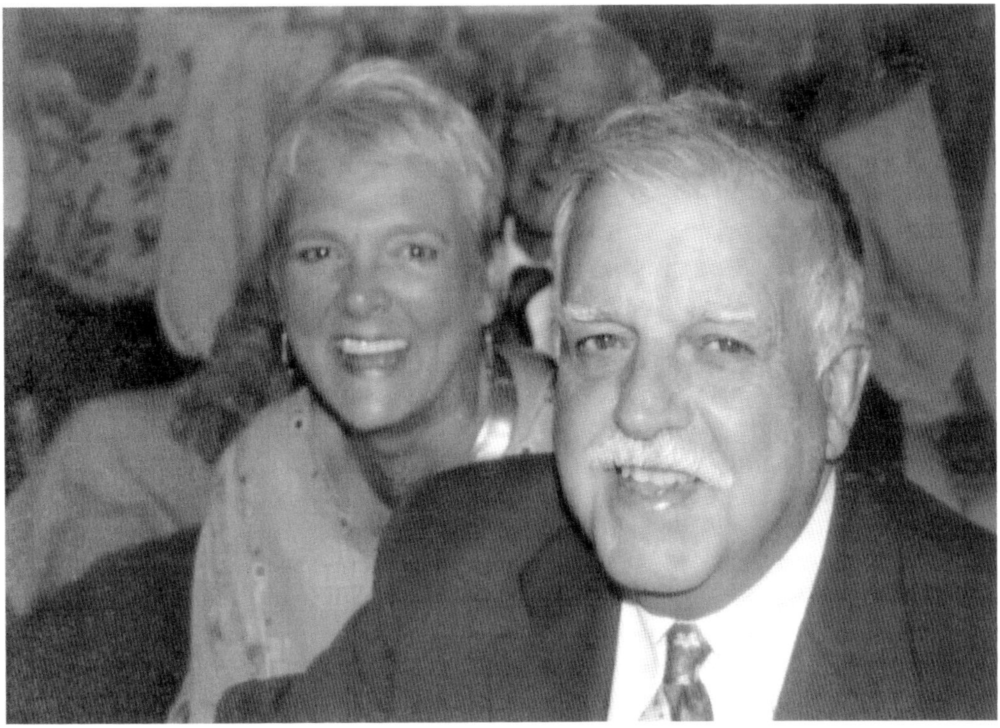

Susan and Bill Hogan

Bill Hogan served five and a half years in the US Air Force and, upon returning home, settled into a career as an investment broker in Wheeling. In 1983, he met Susan Cox Nelson, who was executive director of the Wheeling Symphony. A visit from his son Neil, who had just returned from working for the Peace Corps in Africa, convinced Bill that he had wanted to do the same but had never realized it until that moment. Bill told Susan that he had sent for two applications—she wanted to go, too! They were soon married and set off to Benin, West Africa, where they worked for three years with local residents to improve basic health care, construct facilities, and start small businesses.

Instead of returning directly home, they decided to see the world and traveled to India, Nepal, Thailand, Bali, Hong Kong, and other sites. "I like the people here in Wheeling," Bill said. "Their reputation for friendliness is real. Like in the show *Cheers*, everyone has a neighborhood where they feel they belong. When someone needs help after a flood or fire, people from other neighborhoods are happy to do their part."

Bill's daughter Liza died in a hospice out of state. After experiencing her death, he and his family felt the need to establish such a place in Wheeling. He approached the Sisters of St. Joseph, who donated the land and infrastructure to Valley Hospice and, together, they founded Liza's Place, a warm, friendly environment for the dying.

Susan, meanwhile, was on her own campaign for racial equality. As executive director of the YWCA, she fostered programs promoting diversity and understanding. Her leadership won the Racial Justice Award, a nationwide YWCA honor. Eventually, Susan returned as executive director of the Wheeling Symphony and retired after a total of 17 years. She serves on the West Virginia Commission for the Arts and has been a member of the Wheeling Arts Commission since its inception. "At this time, Wheeling is an empty canvas with a palette of many colors just waiting to create a whole new landscape and lifestyle," she said. She is currently involved in public art throughout the Friendly City. Bill is the father of six children, and Susan is the mother of one son. With Bill's enormous artistic talent and Susan's love for and appreciation of the arts, they are the perfect couple. Their dedication and value to Wheeling is inestimable. (KQ, SH, BH; photograph courtesy Susan Hogan.)

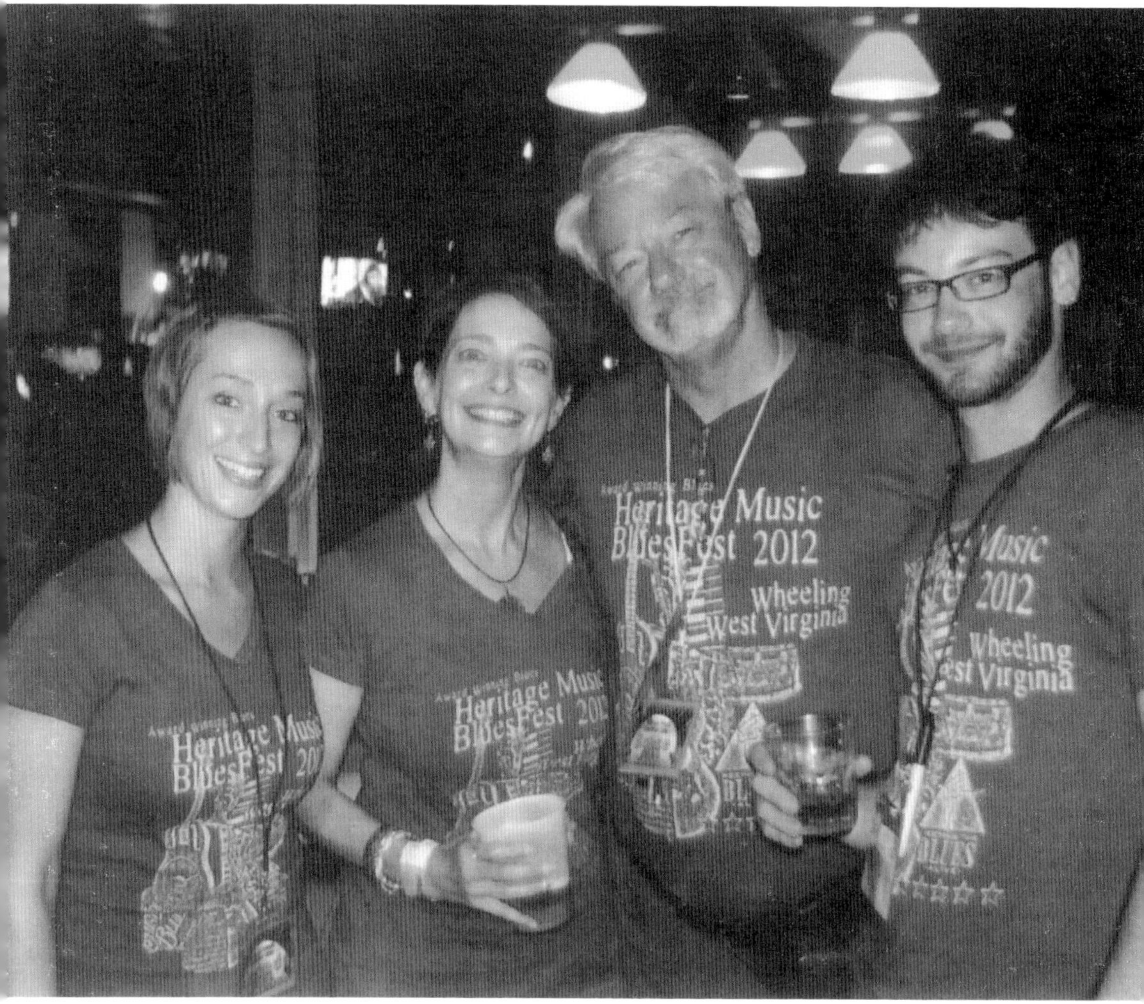

Wheeling Gets the Blues

One night, while sitting on a neighbor's porch, Bruce Wheeler (second from right) was complaining about the lack of activity at a great venue, Wheeling's Heritage Port. Another neighbor challenged him to do something about it. So, he did.

The following summer, Heritage Music BluesFest '01 was born. The crowds were "slight," but the critical acclaim was mighty. Now, blues music lovers come from far and wide—at least 22 states and four foreign countries to date—to enjoy the three-day festival in August. In fact, the group of listeners outside the gate on most nights is as big as the paying crowd that first year. An impressive number of blues legends, such as Buddy Guy and Robert Cray, have appeared at the festival.

In 2010, Heritage Music BluesFest was honored by the Blues Foundation as the "Keeping the Blues Alive" recipient in the festival category. Wheeler does it all, practically single-handedly. He does have the help and support of his wife, Phyllis Sigal (second from left), son Leland A. Wheeler (far right), daughter Amanda Seidler (far left), and son-in-law Chris Seidler, as well as a solid staff of dedicated workers during the festival weekend. (PS.)

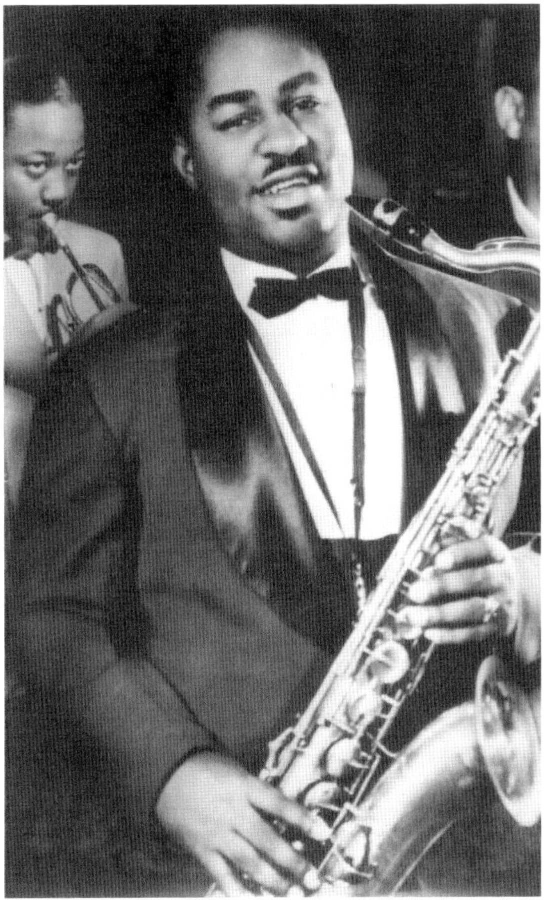

Chu Berry

Leon "Chu" Berry (1908–1941) graduated from Lincoln High School in Wheeling, then attended West Virginia State College, near Charleston, for three years. His stepsister played piano, and Chu became interested in music at an early age, playing alto saxophone at first with local bands. He was inspired to take up the tenor sax after hearing Coleman Hawkins on tour. Although Berry based his style on Hawkins's playing, the older man regarded Berry as his equal, saying, "Chu was about the best."

"It might have been," said a poet, are the saddest of words. In a way, that is part of the story of Chu Berry, a Wheeling native who, during his short life, became the jazz world's dominant tenor saxophone player. Had Berry's life not been cut short when he died at age 33 as the result of an automobile accident, he may have become the most significant jazz saxophonist of the 20th century.

But what he did achieve was enough. Dan Morgenstern, director of the Institute of Jazz Studies at Rutgers University, says of Berry, "Considering the brevity of Chu's life and that his recording career spans a mere decade, it is remarkable that his name continues to loom large in the annals of jazz. Had he lived, there is no doubt that he would be ensconced in the jazz pantheon alongside Coleman Hawkins and Lester Young. He was that good."

Even today, Branford Marsalis, James Carter, and other leading exponents of the tenor saxophone mention Chu prominently among their musical ancestors.

Chu Berry was born in Wheeling on September 13, 1908, the son of Brown Berry and Maggie Glasgow Berry. He died on October 31, 1941, near Conneaut Lake, Ohio, from injuries he received in an accident three days earlier while a passenger in an automobile taking members of the Cab Calloway Band to Canada for a job. (CJ and WHOF, text; photograph courtesy OCPL.)

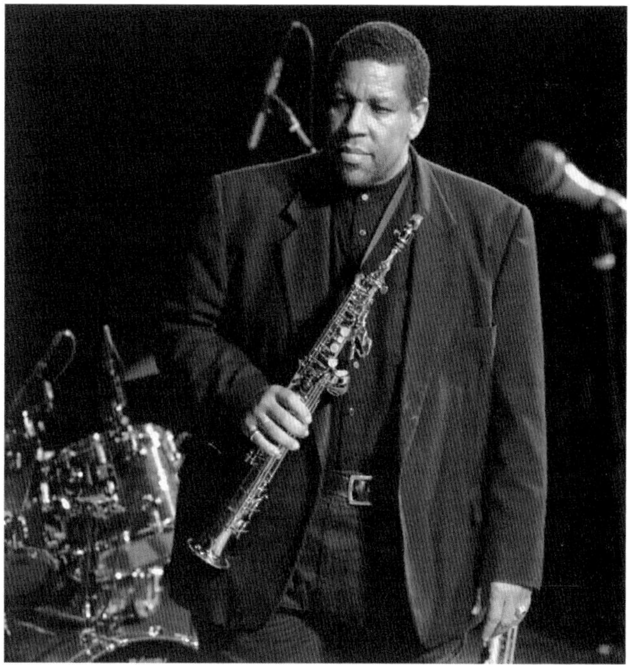

Curtis Johnson

Curtis Johnson taught music at WVU for 20 years. He received his master of music degree in saxophone performance from WVU and his bachelor of music degree from West Liberty State College. He has taught at Slippery Rock University, Washington and Jefferson College, West Virginia Wesleyan, and West Liberty State University. He continues to thrive as a soloist, clinician, and conductor.

Johnson has performed on numerous North American Saxophone Alliance Conference, World Saxophone Congress, and national Saxophone Symposium programs. He has appeared as soloist with the West Virginia Symphony Orchestra and the Pittsburgh Symphony Orchestra and has worked as arranger and performer with the Wheeling Symphony Orchestra and substitute performer for the Pittsburgh Symphony Orchestra.

Johnson is also a renowned rhythm and blues performer, having worked with the likes of Ray Charles, Little Anthony, Aretha Franklin, the Temptations, Chubby Checker, Chuck Berry, Isaac Hayes, Lou Rawls, The Spinners, B.J. Thomas, Dionne Warwick, Martha Reeves, and numerous other stars.

Johnson has been recorded on more than 90 albums featuring jazz, blues, rock, and rhythm and blues. He has also performed on, written for, and produced numerous radio and television commercials. He has recently completed numerous successful tours of Europe and appeared at several international jazz festivals in Russia. Johnson performs with the Pittsburgh Jazz Orchestra under the direction of world-renowned trumpeter Sean Jones. He returns frequently to Europe for festival performances, club dates, and clinics.

As active as he has been as a performer, Johnson has never left the classroom. Jazz education continues to be his forte. He began his career as director of jazz studies at WVU, taking several large ensembles and small groups to regional and national performances. He has conducted numerous all-star high school and college bands, including the 1996 Maryland All-State Jazz Ensemble. Johnson serves as artistic director for the Krakow (Poland) School for Jazz and Contemporary Music Summer Jazz Academy and is an artist/clinician for the Yamaha Corporation of America, band and orchestra division.

"I first came to Wheeling to attend West Liberty State College in 1973," he said. "The local Musicians' Union took me under their wing and allowed me to develop into the musician I am today. Over the next 13 years, while teaching at Wheeling Park High School, Wheeling Middle School, and Clay and Ritchie Elementary Schools, I developed a special place in my heart for the way Wheeling and its residents accepted me. I also forged friendships that continue to thrive to this day." (CJ.)

Doc and Chickie Williams

Doc Williams and Chickie Williams carried the names of Wheeling and West Virginia as they traveled with their country music shows. In their 68 years of marriage, they sang together on thousands of radio, television, and stage appearances with their Doc Williams Show.

Doc came to Wheeling in 1937 to broadcast over WWVA with his group, the Border Riders (which then included his brother Cy Williams). In 1938, they won WWVA's Popularity Concert with 15,877 write-in votes. The radio station's wattage increased from 5,000 to 50,000 in the early 1940s, and the stars of the Saturday night *World's Original WWVA Jamboree* became household names throughout the Northeastern United States and Canada. A fan in Labrador, Canada, e-mailed Doc and Chickie in 2003: "I grew up with your music as my mom would play your LPs every Sunday. Growing up in the 1960s was a hard and harsh time in a small community, but your songs often kept us going."

Early in his career, while playing for a local square dance near Wheeling, Doc met the beautiful Chickie. They were married in 1939, and Chickie would join Doc's show in 1946 after the birth of their three daughters. Over the radio, Doc called them by their nicknames, Peeper, Pooch, and Punkin. They are Barbara (Peeper Williams), Madeline (Pooch), and Karen (Punkin). Doc and Chickie would always give their radio listeners some family news, and his daughters became part of the listeners' families. They even got to travel and sing on some of Doc and Chickie's long-distance road tours. They had a childhood unlike any other.

Devoted parents, Doc and Chickie communicated family values and encouragement through their heart-felt songs. When old age caught up with them and they no longer traveled, their fans came to Wheeling to see them. Beginning in 1977, the family opened Doc Williams Country Store in Wheeling, and there, for many years, the Williamses talked to country music fans from all over the world (and, now, through www.docwilliams.com). Chickie passed on in 2007, and Doc died in 2011 at age 96. "Doc and Chickie Williams, Country Music's Royal Couple" left a legacy of beautiful music and memories to three generations of loyal fans, whom their daughters love. For more information, see *A Country Music Legend: Doc Williams, Looking Back* (Creative Impressions). (BS; photographs courtesy Doc Williams Enterprises.)

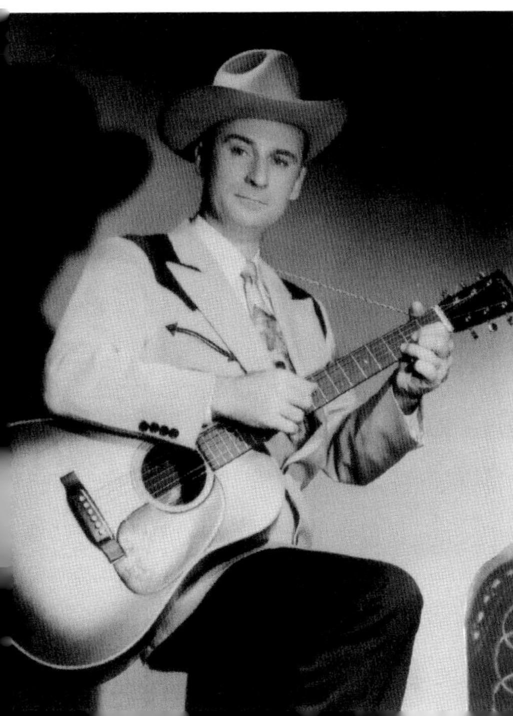

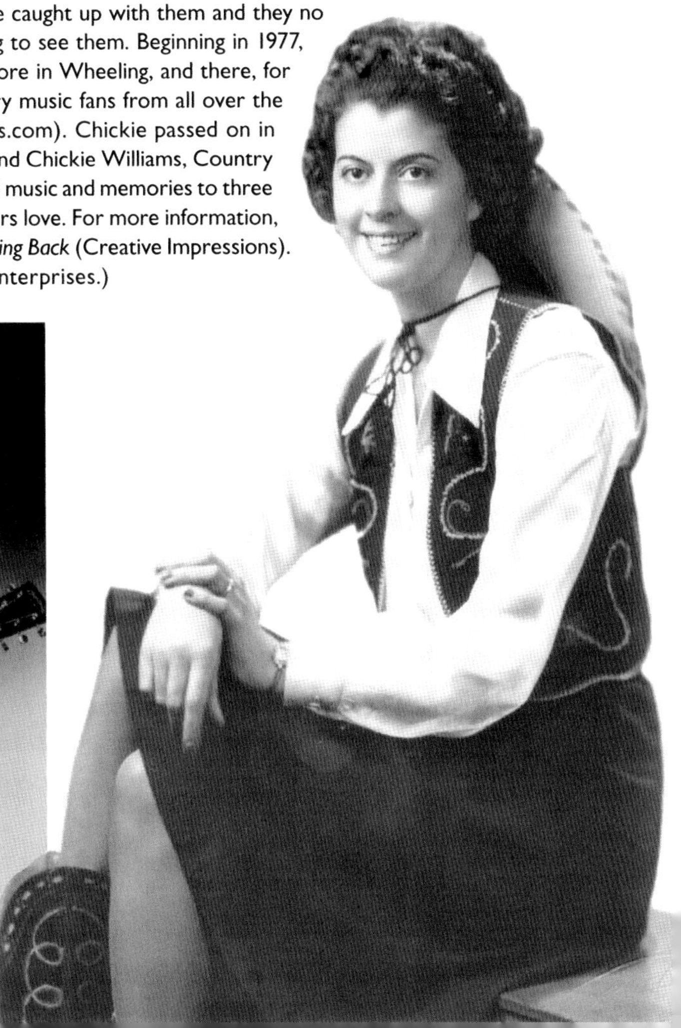

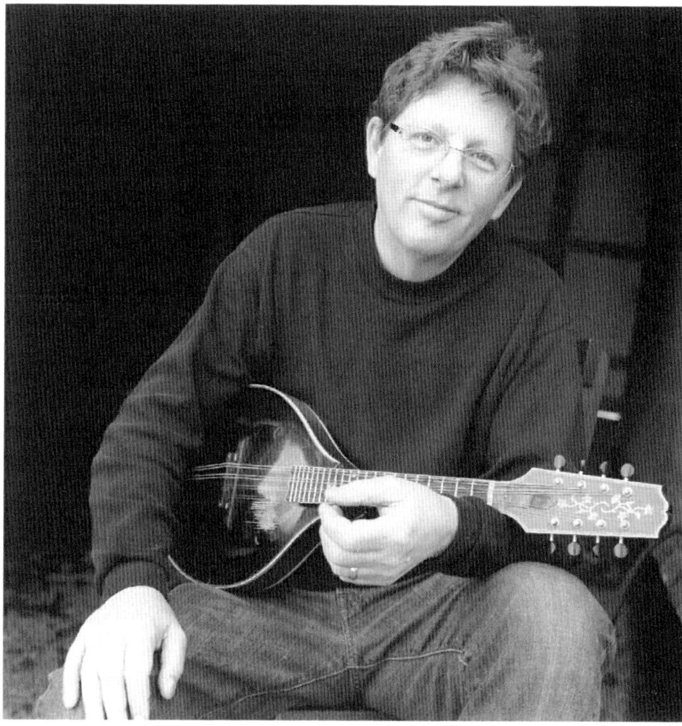

Tim O'Brien

Considered by many to be a national treasure of American traditional music, O'Brien is the cofounder and lead vocalist of the band Hot Rize. In the 1980s, he served as a bridge between the traditional sounds of the hill country and the modern styles of bluegrass. The members of Hot Rize, and their honky-tonk alter ego Red Knuckles and the Trailblazers, remained together for 12 years, receiving critical acclaim and numerous awards from the International Bluegrass Music Association (IBMA), including "Entertainer of the Year" in 1990. Since the band's breakup, O'Brien has continued to expand the music's borders as a powerful solo artist and as a partner with his sister Mollie. In 1993 and 2005, the IBMA named him male vocalist of the year.

He released 13 solo albums through the 1990s and into the following decade, including an album of Bob Dylan covers (*Red on Blonde*), the Grammy-winning *Fiddler's Green*, and the intimate, stripped-down *Chameleon*.

O'Brien has toured extensively in the United States, Europe, Japan, South America, Australia, and New Zealand. He has been featured on the *Grand Ole Opry* and *A Prairie Home Companion*, and he is a perennial favorite at the Telluride Bluegrass Festival, Hardly Strictly Bluegrass Festival, Grey Fox Bluegrass Festival, and Tønder Festival in Denmark. He is also a prolific and celebrated songwriter with recorded hits by Garth Brooks, the Dixie Chicks, Kathy Mattea, Nickel Creek, the Seldom Scene, New Grass Revival, and many others. His song "Look Down That Lonesome Road" won IBMA's "Song of the Year" in 2005. An in-demand record producer, Tim's recent credits include folksingers David Bromberg, Kate MacLeod, and Robin and Linda Williams, as well as Celtic groups the Duhks and Grada. Movie soundtrack work includes *Oh Brother, Where Art Thou?*, *Cold Mountain,* and a biopic on Bill Monroe. In 2008, O'Brien was featured on the BBC's *Transatlantic Sessions* with hosts Aly Bain and Jerry Douglas.

Tim's latest recording, released in April 2012, is called *Reincarnation: The Songs of Roger Miller.* For the current project, under the band name O'Brien Party of 7, he teams up with Mollie O'Brien, her husband, Rich Moore, on guitar, their daughters Brigid and Lucy Moore on vocals and piano, and Tim's sons Jack and Joel O'Brien on vocals, bass, and percussion. *Reincarnation* features all the members singing the wonderful, quirky songs of Roger Miller. (TO.)

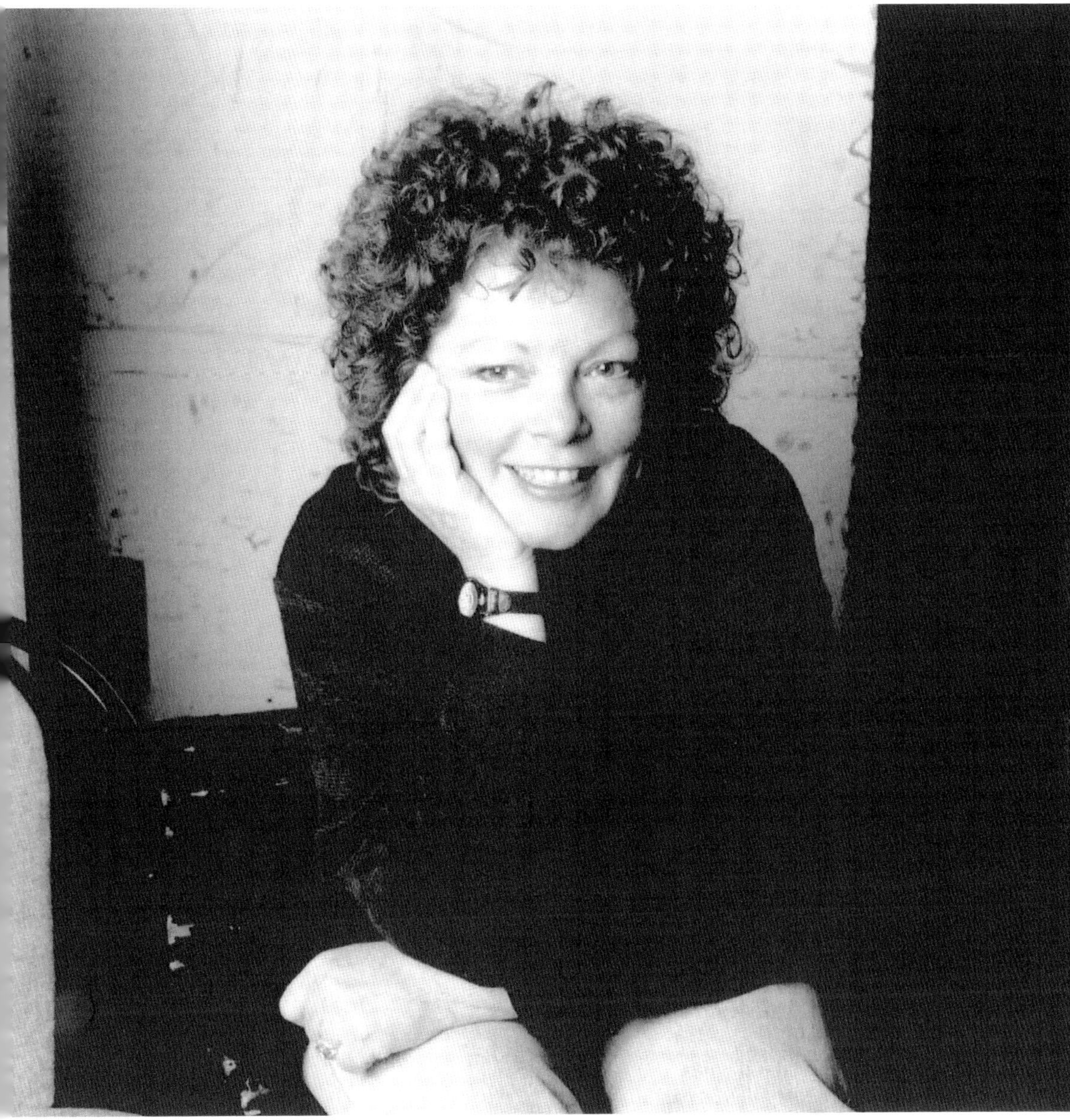

Mollie O'Brien
Born in Wheeling in 1952, O'Brien attended local Catholic schools and got her start in music singing at folk masses, weddings, and parties. She and her brother Tim won first place in the 1969 Oglebay Institute Folk Music Festival. She grew up in a time when her musical heroes, Ray Charles, Count Basie, Dave Brubeck, and Duke Ellington, played live at Wheeling venues like the Capitol Music Hall and the Oglebay Park summer music series. Her first job was working in the ski rental shop at Oglebay in the winter and making hamburgers in the Par 3 snack bar in the summer.

In 1996, she won a Grammy for her work on *True Life Blues: The Songs of Bill Monroe*, and the *Washington Post* called her "one of the best interpreters in American Music today." Because her wonderful voice teacher in high school, Mollie Picchi, taught her the right way to sing, O'Brien is still singing and touring nationally and internationally. (MO.)

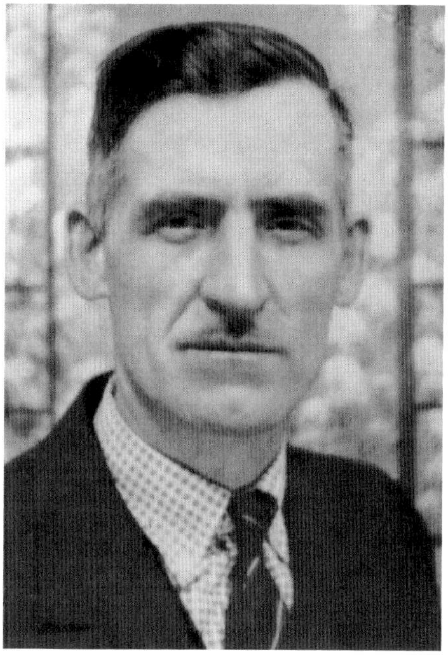

Patrick Sullivan
Sullivan (1894–1967) was an outstanding 20th-century painter of the Primitive style. Moving to Wheeling as a teenager, he worked in the mills, painting in his spare time. During the enforced idleness of the Depression, he had time to apply the laborious technique, rich in personal symbolism, for which he is now known. Sullivan is represented in the Museum of Modern Art in New York by two paintings. Two more are on display at Oglebay Institute's Mansion Museum. (WHOF.)

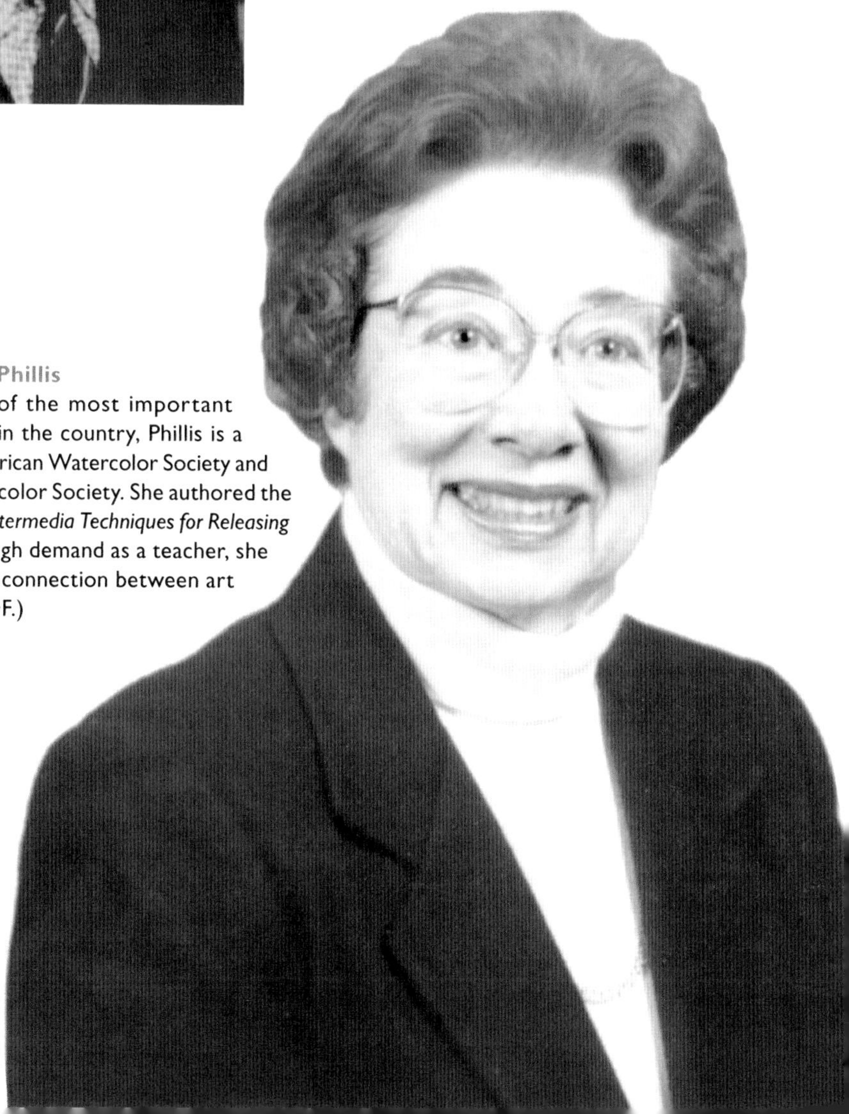

Marilyn Hughey Phillis
Regarded as one of the most important watercolor artists in the country, Phillis is a member of the American Watercolor Society and the National Watercolor Society. She authored the bestselling book *Watermedia Techniques for Releasing Creative Spirits*. In high demand as a teacher, she is interested in the connection between art and healing. (WHOF.)

Harry Holbert

Holbert (1918–1982) was an influential artist and art educator. Through a leadership program fostered by Oglebay Institute, Holbert created art clubs and outreach programs. When television came to Wheeling in the early 1950s, he was named art director at the new station, WTRF. While there, he invented an automatic film processor and became "Uncle Harry" on his own television program about the wonders of art. (WHOF.)

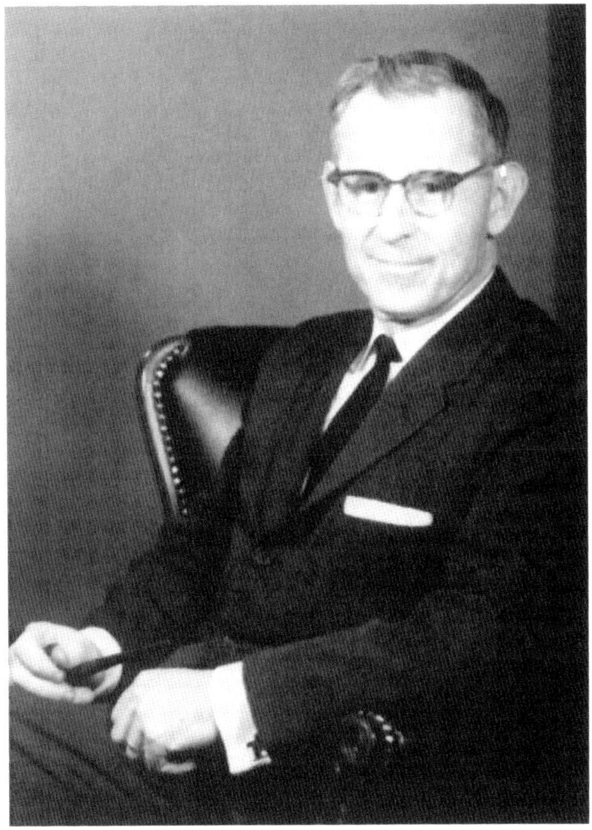

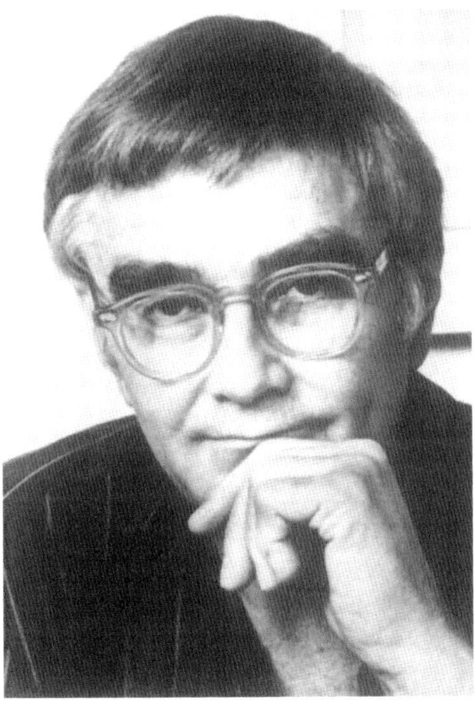

Budd Hopkins

Hopkins (1931–2011) established an international reputation as an abstract artist and sculptor. His work is on display in many of the world's most prestigious art galleries and museums, and he is represented in numerous important private collections. He was also known for his research on the UFO phenomenon, publishing the bestseller *Intruders*. A graduate of Linsly Military Institute and Oberlin College, Hopkins was one of 15 painters featured in a 1963 CBS special on American art. (WHOF.)

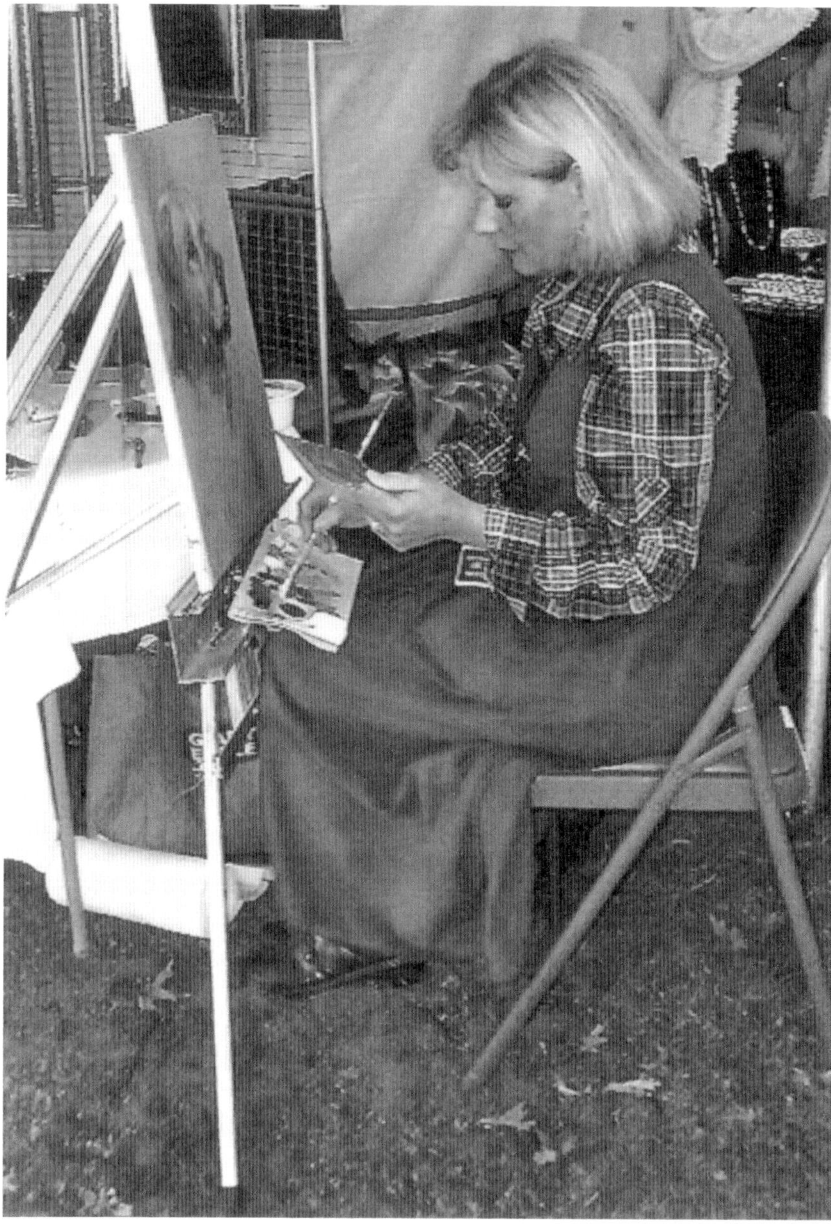

Anne Foreman

Anne Foreman grew up in an environment immersed in a love of history. Her father was James C. Hazlett, a family practice physician whose dedication to his patients was well known in Wheeling. He also researched heavy artillery manufactured and used during the Civil War. "We spent every summer vacation visiting battlefields such as Shiloh, Vicksburg, and Gettysburg," Foreman recalled. "My father collected many items associated with artillery and we thought nothing of the cannon barrel in the living room or the stack of shells beside it. His book on the subject is still in print today and considered the ultimate reference in its field." Anne has loved to draw and paint since she was very young. She was asked to illustrate a book on local Revolutionary War history a few years ago, and ever since, she has depicted many local reenactors who interpret Wheeling's pivotal role in frontier history. (Anne Foreman.)

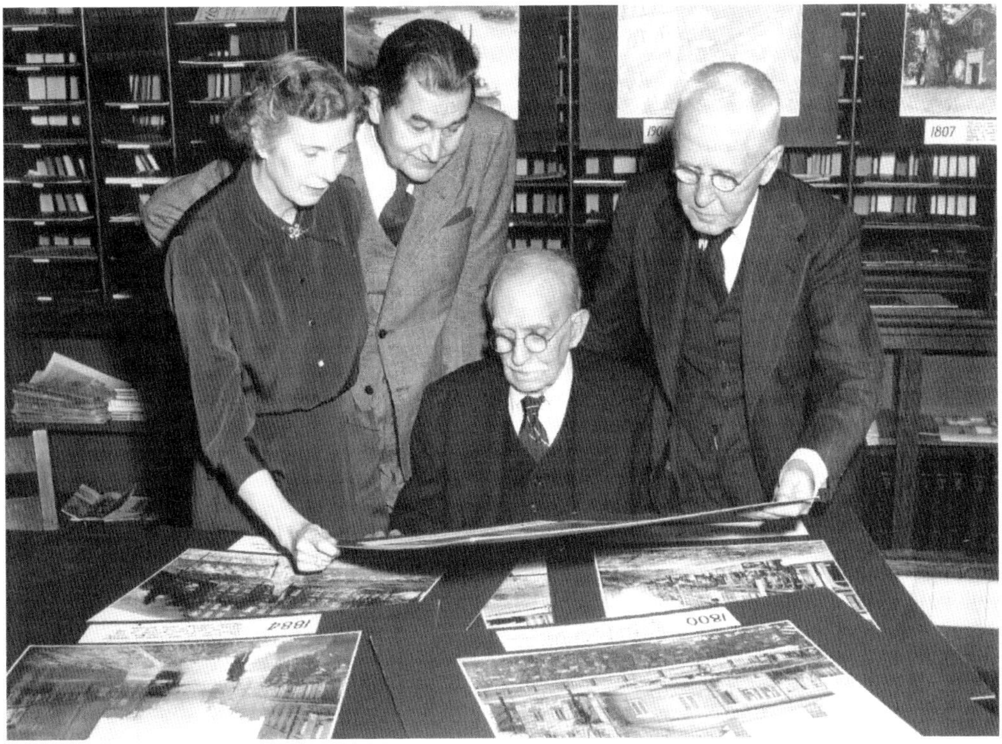

George Kossuth

Kossuth (1886–1960) was a portrait photographer of consummate skill whose avocations covered the spectrum of the arts, from music to woodworking. The gift of a box camera at age 12 sparked his lifelong passion for photography, culminating in international renown. Through the Frazier Concert Society, Kossuth met and photographed every famous musical artist who visited Wheeling in the early and mid-20th century. Pictured from left to right are Ohio County Public Library director Virginia Ebeling, George Kossuth, W.C. Brown, and Mr. McGregor, a library board of trustees member, c. 1950. The Brown Collection is a group of historic Wheeling photographs owned by the library. (WHOF; photograph courtesy OCPL.)

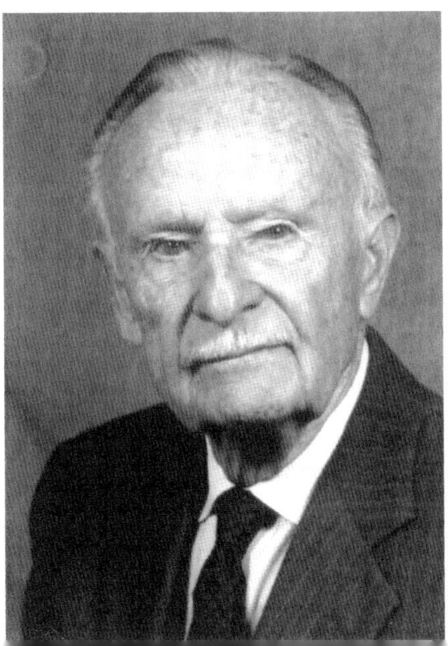

Ellis Dungan

From his youth, Dungan loved adventure. Born in 1909 in the small town of Barton, Ohio, he hitchhiked to California after high school. He studied at USC's first cinema department, then sailed to India in 1935 to direct films for 15 years. He is honored in India as a pioneer in the country's cinema history. Returning to Hollywood after World War II, he worked on jungle adventure films. In 1958, he moved to Wheeling where he met his wife, Elaine, and they raised their son, Chris Bowie. For the next 28 years, Ellis, through his own Ellis Dungan Productions, produced and directed industrial, business, and public relations films for West Virginia University, Ohio Power Company, Wheeling Steel Corporation, Consolidation Coal Company, and the Wheeling Ironmen. He remained a proud resident of Wheeling until his death in 2001. (BS; photograph courtesy WHOF.)

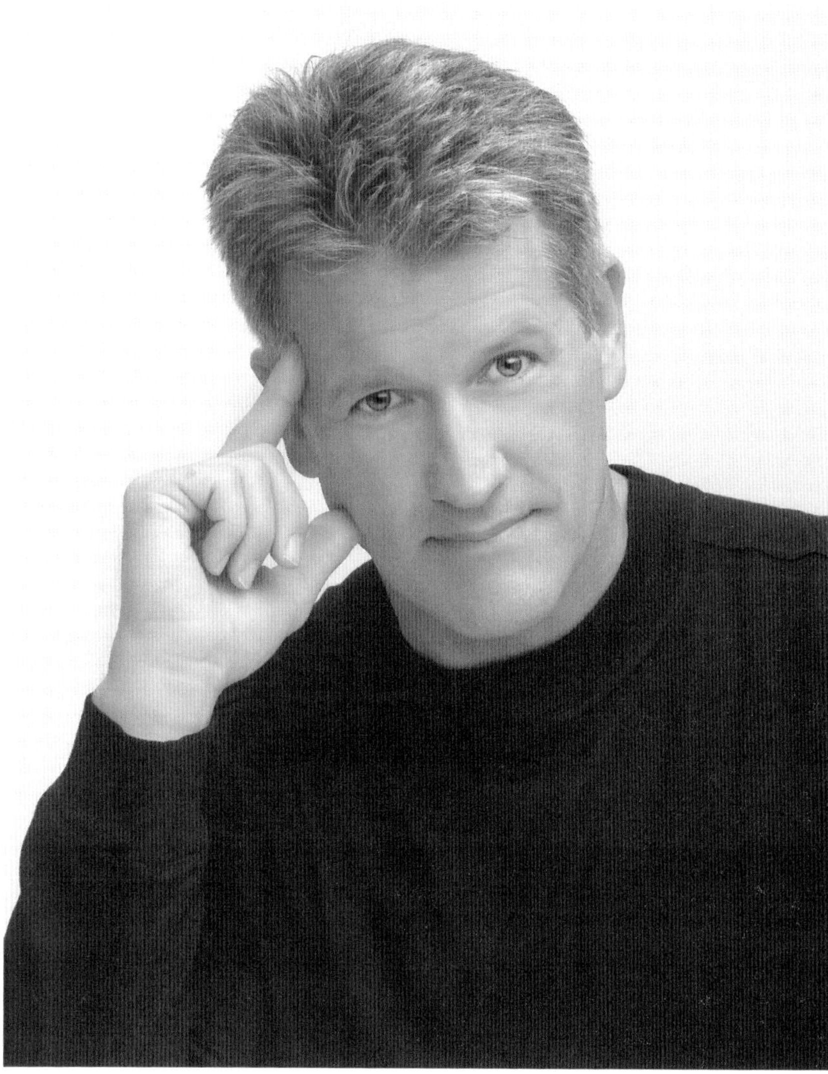

Craig Karges

For more than 30 years, Karges has earned his living as a "mystery merchant." He entertains audiences through the creation of mystery. As an "extraordinist," he simulates, demonstrates, and duplicates the unknown, the unexplained, and the unbelievable. He has conducted more than 5,000 performances in 22 countries on four continents and in all 50 states. He's made over 40 national television appearances, including *The Tonight Show with Jay Leno*. However, some of his fondest memories are of performances in his hometown of Wheeling, West Virginia, in hidden gems of the city located behind plain facades. Among his memorable Wheeling events are the following: performing and shooting a one-hour television special in the beautiful 1904 Victoria Theatre; performing at the extraordinary 1920s-era Capitol Theatre to benefit his alma mater, Wheeling Central Catholic High School, and Oglebay Institute; and performing at the Capitol as part of an opening night celebration after the venue had been shuttered for two years. "It brought tears to my eyes to see her reopened and it brings a smile to my face to know she's thriving," Karges recalled. "With a travel schedule of more than 150,000 miles a year, it's always a joy to get back to Wheeling, my home. Someone once told me to never forget where I was from because that will always be a big part of who I am. I couldn't be more pleased that Wheeling will always be a part of me." (CK.)

CHAPTER THREE

Sports Legends

Wheeling's industrial character has always fostered a gritty determination and work ethic conducive to athletic prowess and high performance. The region's passion for sports is evident to even the casual observer. As a manufacturing center, Wheeling attracted immigrants from all over the world—people of courage, physical strength, and competitive natures. Skilled athletes have emerged, excelling at baseball, basketball, football, wrestling, golf, and numerous other sports. And the Ohio River towns surrounding Wheeling have produced a veritable who's who of American sporting legends, including celebrated collegiate wrestler and Olympic wrestling coach Bobby Douglas (Bridgeport, Ohio), football coaching legend Lou Holtz (Follansbee, West Virginia), NFL stars Bill Jobko (Bridgeport), Lou "The Toe" Groza (Martins Ferry, Ohio), Lance Mehl and Joey Galloway (both from Bellaire, Ohio), NBA legend John "Hondo" Havlicek (Martins Ferry), Major League Baseball pitchers Phil and Joe Niekro (Blaine, Ohio), and third baseman George Brett (Glen Dale). Competitive bodybuilder Eric "the House" Fankhouser qualified for the Mr. Olympia contest in 2010.

Less well known but no less important, Wheeling has produced an impressive array of legendary coaches and sports officials, including Stan Romanoski (West Virginia University track-and-field and cross-country coach), Sam Andy (Wheeling Park High School basketball coach), Jim Thomas (Wheeling Central football coach), Warren Pugh (sports official and swimming coach at Linsly), and John "Streaky" Haloszka (multisport official). Numerous basketball coaches who got their start in Wheeling have gone on to have success in bigger venues, including Dino Gaudio and the late George "Skip" Prosser (Wake Forest University) and Jim O'Brien (Boston Celtics and Dallas Mavericks). A monument on Wheeling Island pays tribute to Hugh E. McConkey, known as the "Dean of Wheeling Sandlot Baseball." Rudy Mumley organized the popular Ohio–West Virginia OVAC Charity Football Classic, mortgaging his own home to fund the first game in 1972.

Skilled sportswriters and commentators, like Bill Van Horne, Nick Bedway, Doug Huff, and George Kellas, have also emerged to chronicle the amazing feats of these Ohio Valleys sports legends. Wheeling is also well represented in new media, as Wheeling Central graduate Mike Florio parlayed a popular football blog, ProFootballTalk.com, into a career as an NFL insider analyst for NBC television, teaming up with *Sports Illustrated's* Peter King.

Wheeling also had a hand in developing America's favorite sports network. Media executive J. William Grimes helped grow ESPN into the nation's largest sports-programming television network, while producer Chuck Scatterday helped launch ESPN2 and ESPNU.

Finally, as part of their passion for sports, many Wheelingites have enjoyed wagering on the results of athletic competition. Gambling has always been an unavoidable reality in Wheeling.

John W. Glasscock

Glasscock (1857–1947) was the first West Virginian to play Major League Baseball. *Sports Illustrated* magazine named him as one of the three best shortstops of all time in 1984. He led the National League in fielding throughout his career and set numerous records without the benefit of a glove. He came home to Wheeling to lead the local team to an Iron and Oil League title. (WHOF; image courtesy Library of Congress.)

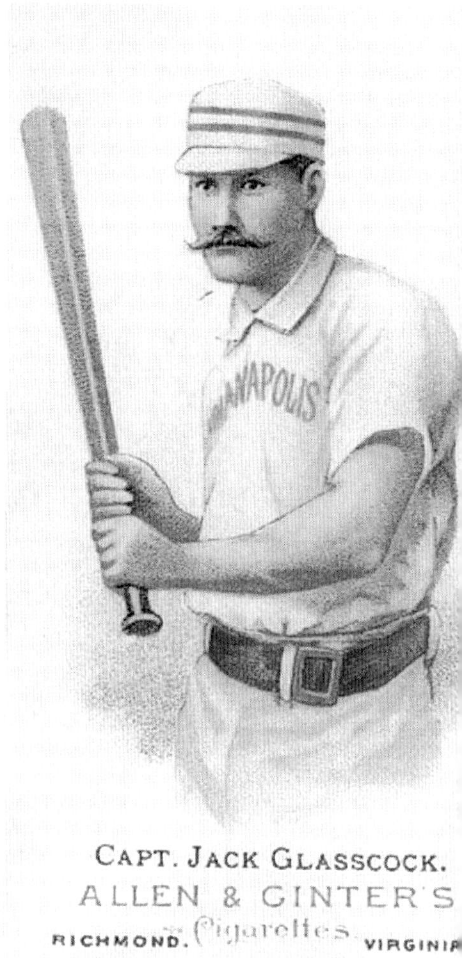

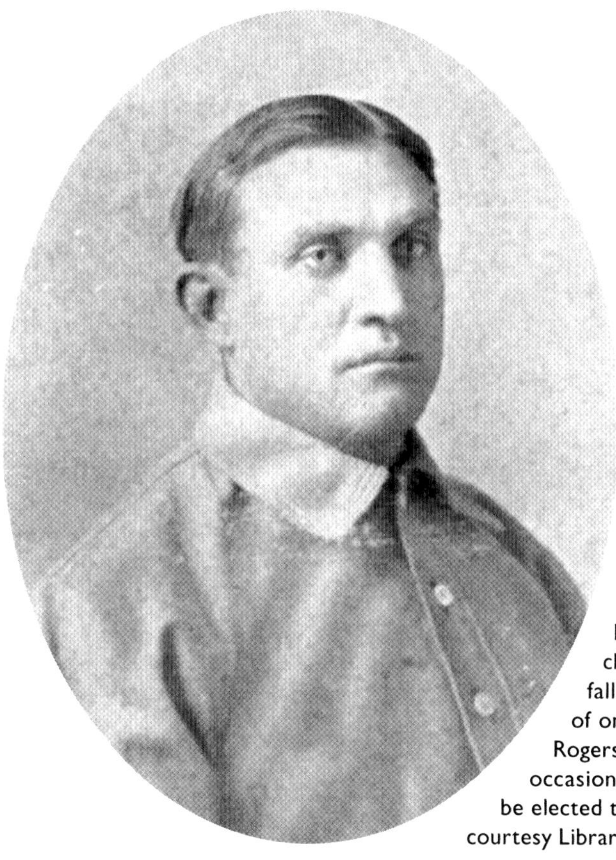

Jesse Burkett

Wheeling Islander Jesse Burkett (1868–1953) played baseball for the New York Giants, Cleveland Indians, St. Louis Browns, Boston Americans, and for Worcester of the New England League. A National League batting champion three times, he hit .342 for his career, falling just 128 hits shy of 3,000. He was one of only three men in history (with Ty Cobb and Rogers Hornsby) to bat over .400 on three different occasions and was the first West Virginia native to be elected to the Baseball Hall of Fame. (WHOF; image courtesy Library of Congress.)

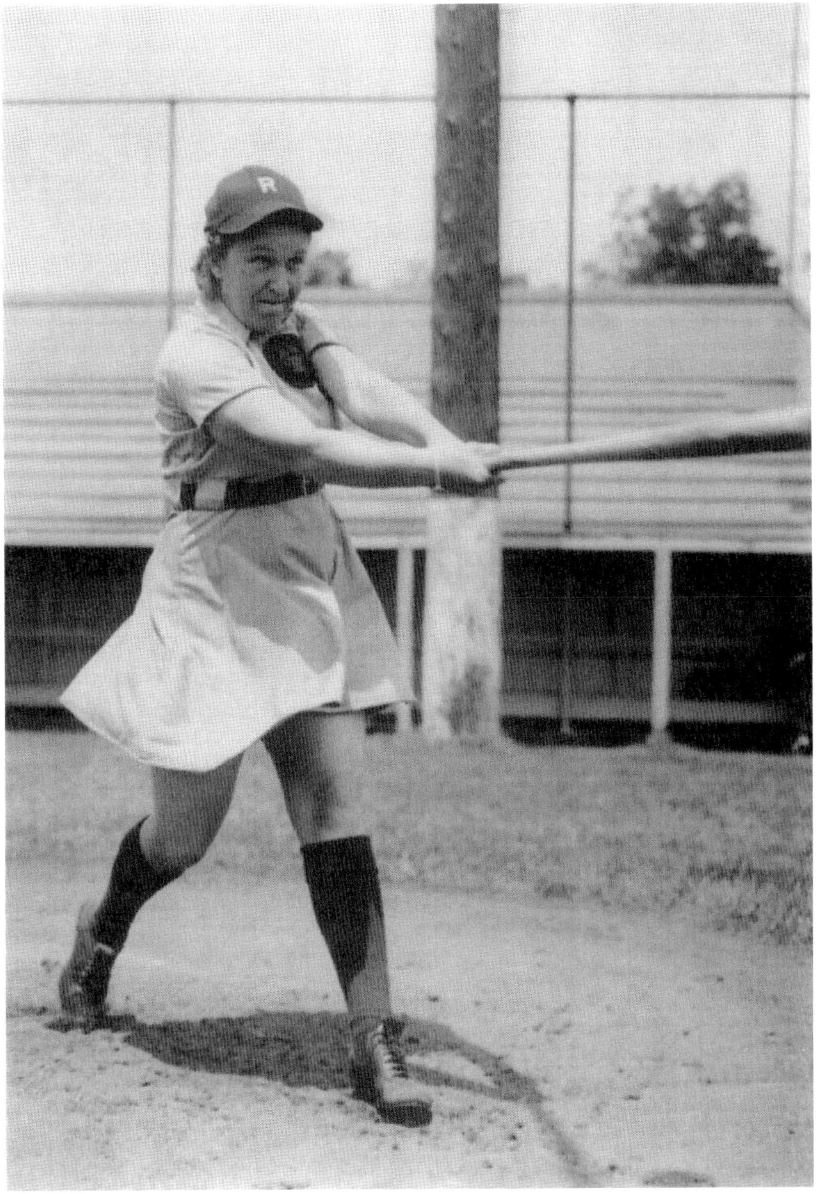

"Rosie Gaspipe"

Rose Gacioch (1915–2004) was a skilled athlete who spent her formative years playing baseball and other sports at Pulaski Field at Forty-sixth Street in South Wheeling. During World War II, while working in a local factory, Rose heard that the All-American Girls Professional Baseball League (organized by Chicago Cubs owner P.K. Wrigley, because so many major leaguers were away at war) was holding a tryout at Pulaski. She made the team and excelled, becoming one of the league's best players as a right fielder and pitcher for the Rockford Peaches. A three-time all-star, Rose hurled a no-hitter in 1953. The inspiration for Rosie O'Donnell's character in the 1992 feature film *A League of Their Own*, Rose was profiled in the book *Women at Play* by Barbara Gregorich. For some now-forgotten reason (perhaps because non-Poles couldn't pronounce her name), she was widely known as "Rosie Gaspipe" in Wheeling. (SD; photograph courtesy Center for History.)

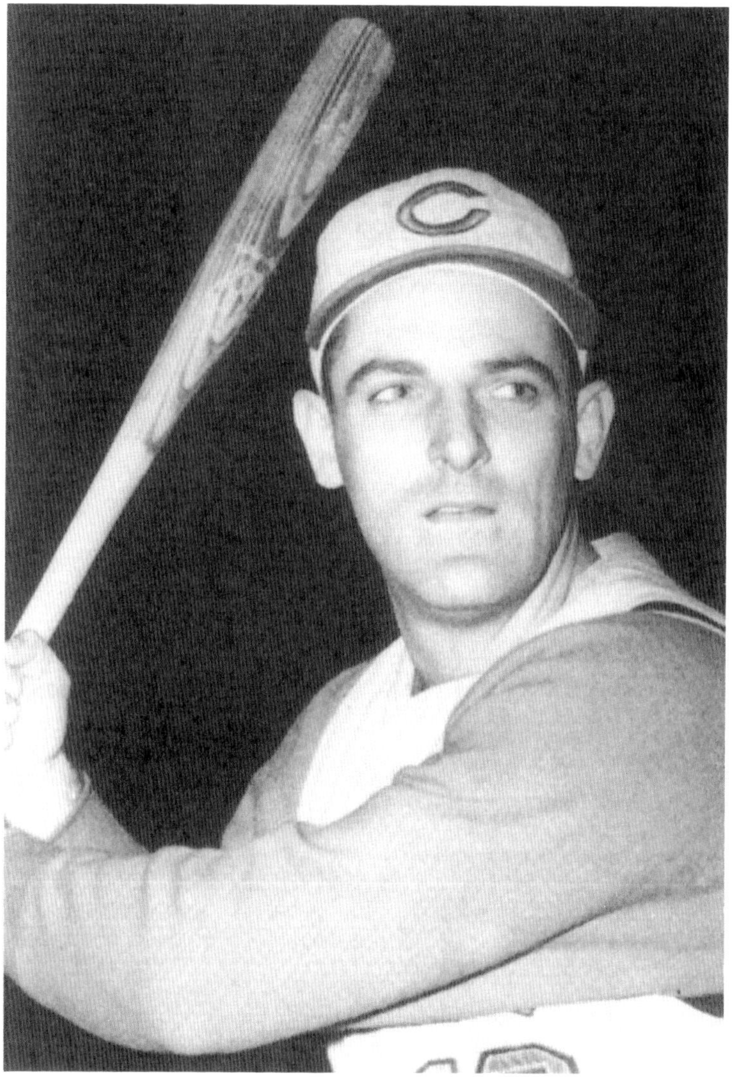

Gene Freese

Eugene Lewis Freese (born January 8, 1934 in Wheeling, West Virginia) was a third baseman in Major League Baseball for 12 seasons (1955–1966). Considered a "journeyman" in professional baseball, he played for the Pittsburgh Pirates (twice), St. Louis Cardinals, Philadelphia Phillies, Chicago White Sox (twice), Cincinnati Reds, and Houston Astros, batting .254 with 115 home runs in 1,115 games. He batted and threw right-handed.

Freese debuted in 1955 with the Pirates and did not disappoint as a rookie. The infielder batted .268 with 23 home runs in 132 games, but it was not until his 1960 season with the Chicago White that his career truly blossomed. In 127 games, Freese batted .273 with 32 doubles and 17 homers. In 1961, he was traded to Cincinnati and promptly played a key role in the Reds winning the pennant while establishing several career bests. Freese batted .277 in 152 games with 159 hits, 78 runs scored, 27 doubles, and 26 home runs.

The following spring, Freese broke an ankle during a spring training game and missed almost the entire 1962 season. He never again played more than 99 games in a single season until he retired following 21 games with Houston. (SN; photograph courtesy WHOF.)

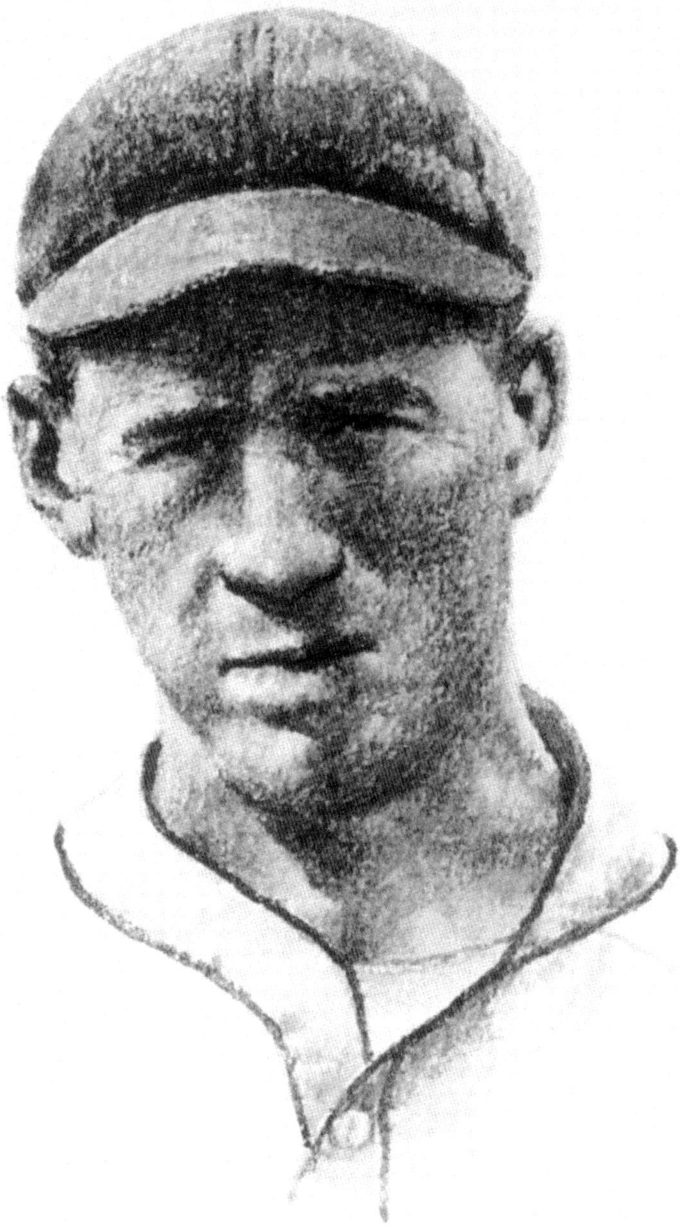

Art Rooney: Wheeling Stogies

Arthur J. Rooney Sr. and his brother Dan, who later became a Franciscan friar and missionary, played baseball for the Wheeling Stogies in the early 1920s. Art was the center fielder, and Dan was the catcher. While playing for Wheeling, the Rooney brothers fought with a whole baseball squad (or as many of them as they could get their hands on) when players from a Frostburg, Maryland, team taunted them with anti-Catholic jibes. Of course, Art is best known as the founder and owner of the Pittsburgh Steelers, but he was also a fine boxer and a solid all-around athlete. He had very fond memories of Wheeling, and his son Art Jr. used this Stogies photograph on the cover of his own book, *Ruanaidh* (Irish Gaelic for "Rooney"), because, as Art Jr. explained, "I knew he would have liked it." (AR.)

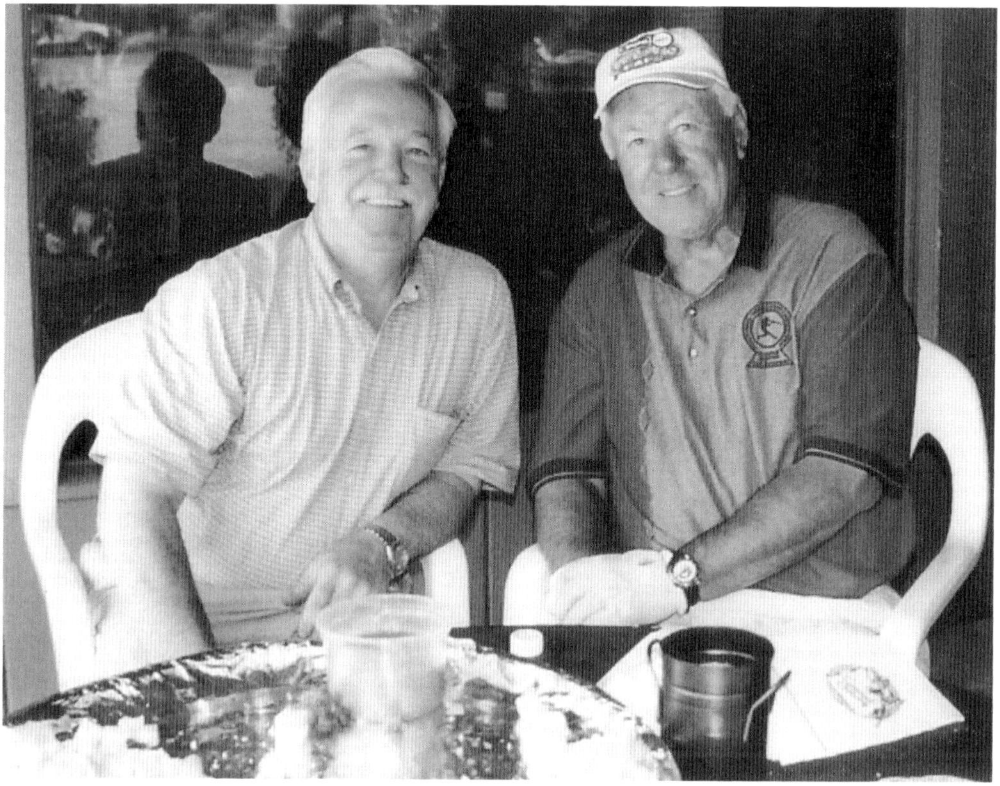

From Wheeling Hospital to Cooperstown

Bill Mazeroski (right) has long been a favorite subject of Pittsburgh sportswriter Jim O'Brien (left), who has written about "Maz" in several of his books and has shared stories about the former Pirate in his appearances at "Lunch With Books" at the Ohio County Public Library. "He is the best kind of sports hero," O'Brien explained, "humble to the core and good company."

"I knew that Maz was born in Wheeling Hospital in 1936," O'Brien continued. "My mother was born at home in Bridgeport, Ohio, on Christmas Eve of 1906. We have relatives there to this day. So I was always aware of athletes from the Ohio Valley." O'Brien has been to the coal patch where Maz walked the rock-strewn paths as a youth. "I used to carry a broomstick and pick up rocks and hit them into the woods," said Maz. "I pretended I was Babe Ruth and I was hitting a home run to win the World Series."

And, of course, that's exactly what Maz did to win the 1960 World Series for the Pittsburgh Pirates over the New York Yankees. He hit the second pitch over the wall to lead off the bottom of the ninth inning in a 10-9 victory in the seventh game. It remains one of the most magical moments in Pittsburgh sports history. Mazeroski is a member of the Baseball Hall of Fame in Cooperstown, a long way from Wheeling.

People in the Ohio Valley remember Maz as a kid they called "Catfish," because he liked to fish in the Ohio River. When O'Brien asked Maz to talk about his beginnings, Maz replied: "My mother went across the bridge to the hospital in Wheeling to deliver me, and then she went back home to Ohio. It was a little place called Witch Hazel . . . back in the hills between Steubenville and Wheeling."

Mazeroski's dad was a promising ballplayer, but lost his chance to turn professional when he lost a toe in a coalmine accident. "He was supposed to go to spring training for the Cleveland Indians that year," Maz recalled. "I wasn't born when he had the accident, and he never talked about it, or about losing his chance to be a big league baseball player. . . . He got to see me play with the Pirates. He liked that. He died in 1959, the year before we won the World Series." After he was a hero in the 1960 World Series, did Maz think about his dad and how proud he would have been to see his son win a World Series? "You always think about things like that, sure." (JO; photograph courtesy www.jimobriensportsauthor.com.)

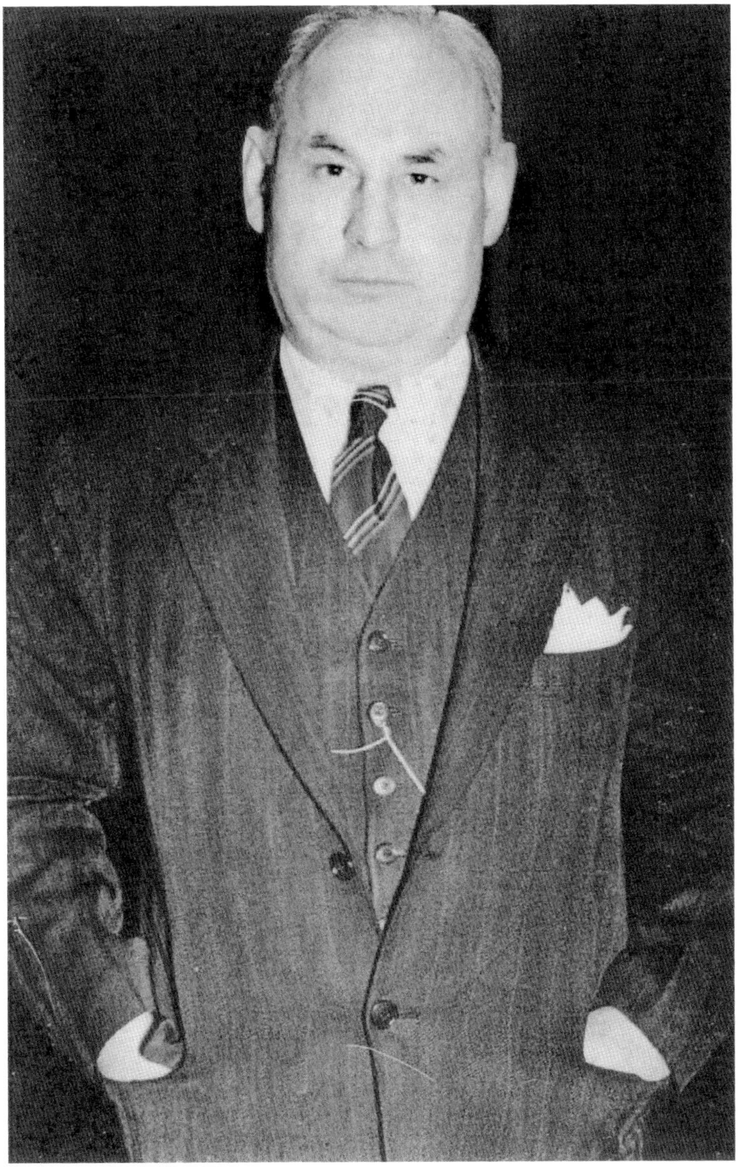

Russell B. Goodwin

Classmates at Wheeling High School nicknamed Goodwin (1893–1968) "Strong Heart" after he played an entire football game with a badly sprained back. While attending Washington and Jefferson College, he was captain and quarterback for the football team, which had a 28-4-1 record and beat the University of Pittsburgh three times during his three-year stint. Olympic athlete Jim Thorpe called Goodwin an "outstanding" player.

After a brief time with the Massillon Tigers, Goodwin graduated in law from Washington and Jefferson, joined the law firm of Judge Frank Nesbitt, and continued his interest in sports by refereeing the Army-Navy Game, the Orange Bowl, and the Rose Bowl. He served on the city council for 16 years before being unanimously elected mayor by the council.

Goodwin had six children and 17 grandchildren on whom he doted and who adored him. They enjoyed his mischievous sense of humor. (KQ; photograph courtesy WHOF.)

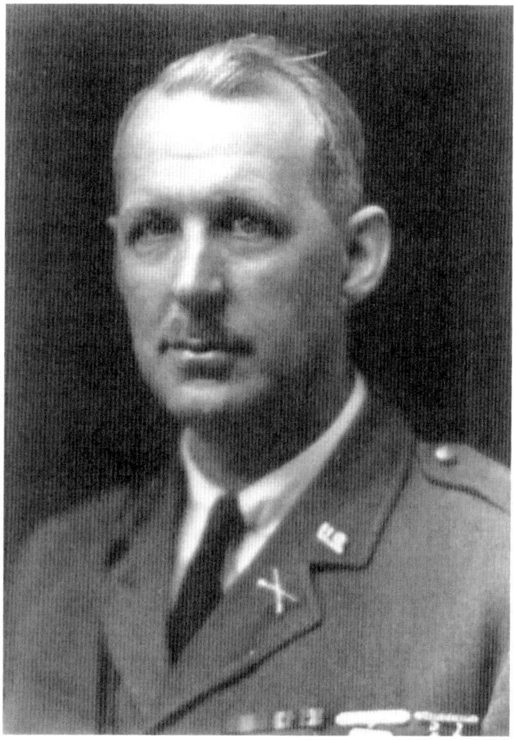

Leland S. Devore
Devore (1889–1939) became Wheeling's first All-American football player, in 1911, while playing tackle for the US Military Academy against the likes of Jim Thorpe and Knute Rockne. Devore also excelled at boxing, wrestling, baseball, and basketball. He accompanied Gen. John J. Pershing on the Pancho Villa expedition and received the Purple Heart as a World War I infantry officer in France. Devore died while still on active duty as a lieutenant colonel in 1939. (WHOF.)

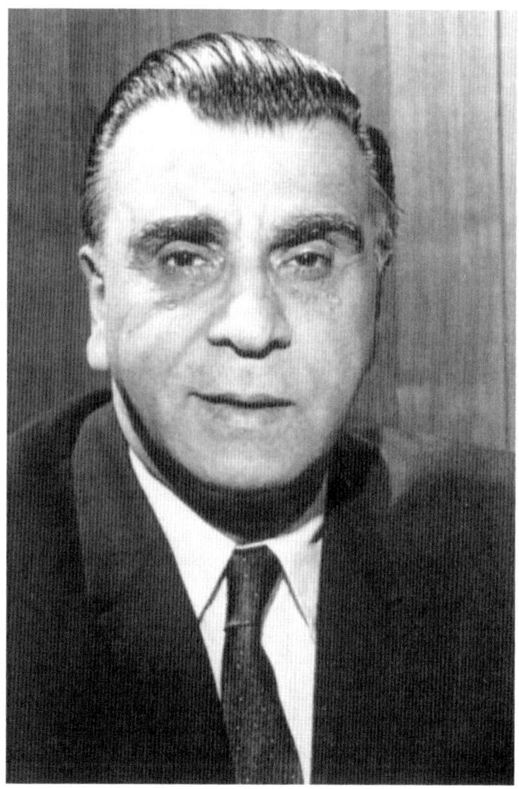

Michael J. Valan
Valan (1910–1986) had a lifelong love affair with sports. In 1948, Valan and business partner Nick Mansuetto founded the Wheeling Puritans (later the Wheeling Blues) of the All-American Basketball Association. Valan is best known as an active founder of the beloved Wheeling Ironmen professional football team. He served as president of the club throughout its existence, from 1962 to 1969. The Ironmen won United Football League championships in 1962 and 1963. (WHOF.)

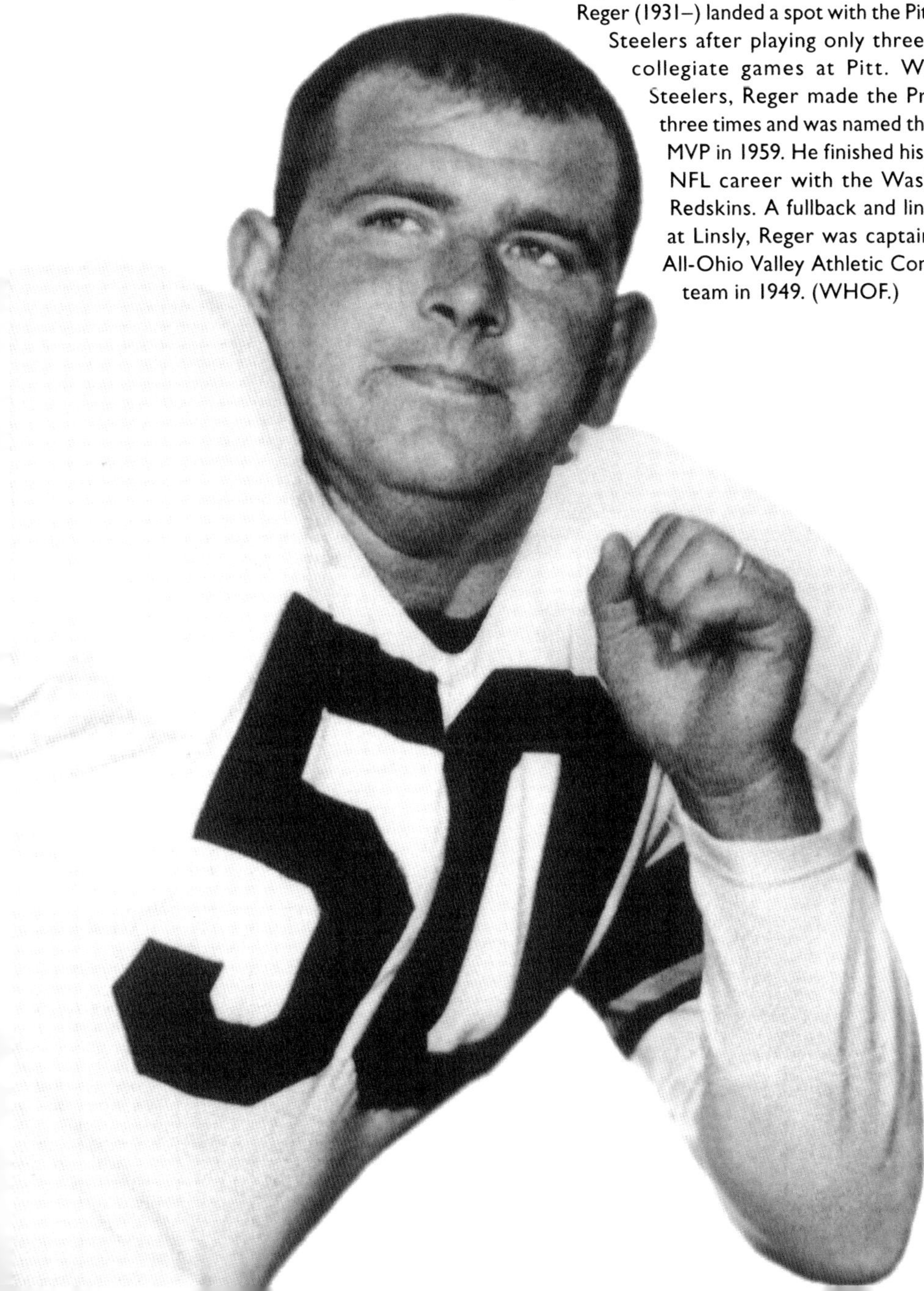

John Reger

Reger (1931–) landed a spot with the Pittsburgh Steelers after playing only three varsity collegiate games at Pitt. With the Steelers, Reger made the Pro Bowl three times and was named the team's MVP in 1959. He finished his 12-year NFL career with the Washington Redskins. A fullback and linebacker at Linsly, Reger was captain of the All-Ohio Valley Athletic Conference team in 1949. (WHOF.)

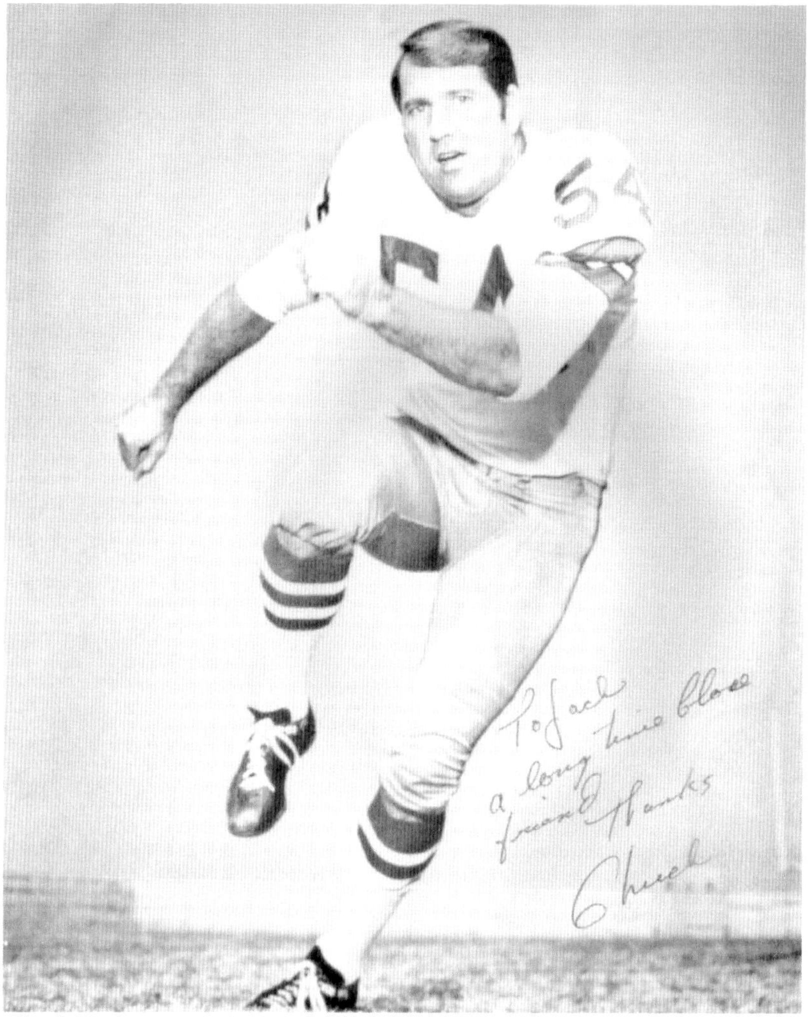

Chuck Howley

An all-state football player at Warwood High School (class of 1954), Howley earned All–Southern Conference honors three times and Southern Conference Athlete of the Year in 1957 at West Virginia University. He made WVU history by starring and lettering in five sports—football, track, wrestling, gymnastics, and swimming. He won the Southern Conference diving championship in 1957. Howley was the first-round draft choice of the Chicago Bears in 1958 and was traded to the Dallas Cowboys in 1961, where he became a six-time All-Pro linebacker, Super Bowl champion, and Super Bowl V MVP. Howley was the first defensive player and the only player from a losing team to be named MVP of a Super Bowl. Noted for his speed, Howley became one of the greatest linebackers to play the game. Legendary Dallas coach Tom Landry once said, "I don't know that I've seen anybody better at linebacker than Howley." He remembered his roots by honoring the top student athlete annually at Warwood High School with the Chuck Howley Award. He was inducted into the West Virginia Sports Hall of Fame, the WVU Athletics Hall of Fame, the Ohio Valley Athletics Hall of Fame, the WVU Academy of Distinguished Alumni, the Ring of Honor at Texas Stadium, and the Texas Sports Hall of Fame. Howley is a successful business owner in Dallas, where he resides with his wife of 54 years, Nancy, also a Wheeling native. They are blessed with two children and six grandchildren. He enjoys raising foundation-bred quarter horses at his ranch in nearby Wills Point, Texas. (MB, TB, MAH; photograph courtesy Jack Schuetz/Chuck Howley.)

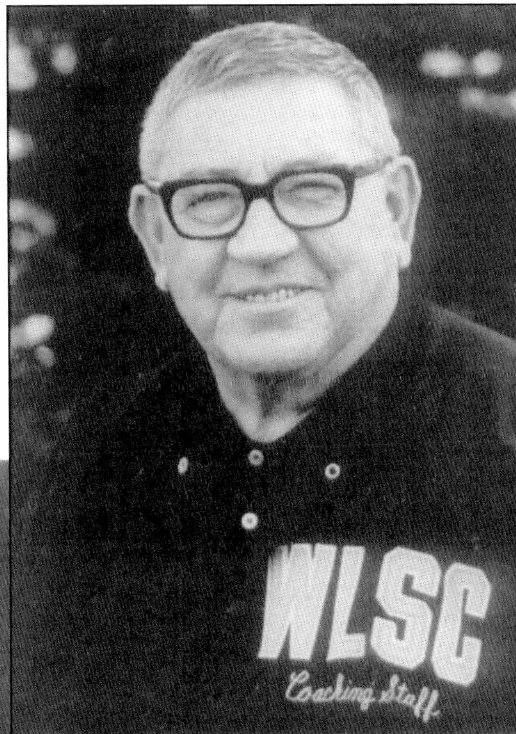

Bob Roe
Bob Roe (1908–1984) coached football for 44 years at Warwood and Wheeling High Schools and at West Liberty State College, winning a total of 232 games. He mentored many players who went on to collegiate and professional careers. Roe also piloted West Virginia to a 13-7 victory over Ohio at Wheeling Stadium in 1940 in the first Ohio–West Virginia All-Star Game. The versatile coach also led the 1946 Warwood track team to a state championship. (WHOF.)

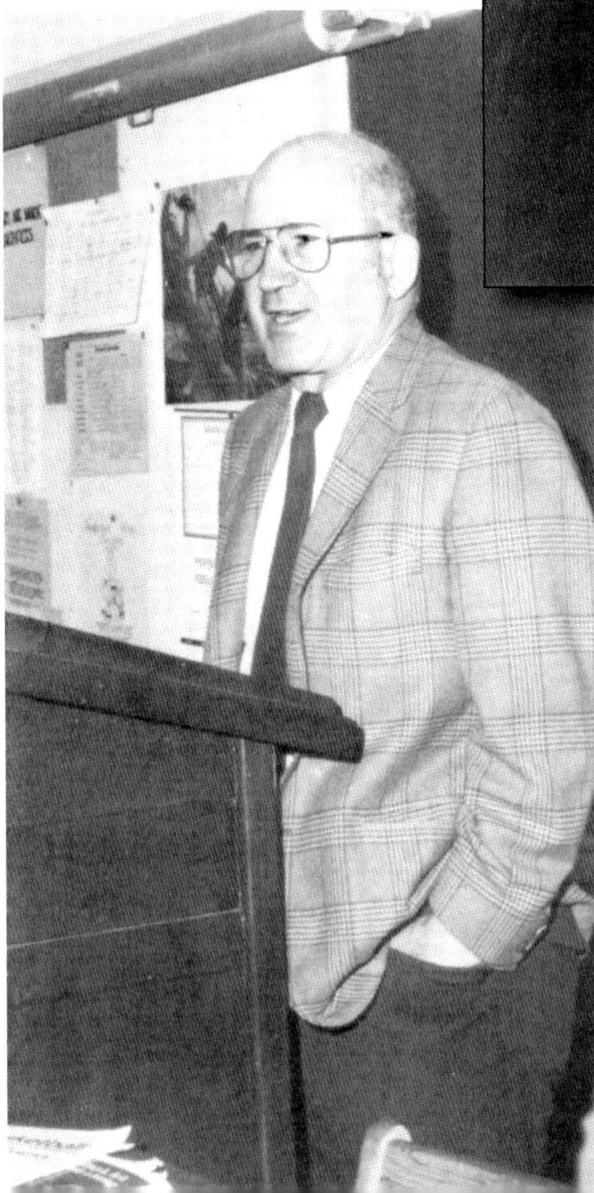

Jim Foti
A basketball coach for 38 years, Jim Foti (1910–2004) compiled an impressive 466 victories. The Jamestown, New York, native came to Wheeling to coach basketball and football at Central Catholic High in 1942. Known as "the Little General," Foti led five Central basketball teams to state Catholic championships, and his Warwood teams appeared in the state tournament seven times. While coaching football at Warwood, Foti mentored NFL legend Chuck Howley. In 1947–1948, he piloted the professional Wheeling Puritans basketball team. (WHOF; photograph courtesy Warwood High School.)

Bernie Mehen

Bernard "Bernie" Mehen (1918–2007) played on two state championship basketball teams at Wheeling High (1936 and 1938). In his senior year, when younger brother Dick joined him, the Gold and Blue went 24-0. Coach Everett Brinkman called the Mehens "the greatest players I ever coached." Bernie went on to play for the Youngstown Bears and the Center Wheeling Merchants, where Jule Rivlin was among his teammates. When Rivlin was made player-coach of the Toledo Jeeps of the National Basketball League, he sent for the Mehen brothers. (WHOF.)

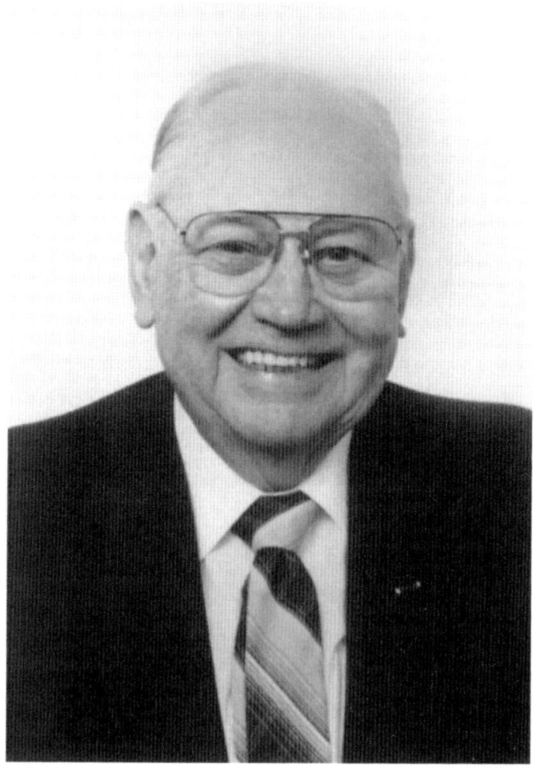

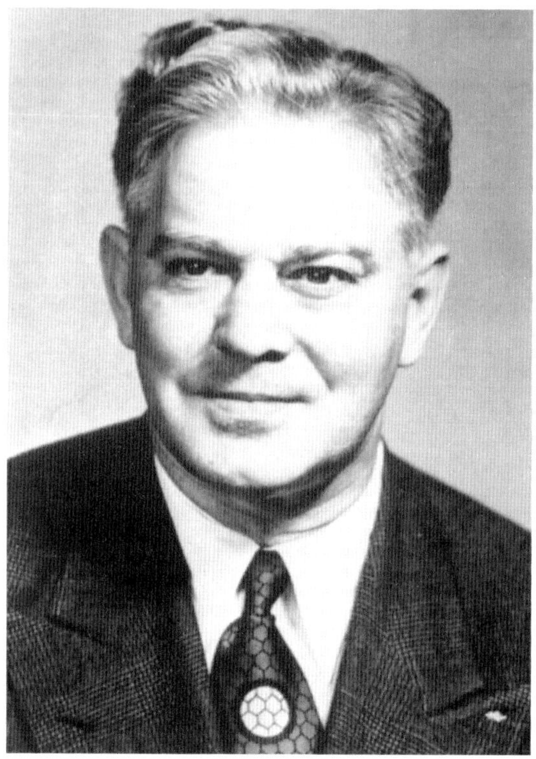

Everett Brinkman

With 405 career wins, Brinkman (1902–1972) was a master coach. A strict disciplinarian, "Brinkie" was a pioneer of the two-handed jump shot and the fast break. His Wheeling High basketball teams won five state championships. Moreover, the South Wheeling native was an outstanding football coach, and teams he piloted laid claim to four state crowns in the autumn sport. He coached the first Wheeling football squad to play under lights. (WVHOF.)

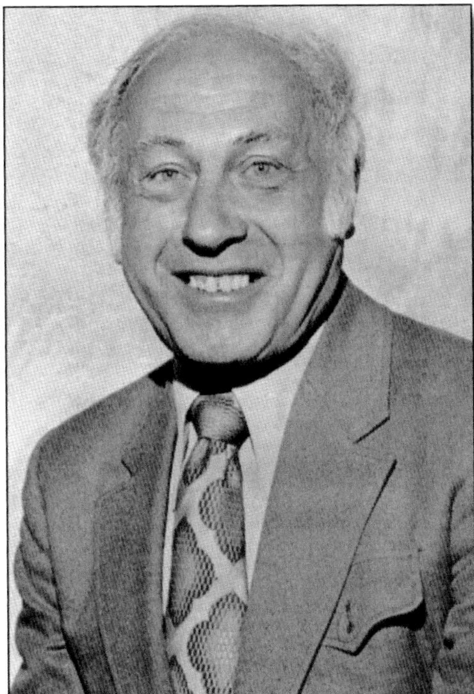

Jule Rivlin
An all-state basketball guard for Triadelphia High School, Rivlin (1917–2002) set a Marshall College season scoring record with 530 points. He later coached Marshall to two Mid-America titles. Rivlin played professionally with the Toledo Jeeps and the Wheeling Blues. In 1947, he was the most valuable player in the World Tournament in Chicago, which featured the nation's best professional teams, including the Harlem Globetrotters. (WHOF.)

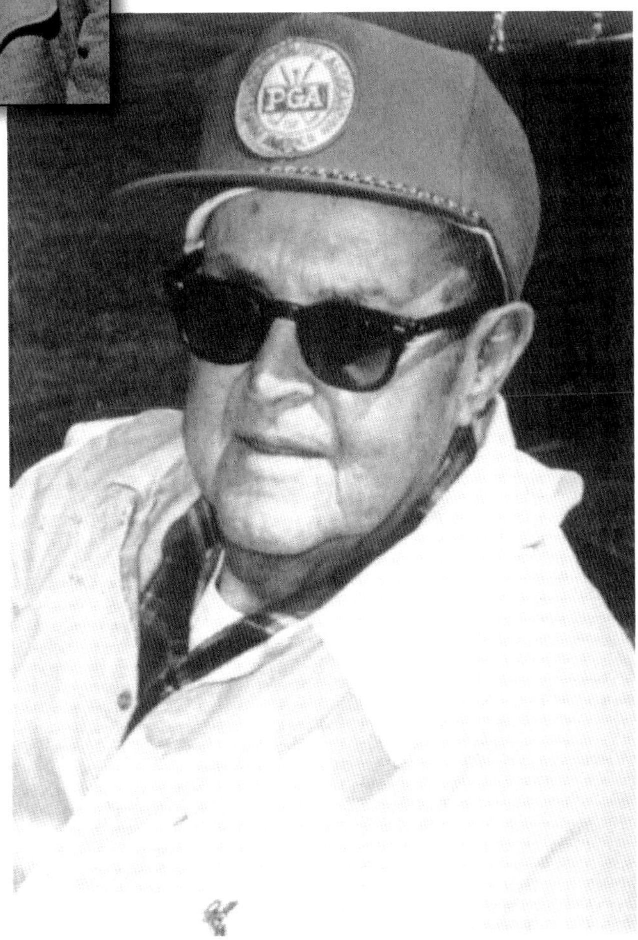

Bob Biery
After spending his childhood years as a caddy, Bob Biery (1901–1991) developed into West Virginia's first native golf professional. As a protégé of golf architect Emmett Deveroux, Biery helped build the Wheeling Country Club course. In 1925, he built the course at Wheeling Park, using "mules and scoops." He built Oglebay Park's Crispin course in 1927 and founded Oglebay's Caddy Camp. In later years, Biery cruised Oglebay's Speidel course in a golf cart as a ranger. (WHOF.)

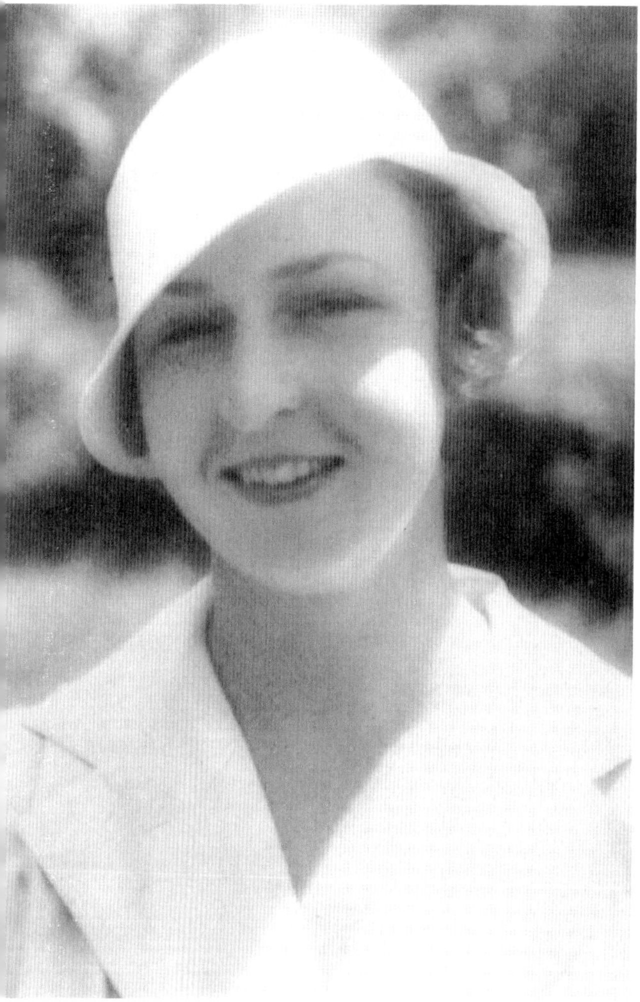

Mary E. Stifel Quarrier

"Fritzi" Stifel Quarrier (1904–1967) won 10 West Virginia amateur women's golf championships and competed in the US Amateur Championship 10 times, reaching the semifinal round in 1935. A finalist in the 1927 Canadian Amateur, she won the Mason-Dixon Amateur in 1934. Also an accomplished musician, Stifel Quarrier holds the distinction of being the first woman elected to the West Virginia Sports Hall of Fame. (WHOF.)

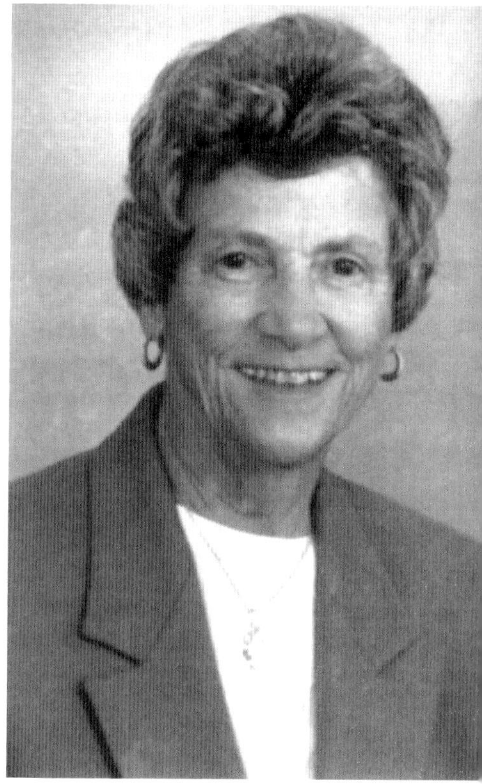

Sally Carroll

Carroll (1926–2012) was a seven-time West Virginia Women's Amateur golf champion and six-time runner-up. A schoolteacher, Carroll advanced to the fourth round of the British Amateur in 1964 and was the second-lowest amateur in the US Open twice. Chair of the USGA's National Girl's Tournament for 10 years, Carroll won the Card Walker Award in 1984 for her contributions to junior golf nationally. (WHOF.)

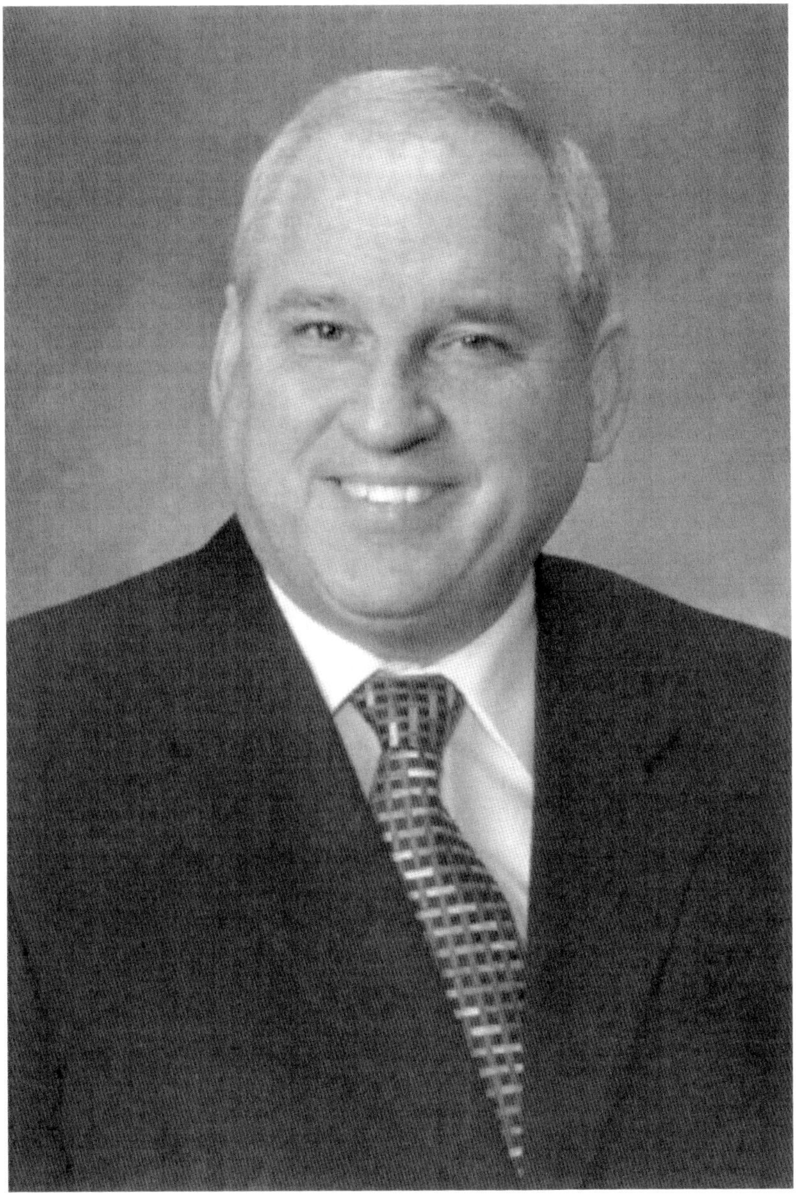

Denny Magruder

Life has not always been easy for Denny Magruder, executive director of the Greater Wheeling Sports and Entertainment Authority. Born on Wheeling Island and raised in Center Wheeling, he learned the meaning of hard work at an early age, and he experienced the cruelty of life when he lost three members of his family to a house fire on New Year's Eve. Denny kept a full-time job at the *Wheeling Intelligencer* and worked a split shift in the mail room while putting himself through West Liberty College.

"I'm a believer in people's lives touching each other. I am so lucky to have had all the right breaks. I feel blessed that my three children live within walking distance of my home and the joy of seeing my grandchildren brings me such happiness. I love Wheeling . . . we have the best schools, post-graduate schools, and park system. We celebrate all four seasons here. Our Capitol Theatre is a jewel in our crown." (KQ; photograph courtesy WHOF.)

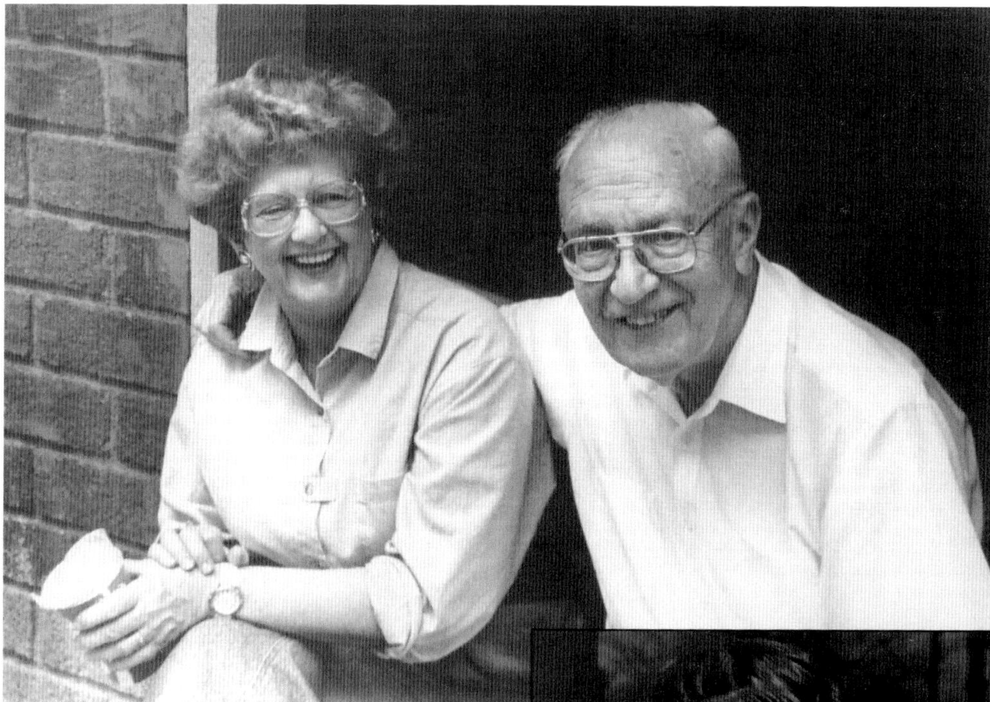

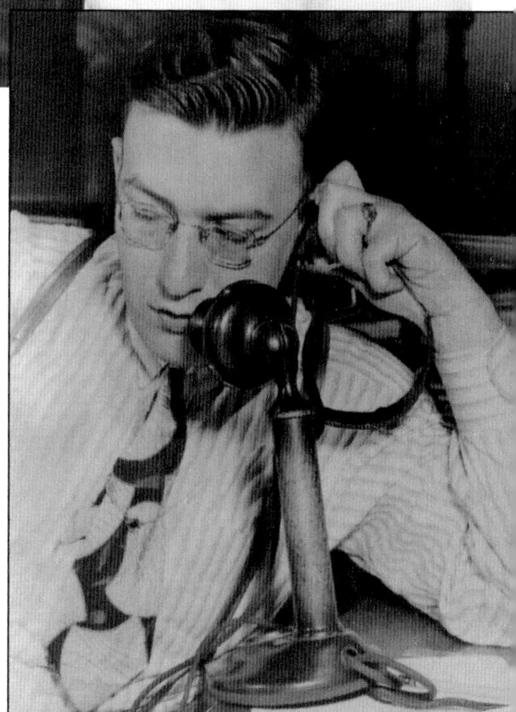

Bill Van Horne

For decades, Bill Van Horne was sports in the Upper Ohio Valley. Most knew him from his weekly columns in the *Times-Leader* and *Wheeling News-Register*, where he covered everything from WVU football to prep wrestling to the Pittsburgh Pirates' 1960 World Series championship.

Others knew him as a key ingredient in the success of Wheeling's sports teams, from the semipro Wheeling Ironmen of the 1960s to today's Nailers hockey club. His friends knew him as a loving husband; he shared a life, from newsroom to living room, with his cherished wife, Gladys. She is an Ohio Valley institution in her own right; her work appeared just a few sections down from Bill's in the Sunday papers. He was a loving husband, a dedicated newspaperman always quick with a kind word of encouragement, and, above all, a man who was fair, honest, and beloved by all who knew him. (PR; photographs courtesy Gladys Van Horne.)

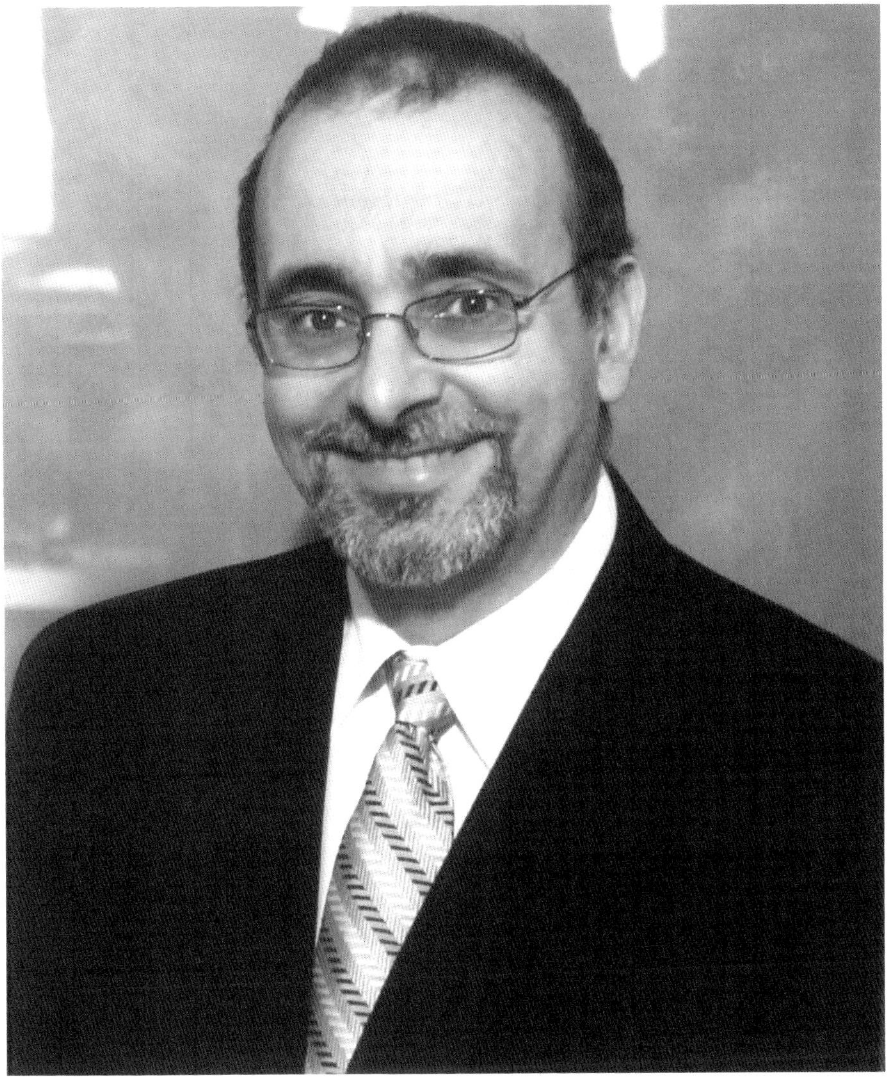

George Kellas
Kellas (1956–2009) started hosting radio and television shows during his teenage years at Wheeling Park High School only because he asked if he could. He presented his idea to former Patriots head basketball coach Sam Andy. "No one had ever asked me that question before George did. I told him if he could do it well, to go ahead and do it."

Following his graduation from West Liberty University, Kellas provided the Wheeling-Steubenville television and radio markets with an ESPN-like style of delivery before that cable network launched in September 1979. He began his career in radio in 1977, and spent 12 years at WTRF-TV and eight years at WTOV-TV as a sports anchor and commentator. He founded and co-owned the Ohio Valley Greyhounds arena football team, which won the national title in 2002 and 2003.

He hosted the *George Kellas Radio Talk Show* for WKKX from its inception in September 2004. "His three children meant everything to him, and his wife Sherri was the backbone of who he was," John Blackmore told the Wheeling media. "He said that to me many times. He was the most wonderful, genuine person I knew. He wore his emotions on his sleeve, and he wouldn't lie even if it was the easy thing to do. He would say it how it is." (SN; photograph courtesy WKKX.)

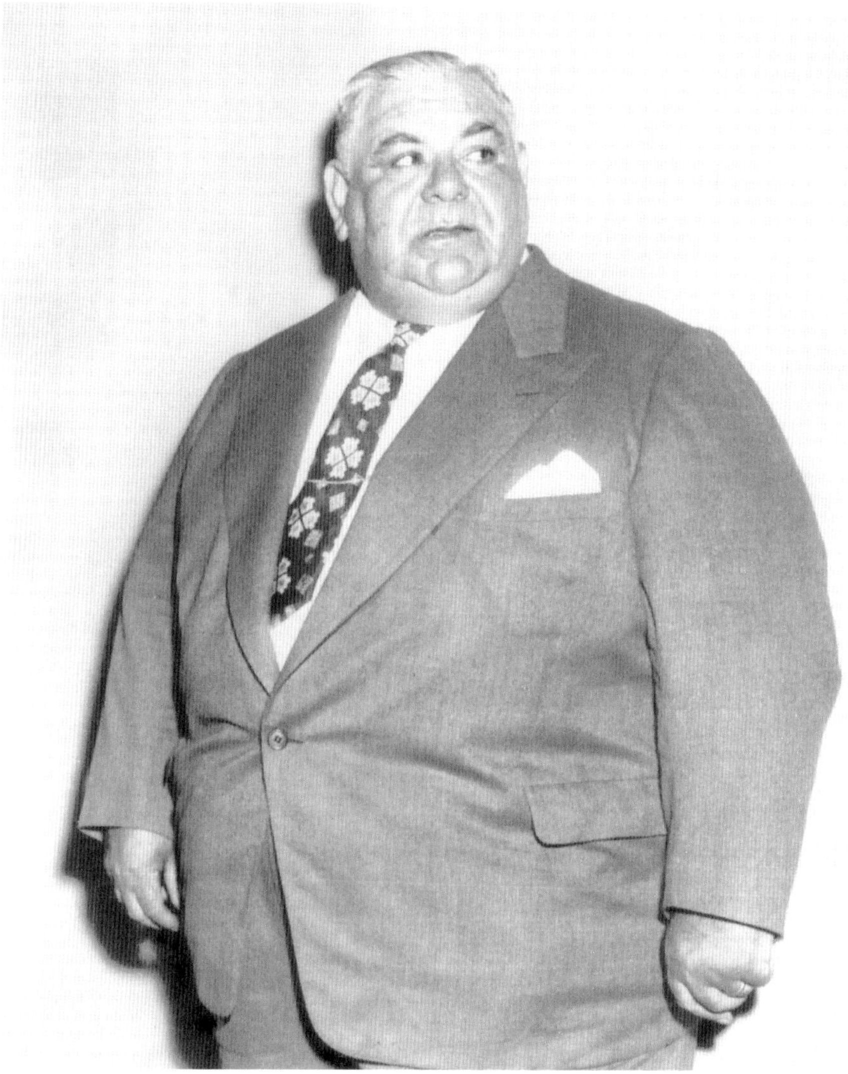

William G. Lias

"Big Bill" Lias (1900–1970) was born in Greece; at birth, he weighed 12.5 pounds. He was called "Butt Boy" in school (though, not to his face). Lias controlled the illegal rackets in Wheeling with an iron fist and an extensive web of mob ties. The rotund racketeer was associated with the Purple Gang of Detroit and was also the subject of a *Life* magazine article. He had four convictions and served a couple of prison terms for illegal booze, though many acquaintances hint that he got away with much more than those charges. He was questioned in the death of his first wife, Gladys, the explosion at Nick Frank's Coffee Shop, the bombing of "Skinny" Thorton's home, the fire at Sam Grossfield's, and the car bombing of rival gangster Paul Hankish. He was suspected of being behind the shooting of his cousin Mike days before he was to testify against Lias. Big Bill owned or had interests in the Wheeling Downs Race Track, Zeller's Steak House, Club Diamond, White Front, The Bachelor's Club, and the Roosevelt Restaurant. In 1948, Lias was charged with tax evasion and, four years later, his beloved Wheeling Downs was seized. In 1953, the federal government failed in its attempt to deport Wheeling's most infamous citizen. Lias mimicked an Al Capone gimmick to garner public support, giving away turkeys to Wheeling's poor citizens during Thanksgiving. (BC.)

CHAPTER FOUR

Business and Industry

As a frontier outpost located on the Ohio River, Wheeling developed into a transportation hub and a bustling trading outpost. The river brought rough-hewn characters like legendary keel-boatman Mike Fink to Wheeling's ports. The town is known as the "birthplace of the American steamboat," as Henry Shreve built the *Washington* on the north bank of Wheeling Creek in 1815, and innovative steam engine builder Arthur Phillips was operating his boat works in North Wheeling by 1832. The National Road and B&O Railroad brought even more opportunity to town.

Farmers from all over the valley brought their produce and livestock to market in Wheeling, where butchers, grocers, and bakers turned raw materials into food products, and entrepreneurs made everything from glass and nails to stogies and beer. Small dry-goods wholesalers and retailers founded Wheeling's great department stores. After the Civil War, Wheeling grew into a major steel-making center and helped supply the US military through two world wars.

The modern era brought difficult changes, and Wheeling's entrepreneurs are a tough, creative group—survivors determined to reinvent their hometown while honoring its fascinating past.

Gary E. West, for example, established Valley Welding Supply Company, which grew into a multistate, multi-million-dollar corporation. Alan Lestini operates Words and Music, one of the last independently owned bookstores in the area, still selling "real books" in the digital age. Dominic Agostino and Howard Long made their fortunes in large-scale food processing. Agostino rose from pastry chef to founder of Aladdin Food Management, managing food services for local colleges, while Long went from grocery delivery boy to founder of Coronet Foods, an international vegetable processing company. A fitness enthusiast, Long's generosity made possible the Howard Long Wellness Center at Wheeling Hospital. Ernie Pandelos founded Ernie's Esquire Restaurant and Lounge along Bethlehem Boulevard in the 1950s. It grew into one of Wheeling's fine old supper clubs, hosting national music acts, including Tom Jones, Tanya Tucker, and John Corbett.

Wheeling has always been well known for its distinctive foods (often reflecting its immigrant heritage), including sweet culinary memories like the family-friendly Elby's Big Boy (the Boury family), Green's Donuts, Louis (Mamakos) Famous Hotdogs, and Saseen's Diner, as well as surviving stalwarts like Dicarlo's Pizza, Coleman's Fish, Figaretti's Italian Restaurant, and the Fadoul family's Lebanon Bakery. Whether managed by the Miller family or by Charlie Schlegel, the Ye Olde Alpha has been a favorite eatery and watering hole for decades. And the tradition is continued by restaurateurs like Susan Haddad (Later Alligator) and Martin Tse (Golden Chopsticks).

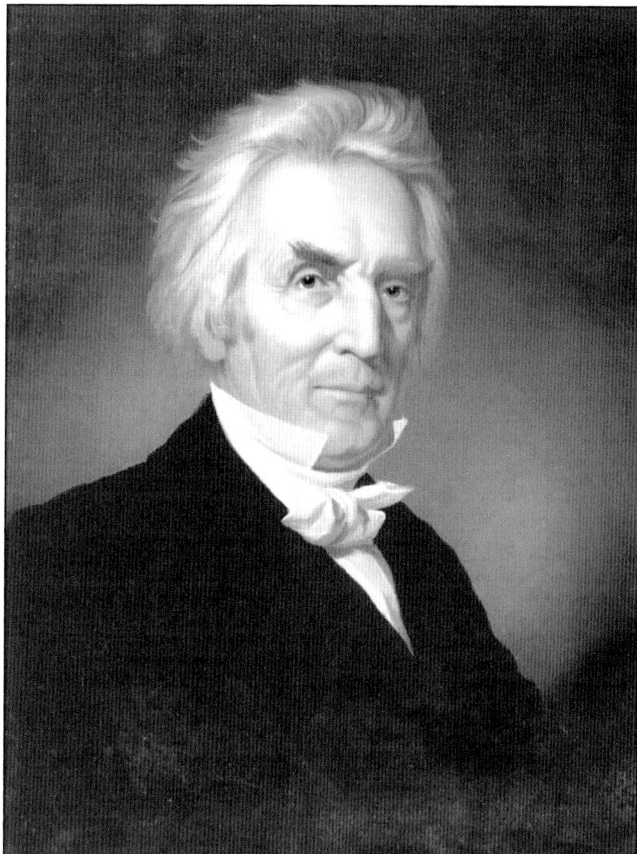

Alexander Campbell
Born in Ireland and educated in Scotland, Campbell (1788–1866) came to America and was ordained a minister in 1812. He was among the founders of the Disciples of Christ and Churches of Christ, and in 1840, he founded Bethany College. In 1823, he set up a printing shop, where he published his own books as well as the journals *The Christian Baptist* and the *Millennial Harbinger* until his death in 1866. (EP; image courtesy Library of Congress.)

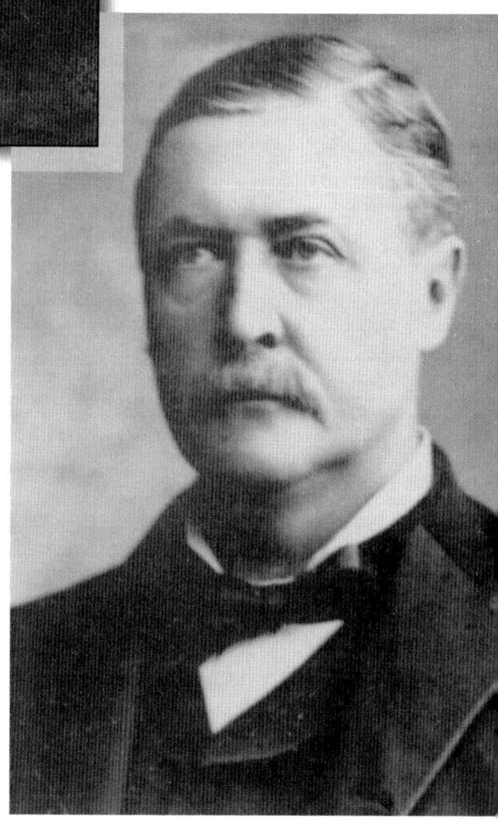

Archibald W. Campbell
Archibald Campbell (1833–1899), the nephew of Alexander Campbell, was educated at Bethany College. He purchased the *Wheeling Daily Intelligencer* in 1856, became its editor, and used the paper to express his abolitionist views. A staunch Unionist and early member of the Republican Party, he supported Abraham Lincoln for president. By 1861, Campbell was one of the most influential leaders in the West Virginia statehood movement. He served as Wheeling postmaster during the Civil War. (EP; photograph courtesy WHOF.)

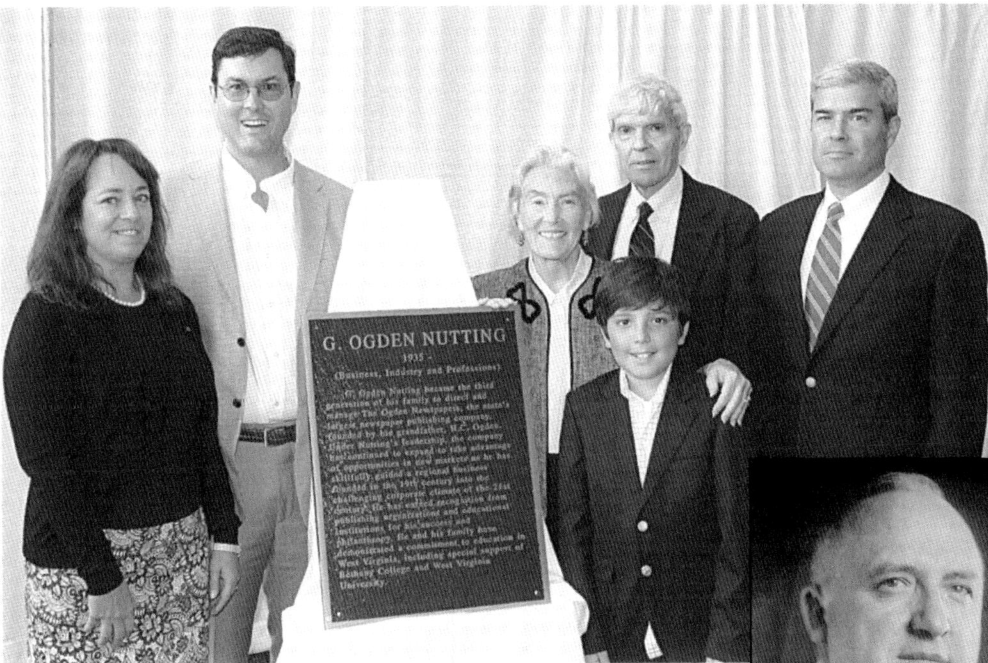

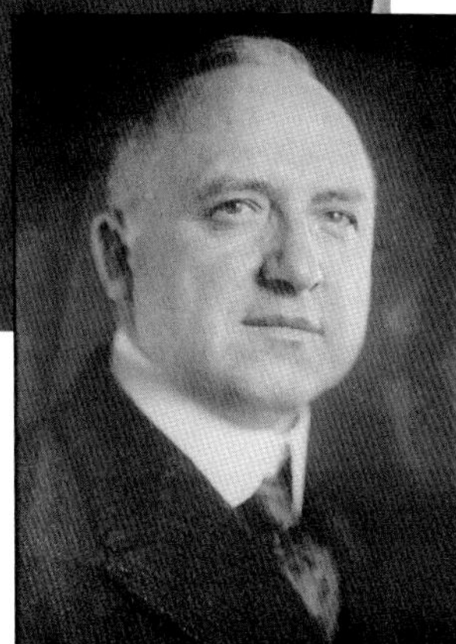

The Ogden Family

For more than 200 years, members of the Ogden family have been proud West Virginians with a deep commitment to the state. H.C. Ogden (inset) was just 21 years old when, in 1890, he founded his first newspaper, the *Wheeling Evening News*. In 1904, he bought the *Intelligencer*, and in 1935, he merged the *Wheeling Register* with his *Evening News*. He pursued the causes of tax reform, worker protection, and the advancement of humanitarian legislation, and he campaigned for the city's first public high school. H.C Ogden helped find a modern home for the public library and led the fight for the acceptance of the gift of Oglebay Park. He was a founding member of Oglebay Institute.

Subsequent presidents and publishers of Ogden Newspapers included H.C. Ogden's daughters Frances Ogden Stubblefield and Margaret Ogden Nutting, his grandson G. Ogden Nutting and, now, his great-grandsons Robert McLain Nutting (second from left) and William Ogden Nutting (far right), whose parents are G. Ogden (fourth from left) and Betty Woods "Snookie" Nutting (third from left).

Great-grandsons Bill and Bob Nutting have carried on the family tradition of contributing to the community. Robert is president and chief executive officer of Ogden Newspapers, chairman of the board of the Pittsburgh Pirates, chairman of Seven Springs Resort, and serves on the boards of Linsly and Bethany with his father. In 2010, he received the YMCA Light of the Valley Award. Bill is vice president of Ogden Newspapers, president of the Southern Newspaper Publishers Association, and serves on the board of governors of WVU. Their parents remain very active in the community, and G. Ogden continues the family's interest in Oglebay, serving as a Wheeling park commissioner.

Betty "Snookie" Nutting is yet another Wheeling treasure. An art major at Mary Washington College, her interest in historic houses began when she became involved with the home of George Washington's mother in nearby Fredericksburg. Her interest in preservation led her to buy a house in North Wheeling. Working alongside carpenters and electricians, she learned how to convert the beautiful but unwanted house into a jewel. Snookie became a founding member of Friends of Wheeling (the oldest preservation group in the state) and served for nine years on the board of advisors of the National Trust for Historic Preservation. She was the first president of the Preservation Alliance of West Virginia. (KQ; photograph courtesy of Gail P. Atkinson, inset courtesy of WHOF.)

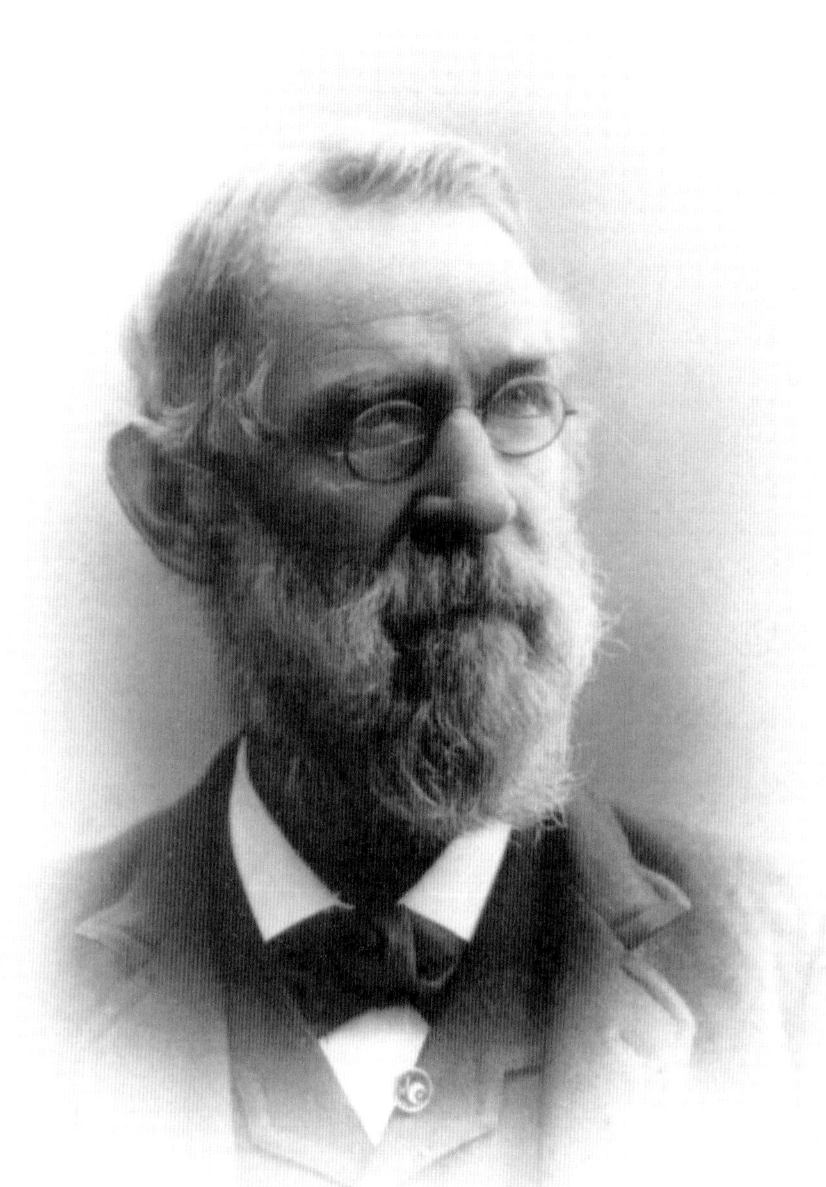

Andrew Sweeney

Andrew James Sweeney (1829–1893), an innovative businessman, brought electricity to the city of Wheeling; served as a militia colonel in the Civil War; manufactured engines, mill machinery, foundry castings, and steamboats; incorporated the Citizens Railway Company, and served nine terms as mayor. An inventor with a number of patents, Sweeney was noted as a hard worker who, at the close of day, was as "grimy as the humblest man in his employ." Twice married, Sweeney fathered 13 children and was dubbed one of "the most popular men" in the city. At 66 years of age, he died in his North Main Street home on Valentine's Day and was buried in Greenwood Cemetery (which he helped to incorporate). He was intimately connected with community improvements, including street, railway, paid fire department, fire alarm telegraph, and many new bridges and shipping facilities. (CJu; photograph courtesy WHOF.)

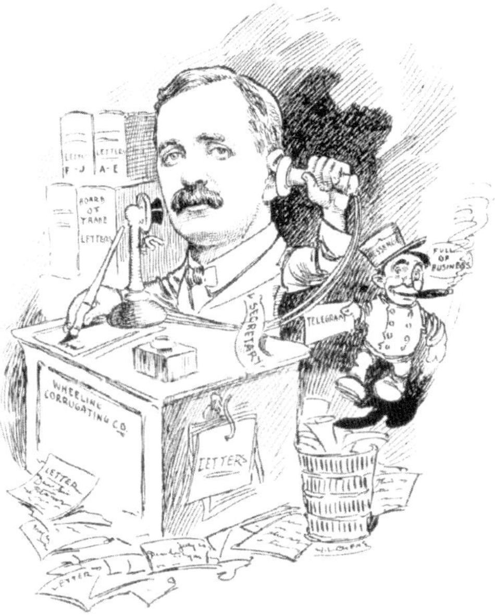

ALEX. GLASS
Secretary Wheeling Corrugating Co.
Wheeling, W. Va.

Alexander Glass

Glass (1858–1941) envisioned a new, lightweight metal building material: sheet steel coated with zinc to protect it from rust and then corrugated to increase its strength. Wheeling Corrugating Co. was established in 1890. Under the guidance of the energetic Glass, the company diversified, producing various light metal products, including roofing, metal ceilings, and tin plate. Glass later merged the LaBelle Iron Works, Whitaker-Glessner Co., and the Wheeling Steel and Iron Co. into the Wheeling Steel Corporation. (WHOF; image courtesy OCPL.)

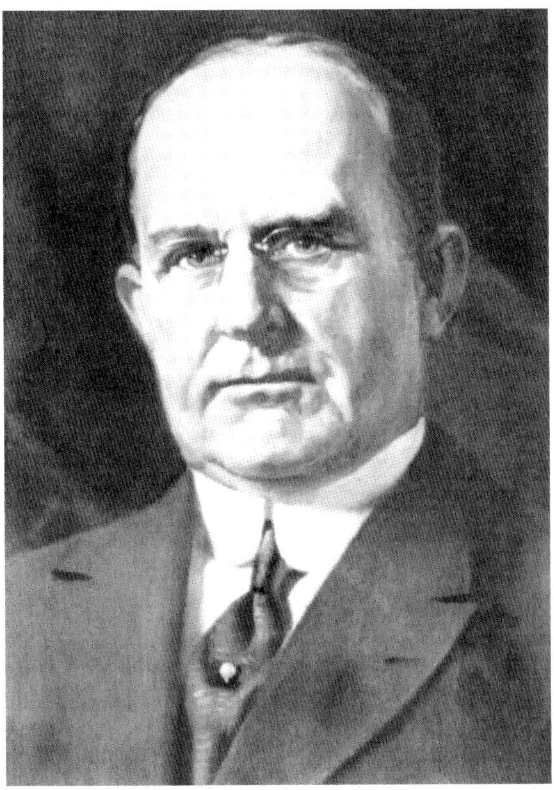

Earl Oglebay

Earl William Oglebay (1849–1926) worked in his father's grocery business, became a bank president, and acquired iron ore mines. He bought Waddington farm in Ohio County and raised blooded horses and cattle. The farm was a center for scientific agricultural research, particularly in the breeding of sheep and dairy cattle. Oglebay deeded his farm to the City of Wheeling, and it was transformed into the beautiful Oglebay Park. His nephew Crispin Oglebay founded Oglebay Institute, and his grandson Courtney Burton continued the family interest. (WHOF; image courtesy Museums of Oglebay Institute.)

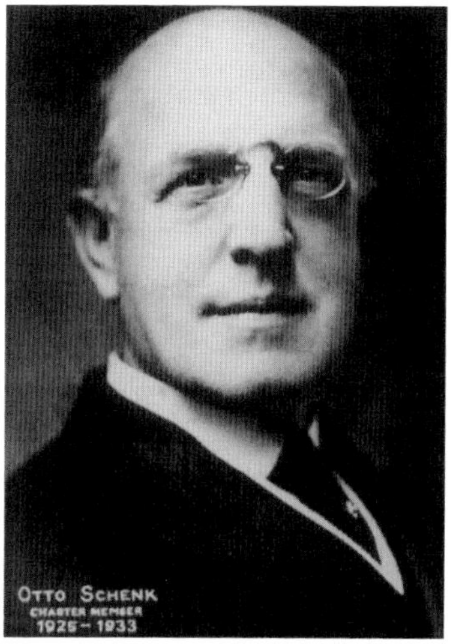

Otto Schenk

Schenk (1863–1933) started in the meatpacking business, then led insurance companies, banks, and other businesses. He was the first chairman of the Wheeling Park Commission and, along with W.E. Stone, helped raise the funds to acquire what would become Wheeling Park. A plaque at the park dedicated to Schenk reads, "His devotion to the cause of public recreation distinguished him most in the eyes of people who enjoyed, and who will enjoy in perpetuity, the things his kindness and interest helped make possible." (WHOF.)

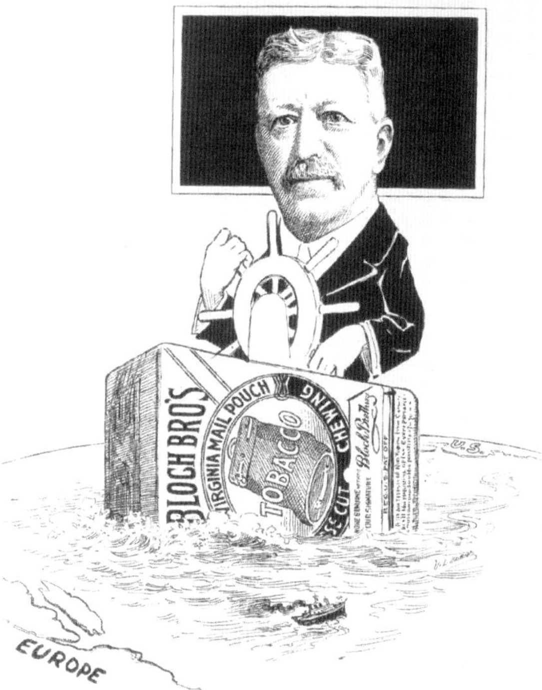

SAMUEL S. BLOCH
President of Bloch Bros. Tobacco Co.
Wheeling, W. Va.

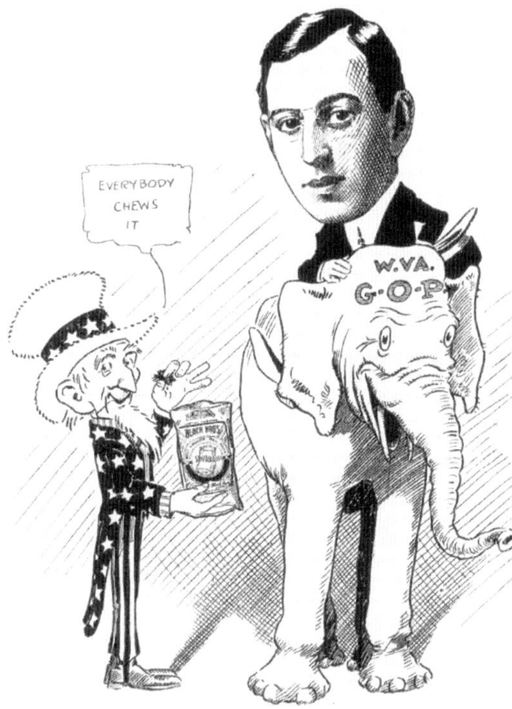

JESSE A. BLOCH
First Vice President Bloch Bros. Tobacco Co.
Wheeling, W. Va.

Bloch Brothers

Samuel S. Bloch (1850–1937) cofounded Bloch Brothers Tobacco. The company was known for using scraps of tobacco from its stogie-making, packaging the tobacco in a paper pouch, and advertising the resulting product as Mail Pouch on hundreds of painted barns across the nation. Samuel's son Jesse A. Bloch (1879–1951) was elected to the state senate, where he championed labor laws and women's suffrage. Samuel's great-grandson Stuart F. Bloch was the last Bloch to run Bloch Brothers. He also served as president of the United States Golf Association. (WHOF; images courtesy OCPL.)

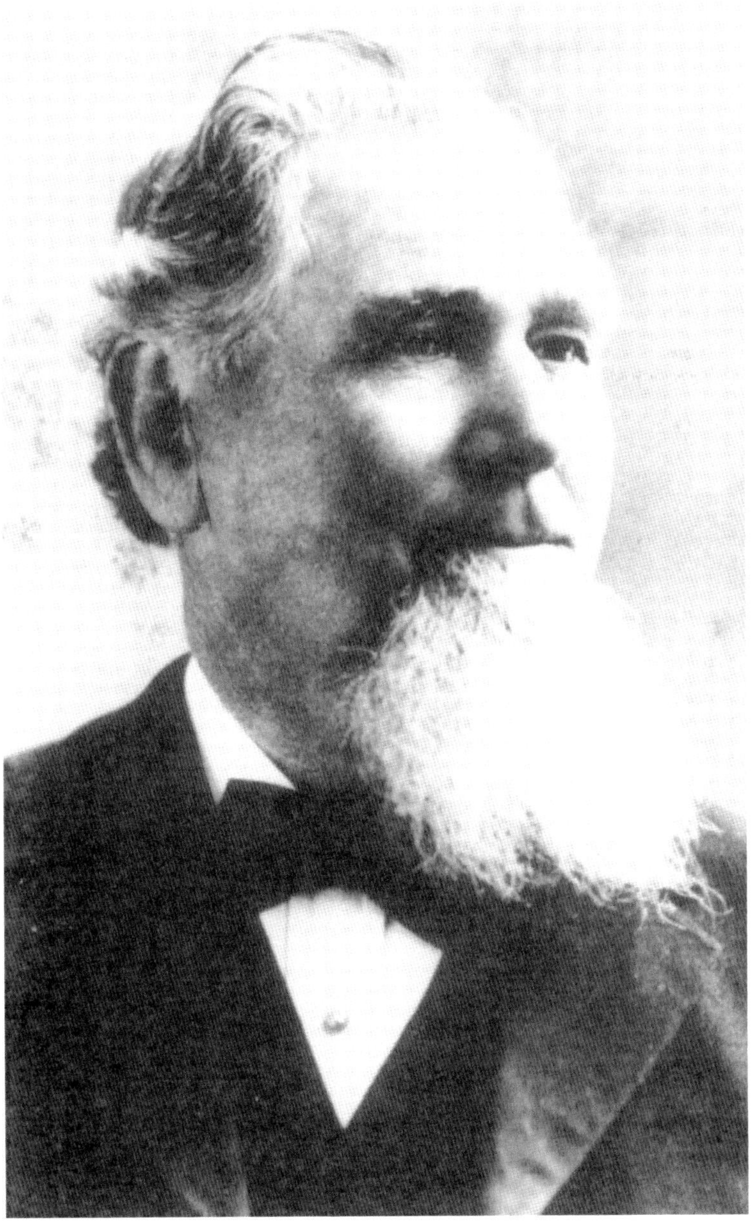

Mifflin Marsh

Mifflin Marsh started Marsh Stogies in 1840, selling cigars out of a basket at the Wheeling waterfront. He sold his hand-rolled stogies to anyone who stepped off a riverboat: steamboat captains, dockworkers, and high-society passengers. Mifflin Marsh made sure that each Conestoga wagon driver on the National Road had a stogie in hand. His famous cigars have reportedly been smoked by President Lincoln, Senators Henry Clay and Daniel Webster, Generals Sam Houston and Santa Anna, P.T. Barnum, John Wayne, Annie Oakley, and Andrew Mellon. Mark Twain said of the product, "Then once more, changed off, so that I might acquire the subtler flavor of the Wheeling Toby. . . . I discovered that the worst cigars, so called, are the best for me, after all." Marsh's iconic cigar boxes have also appeared in several movies, including, *Jaws*, *Missing*, *Fool's Parade*, and *The Green Mile*. (BC.)

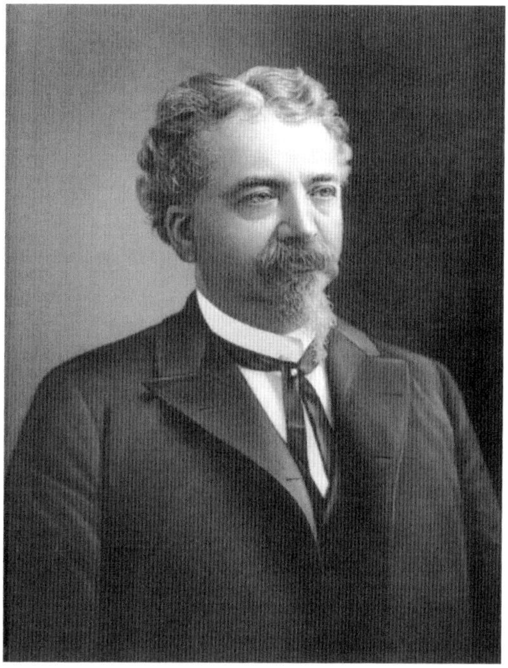

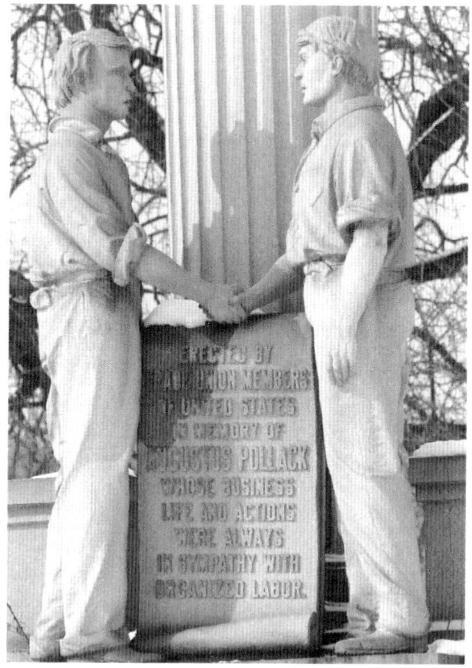

Augustus Pollack

Pollack (1830–1906) established a notions and fancy-goods business in Wheeling in 1854. A German Jew, Pollack was an active member of Wheeling's large German immigrant community. He helped establish a German American volunteer company during the Civil War and, later, a German-language newspaper. He also helped raise money for widows and orphans of German soldiers killed in the Franco-Prussian War (1870–1871). Pollack served on the board of the Wheeling Library Association (precursor to the Ohio County Public Library) and was named president of Wheeling's 1885 Saengerfest (a German singing festival).

Founded in 1871, Pollack's signature business, Crown Stogies, grew to become West Virginia's largest cigar manufacturer. When built, his factory, spanning Eighteenth and Nineteenth Streets from Chapline Street to Eoff Street, was one of the largest cigar factories in the world. In his 1906 obituary, the *Wheeling News-Register* declared, "no one deserves more credit for the Wheeling stogie's prestige."

Pollack did not ask or expect more of his employees than he did of himself. He paid them well for the period, and maintained an open-door policy regarding employee concerns over work conditions, hours, and wages—an unusually progressive attitude for a 19th-century entrepreneur. While his contemporaries in steel and coal faced regular and often violent struggles over labor issues, Pollack's employees remained comparatively loyal and content. His policies influenced other local stogie manufacturers. Pollack refused, as he pondered retirement, to sell his factories to buyers who would not honor the pact he had made with his employees regarding their labor concerns.

After his April 23, 1906, death, the Ohio Valley Trades and Labor Assembly called a special meeting to encourage all the members of local trade unions to attend Pollack's funeral. The pallbearers were chosen from his employees, who, along with their union brethren, publicly demonstrated their affection for him in an unusual manner. The Garfield Assembly of International Stogie Makers spearheaded a collection of donations to erect a large monument in Pollack's honor. Depicting a handshake between employee and employer, the monument was placed in a prominent position on the grounds of Wheeling's city building. It was later moved to its current home on Main Street near the Fort Henry Bridge. The monument's inscription reads: "Erected by Trade Union Members of United States in Memory of Augustus Pollack Whose Business Life and Actions Were Always in Sympathy with Organized Labor." It is thought to be the only monument ever built by labor in honor of a business owner. (SD; photographs courtesy OCPL.)

70

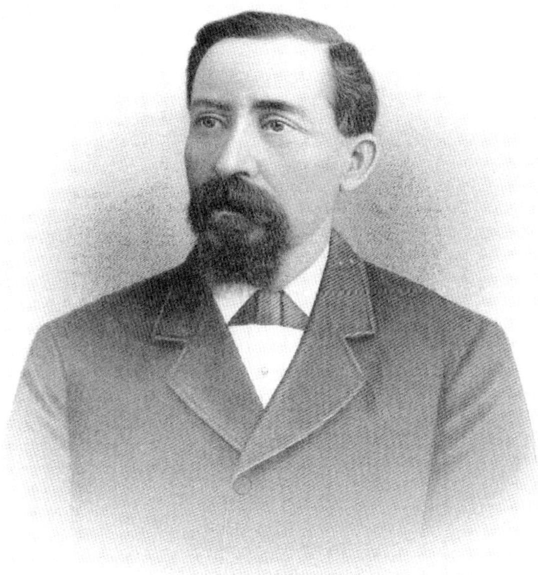

Anton Reymann

Brewer and philanthropist Anton Reymann was born in Gaubickelheim, Germany, on September 15, 1837, and immigrated to the United States in 1853. The family landed in New Orleans and came up the Mississippi River, settling in Galena, Illinois. They soon left due to an outbreak of chills and fever. The family then made its way east to Wheeling, where Anton's father, George, partnered with Peter Paul Beck, a brewer who operated The Franklin Brewery at 31 Main Street. Combining their interest, the two men started a summer garden across the creek in East Wheeling along Rock Point Road.

At the age of 17, Reymann became Beck's apprentice and studied brewing in Cincinnati and St. Louis. In 1862, he returned to Wheeling and considered enlisting in the Union Army but was persuaded otherwise by friends and family. Also in 1862, Reymann married Thusnelda, Beck's daughter. Upon his father's retirement and Beck's death, Reymann partnered with Beck's widow a short while before purchasing the entire business and moving the brewery to the site on Rock Point Road. With a freshwater supply, cold storage caves, and new buildings, Reymann's business grew to be one of the largest in the state. It catered to the tri-state area, as did Reymann's main competitor, Henry Schmulbach.

As Reymann was establishing his brewery, he also began expanding his business interest. He was president of the Wheeling & Elm Grove Railroad and made investments to move from the old horse-drawn system to electrification and steam engines. He also served as president of the West Virginia State Fair association and was vice president of the German Fire Insurance Company, a founder of the German Bank of Wheeling, and a stockholder in Warwick China and North Wheeling pottery. Known as an upstanding member of the community, Reymann was also a philanthropist. He started the Wheeling Park Company, where he created a German beer garden getaway with amusement rides, a swimming pool, and a casino. Reymann was also responsible for the creation of Altenheim, which served as a home for women who had spent their lives as domestic servants but who, in their old age, had no one to take care of them. Just as the grounds of Wheeling Park are still enjoyed today, Altenheim still serves as a home for elderly women. Long after his death in 1924, Reymann's legacy is still present in Wheeling. (RS; image courtesy OCPL.)

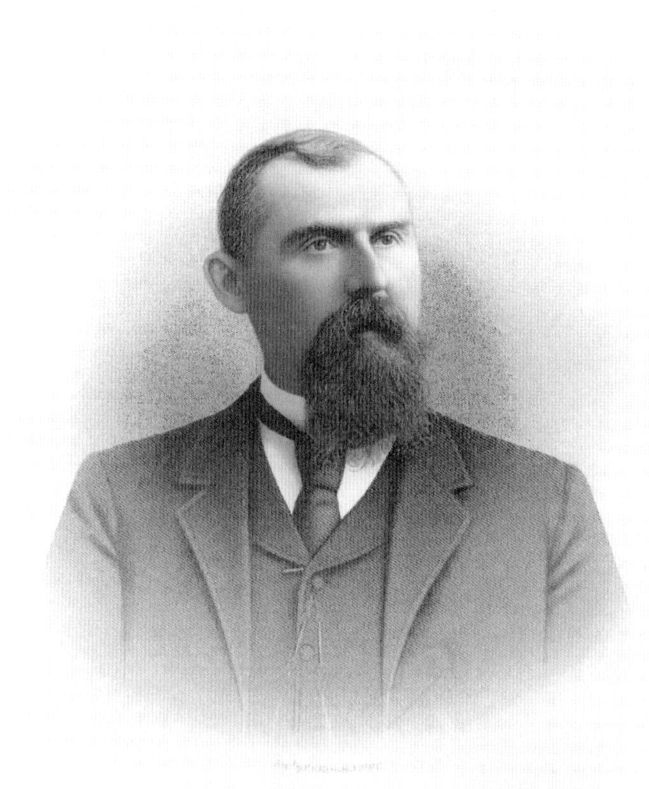

Henry Schmulbach

Schmulbach was born in Germany on November 12, 1844, and immigrated to Wheeling in 1852. At an early age, he began working on packet boats, where he learned the art of entrepreneurship. By age 20, Schmulbach had invested in several packet boats, but during the Civil War, he shifted his interest to the wholesale grocery business with his uncle George Feller and, later, the wholesale liquor business.

In 1873, Schmulbach purchased a home at 2311 Chapline Street that still stands today. Here, he lived with his two sisters and continued to expand his business interests and stock purchases. Socially, Schmulbach led a life of bachelorhood, enjoying gambling and participating in Wheeling's nightlife.

He made headlines in 1878, when he was involved in an altercation at a tavern in which he struck a man for over-racing his horses. The man died as a result of the blow, and Schmulbach went on trial for murder. He was acquitted, but this event added to his reputation.

In 1882, Schmulbach became the leading stockholder of the Nail City Brewing Company; soon after, the name was changed to the Schmulbach Brewing Company. Schmulbach expanded the brewery, which eventually became one of the largest in the state. Aside from the brewery, Schmulbach also held interests in numerous iron and nail companies, steamboats, railroads, and public projects. Throughout his career, it was said that his proudest accomplishment was serving as president of the German Bank of Wheeling.

The book *Prominent Men of West Virginia* (1890) described Schmulbach as a man "possessing many elements of solid popularity." This description stems from the fact that Schmulbach was very civic minded. One of his most notable contributions was the construction of Mozart Park, a hilltop resort above South Wheeling. The park was accessed by an incline railway; along with majestic views, the resort boasted a dancing pavilion, casino, bowling alley, bar, restaurant, and bicycle track. Schmulbach was also responsible for building Wheeling's first skyscraper, the 1905 Schmulbach building on Market Street, which still stands today. Shortly after his brewery closed due to Prohibition in West Virginia, Schmulbach died in 1915 at his mansion at Roney's Point. (RS; image courtesy OCPL.)

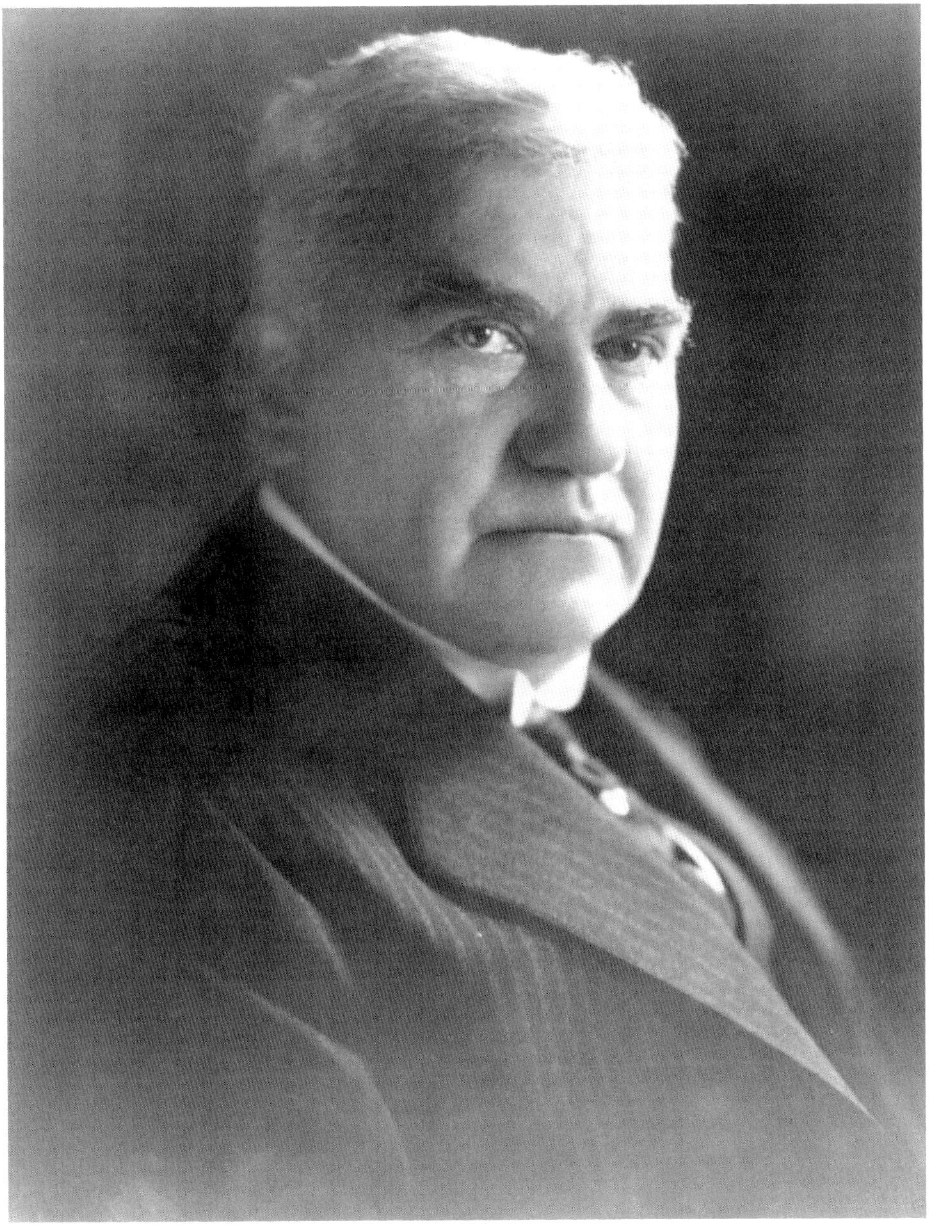

Michael Joseph Owens
Owens (1859–1923) revolutionized the American glass industry. He was born in Mason County, Virginia (now West Virginia), and his family moved to Wheeling in 1869. Mike Owens began work at the Hobbs-Brochunier glass plant and, by age 15, had become a glassblower. In 1888, Owens moved to Toledo, Ohio, to work for Edward D. Libbey at his glass factory. Owens was a mechanical genius who began to chum out the inventions that would earn him 49 patents. His efforts eliminated child labor in the glass industry. His most important invention was the automatic bottle blowing machine, consisting of 9,000 separate parts and developed between 1895 and 1904. Owens also helped produce continuous flat-sheet glass. His name has been associated with multiple companies, including Libbey-Owens-Ford, Owens-Illinois, and Owens Corning. (MBr.)

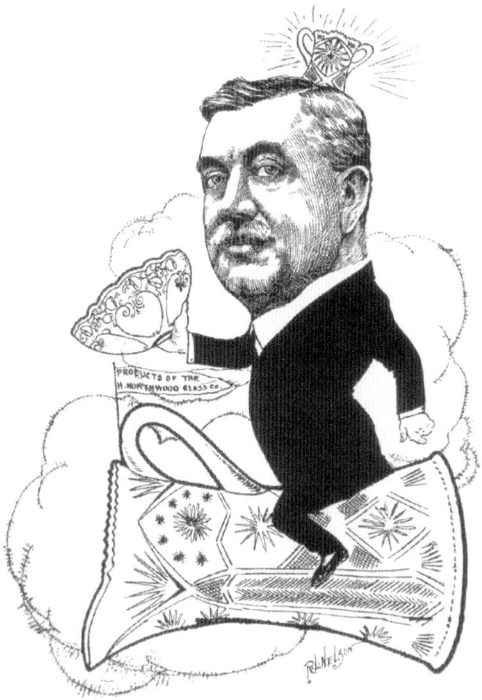

HARRY C. NORTHWOOD
General Manager H. Northwood Glass Co.
Wheeling, W. Va.

Harry Northwood

English-born Harry C. Northwood (1860–1919) was employed at the Hobbs-Brockunier Plant as a glass etcher. In 1901, he established a glass tableware plant in the Hobbs-Brockunier factory. The company produced tableware, novelty items, and lighting fixtures in an array of opaque, translucent, and high-colored glass, much of which was pressed rather than blown. The most famous Northwood product was carnival glass. Northwood's glassware is now treasured and prominently displayed at the Oglebay Institute Glass Museum, among other places. (WHOF; image courtesy OCPL.)

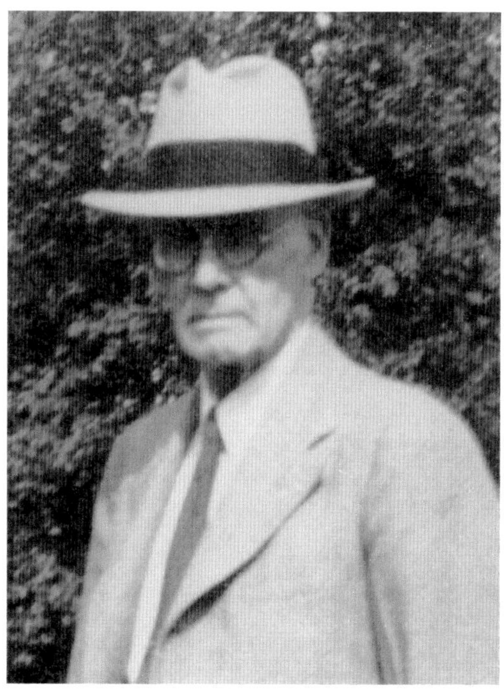

Ralph Reed Spears

Spears (1859–1943) gained recognition while building an oil distribution empire in South Wheeling. He established Fleet-Wing as the first jobber brand of oil products and pioneered the development of tetraethyl anti-knock gasoline. (WHOF.)

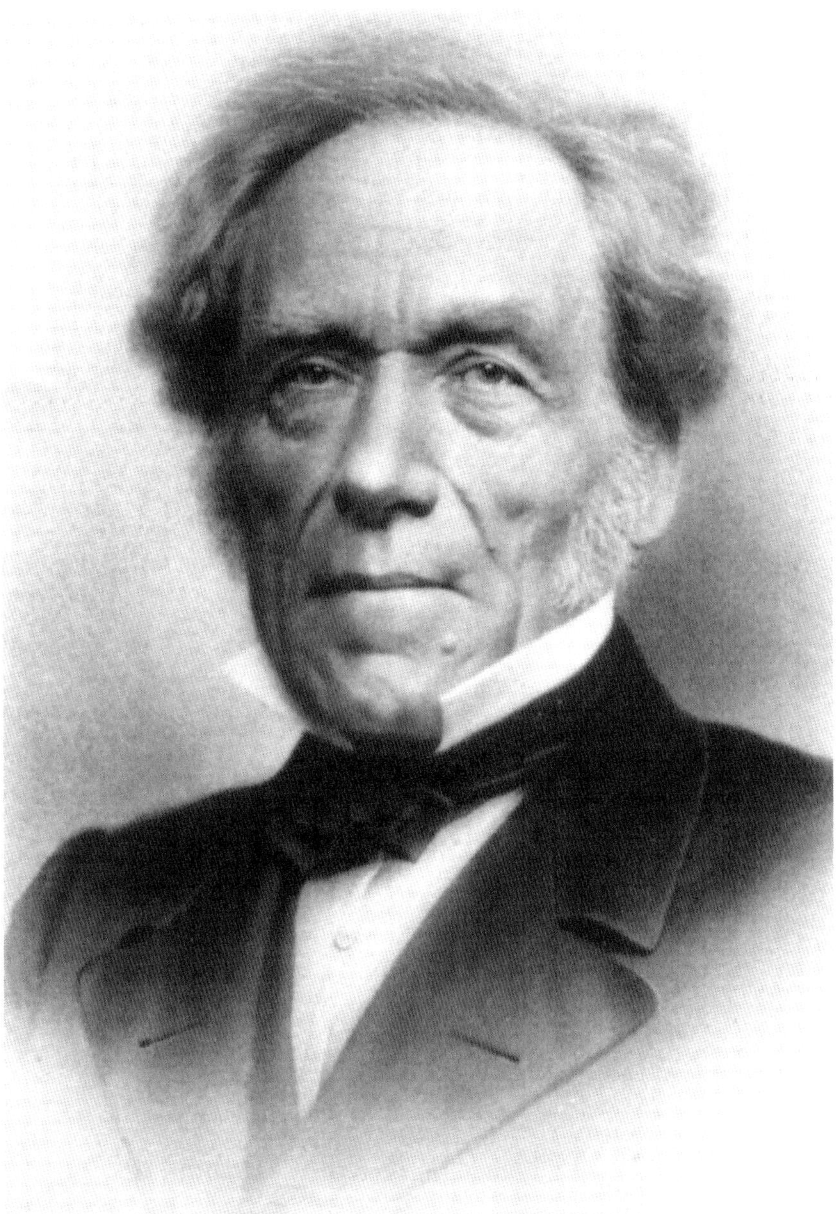

Johann Ludwig Stifel

Stifel (1807–1881) contributed greatly to the industrialization of Wheeling. Two years after arriving in America from his native Germany in 1833, he began producing quality indigo-dyed cloth known as calico. He married Barbara Becht, a German immigrant, in 1837, and their two sons eventually joined the family business in 1859. The business lasted for more than 120 years and at its peak produced 3.5 million yards of cotton cloth a month. Johann participated in many business ventures that spurred Wheeling's development. He founded the first German newspaper in Wheeling and served as an investor and officer in local banking, railroad, iron manufacturing, and bridge companies. Politically, he favored the Republican Party, supported the Union during the Civil War, and he served as a delegate to the first Wheeling Convention when Virginia joined the Confederacy in 1861. (JL; image courtesy WHOF.)

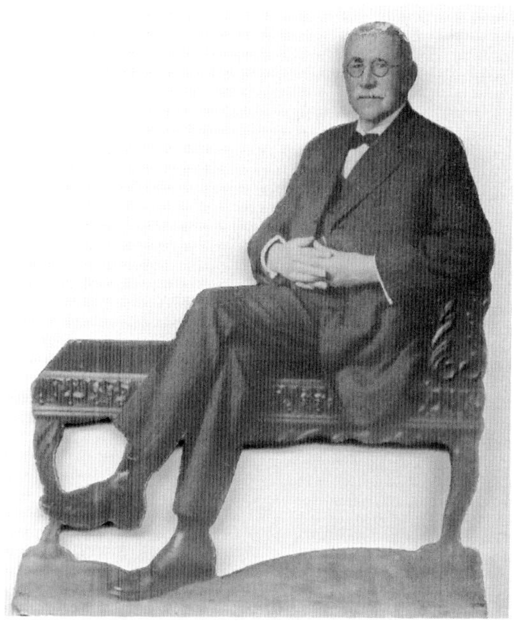

Lee Samuel Good

Lee Samuel "L.S." Good (1855–1927) left Germany for Texas as a penniless 17-year-old. He traveled to Wheeling (legend has him walking the whole way) and began buying and selling dry goods from a cart. He saved enough money to found L.S. Good & Co. People still remember the store's famous talking Christmas tree. Good was a progressive executive, beloved by his employees. Many of his fiercest competitors closed their doors during his funeral. (SD; image courtesy Larry Good.)

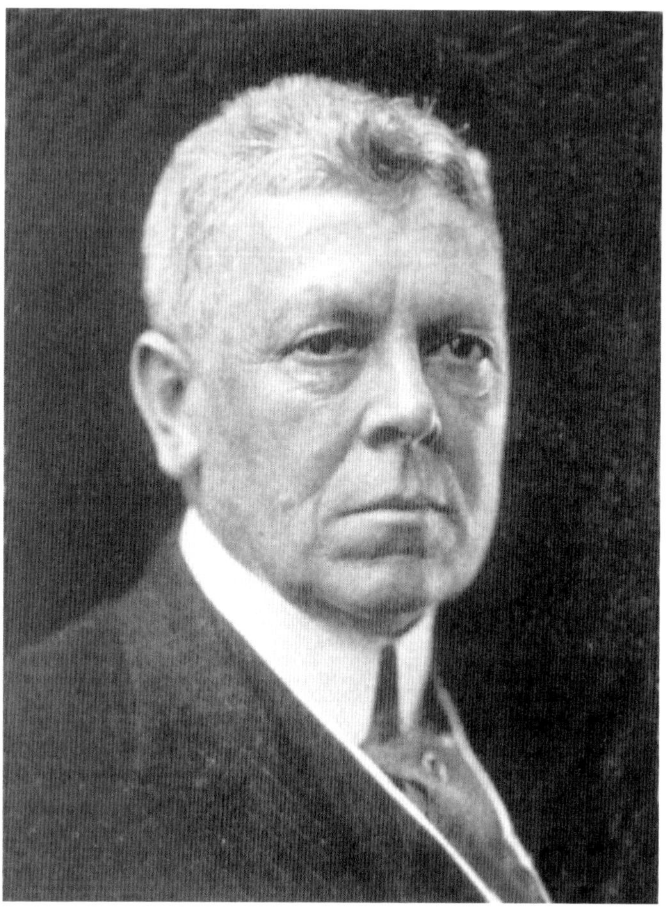

Wilbur E. Stone

Wilbur Stone (1863–1938) helped make Stone & Thomas, the mercantile business established by his father and uncle, West Virginia's largest department store chain. He helped found the Wheeling Board of Trade and helped create the Board of Trade Building and the Market Auditorium. Along with Otto Schenk, Stone led the drive to purchase Wheeling Park for the city and to create the Wheeling Park Commission in 1925. (WHOF.)

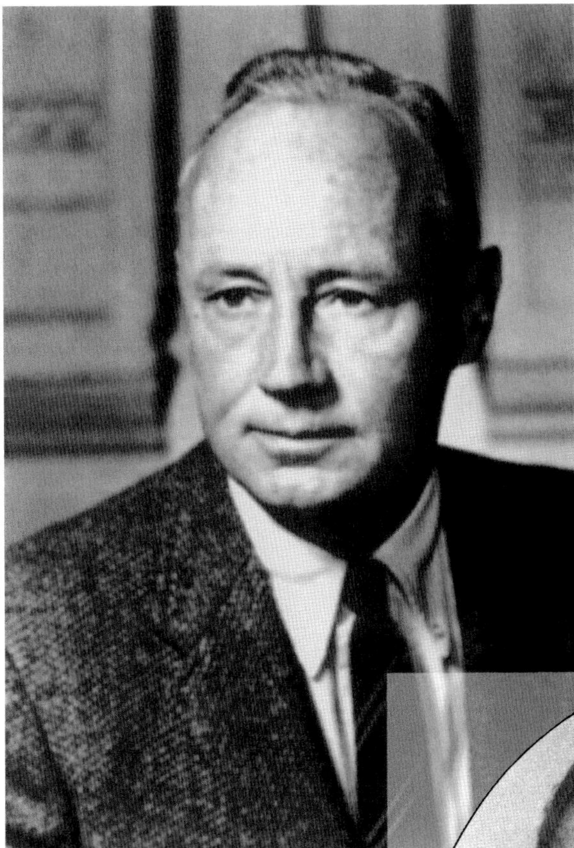

Wilbur S. Jones
An Army colonel in World War II, Jones (1909–1977) was a department store executive and longtime chairman of the Wheeling Park Commission. Hospitals, parks, schools, and businesses throughout the community benefited from his tireless efforts. (WHOF.)

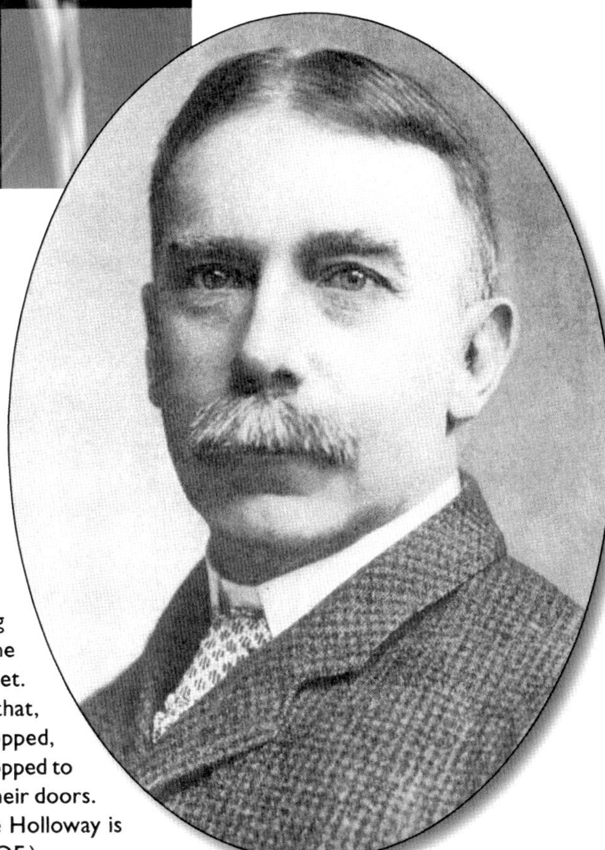

B. Walker Peterson
Peterson (1851–1925) owned several businesses, including Warwood Tool Co. and the Wheeling Traction Co. As president of the Wheeling Dollar Bank, he never turned his back on any business formed in Wheeling or intending to build in Wheeling. He was one of the first presidents of Ohio Valley General Hospital. In 1920, he gave the Wheeling Public Library a statue of Ethan Allen, which many Wheeling citizens remember standing guard in the lobby at the old library on Market Street. Peterson was held in such high regard that, on the day of his burial, trolley cars stopped, foundry whistles sounded, flags were dropped to half-staff, and stores and banks closed their doors. Contemporary community leader Pete Holloway is a direct descendant of Peterson. (WHOF.)

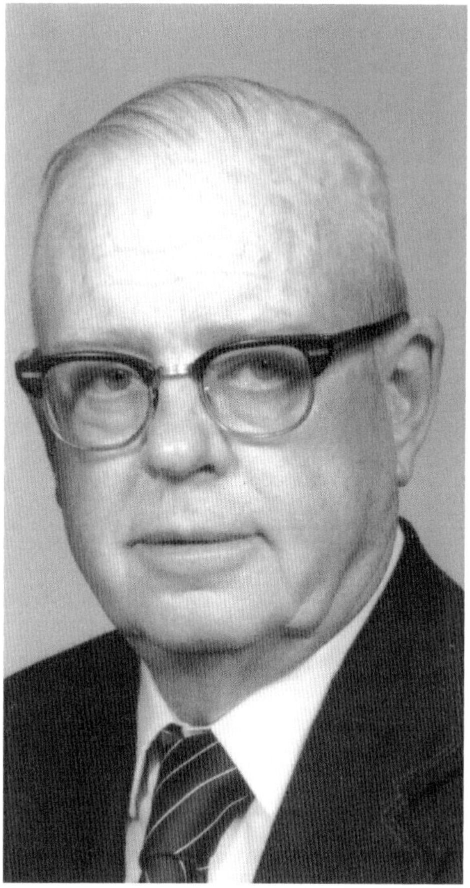

Robert C. Hazlett

As president of Wheeling Dollar Bank and the West Virginia Banker's Association, Hazlett (1910–1996) was the prime force in bringing branch banking to West Virginia. He served on the board of the Pittsburgh branch of the Cleveland Federal Reserve Bank, as president of the Ohio County Board of Education, and as chairman of the Wheeling Park Commission. Hazlett married his best friend, Susan Bradshaw Arbenz, and they loved their five sons. His avocations included gardening, golf, duplicate bridge, and rooting for the Pittsburgh Pirates. (HZ; photograph courtesy WHOF.)

Jesse Wheat Speidel

The Speidel golf course in Oglebay Park is named for Jesse Wheat Speidel. The land was once Jo Betty Farm (named for Speidel's daughter, Elizabeth) and was a gift from the Speidel family to the park. Jesse (1879–1969) graduated from Yale and entered the banking and brokerage business. He was general manager of the City & Elm Grove Railway and the City Railway Co. (KQ; image courtesy OCPL.)

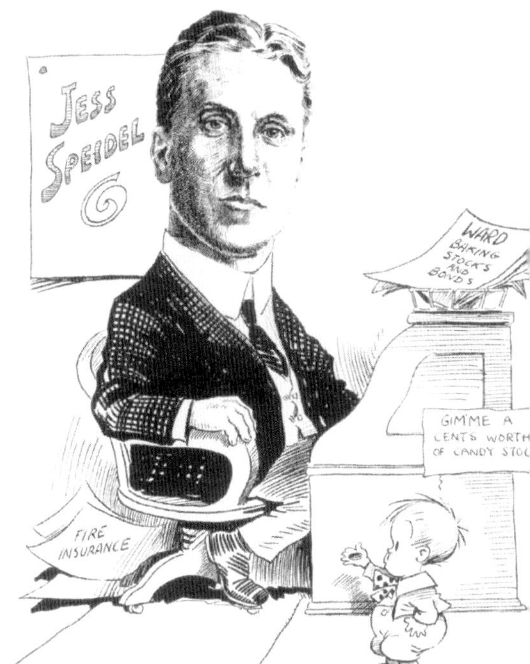

JESSE W. SPEIDEL
Stock Broker and Insurance
Wheeling, W. Va.

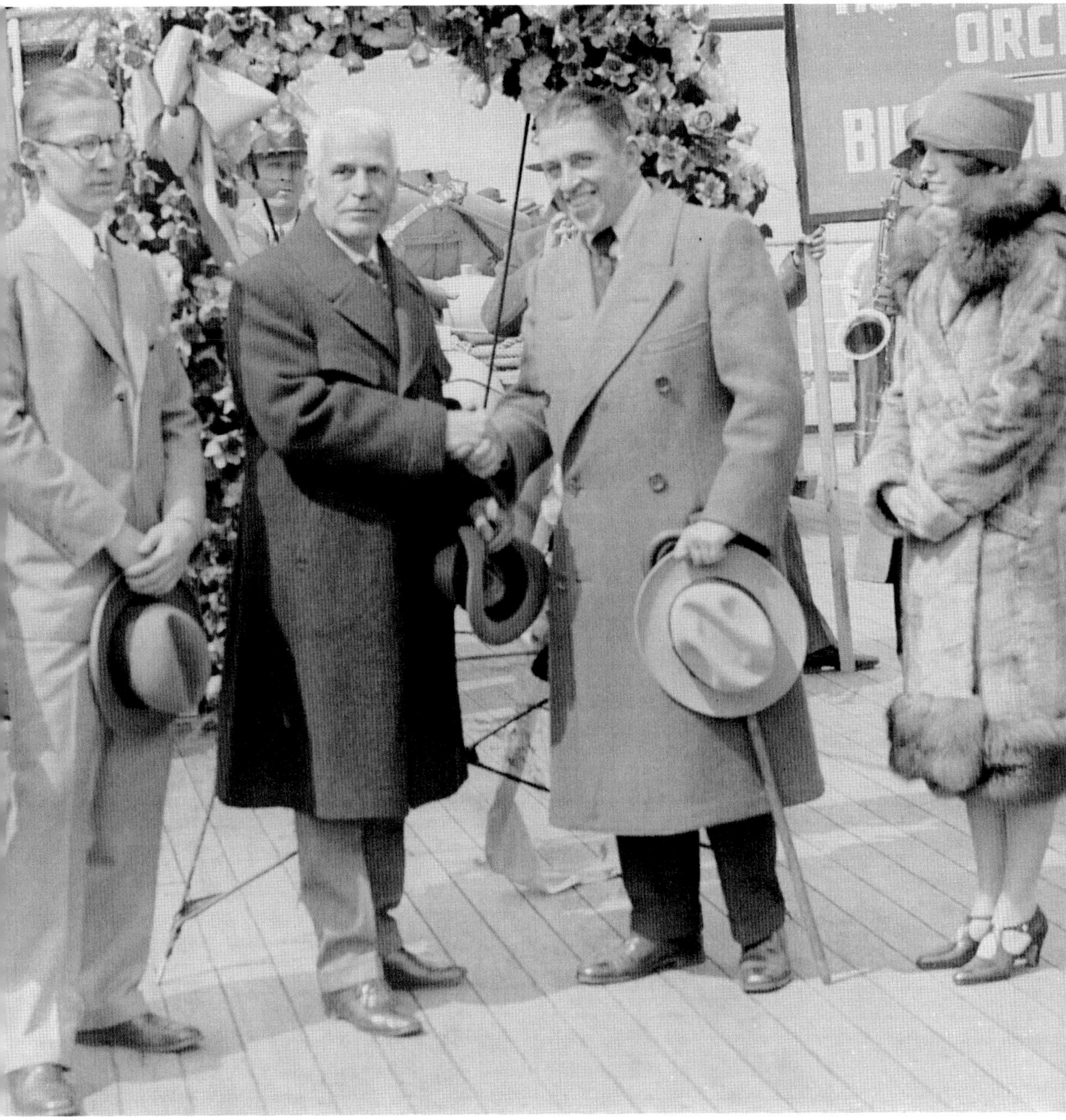

Ellsworth Milton Statler

Working from the time he was nine years old, E.M. Statler (1863–1928) became a bellboy at Wheeling's McLure House when he was 13, earning $6 a month. Nicknamed "the Colonel," Statler pioneered customer-focused hotel innovations, including a bathroom, circulating ice water, closets (with lights), redesigned keys, full-length mirrors, free newspapers, telephones, and radios in each guest room. A plain, rugged, self-made man with only a second-grade education, Statler coined the slogan, "The customer is always right." He staunchly maintained that "people want good beds, decent food, and cleanliness." His boyhood wish to own a hotel was fulfilled in 1907 in Buffalo, New York, and future hotels opened in Boston, Cleveland, Detroit, New York City, and St. Louis. At age 64, Statler, who began work in a glass factory for 50¢ a day, was managing hotels worth $25 million. He is pictured here, second from left, shaking hands with bandleader George Olsen. (CJu; photograph courtesy LOC.)

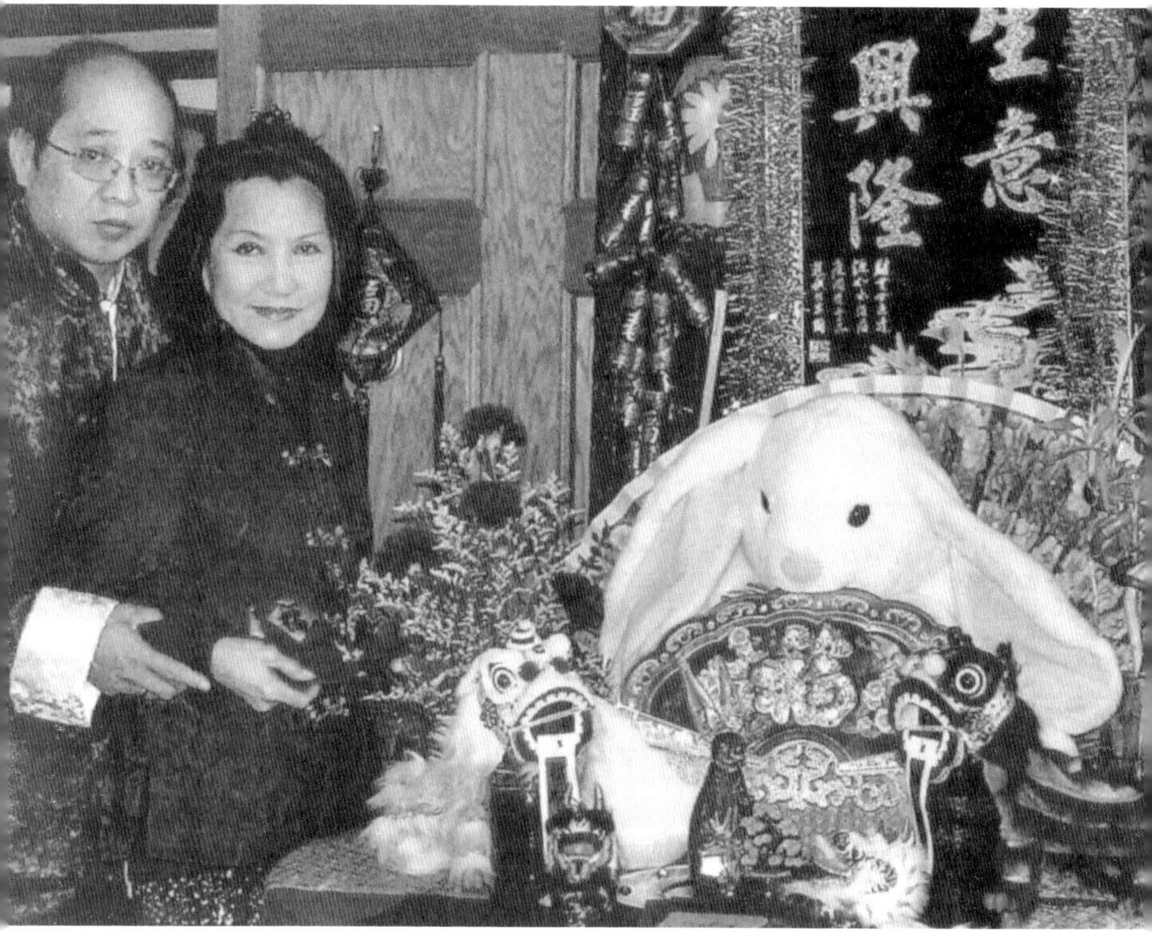

Martin Tse

Martin Tse (pictured here with his wife, Pom) is an example of the classic American success story. He was born in Hong Kong to a large family, including 17 brothers and sisters. His father, Sir Jim Tse, was knighted by the Queen of England for his business work in the community, and young Martin learned from him the lessons of hard work and seizing every opportunity to improve relationships with one's customers. His father promised him love and an education—the rest would be gained through hard work. Martin immigrated to the United States in 1975 on a British passport. He first attempted college in California, but stayed only three days due to "culture shock." Martin never felt at home in such an impersonal place. He transferred to West Liberty State College in 1975 in order to study economics and management. After graduation, he began working as a waiter for Ernie's Esquire. In 1982, Dorothy Chang hired him to work at the Peking Garden on Twelfth Street. He learned much from Dorothy and, in 1994, decided to strike out on his own, opening Golden Chopsticks on Wheeling Island. He also became an American citizen in that same year. Tse declares that the promise of opportunity and individualism are what brought him to America, and that the sense of community and caring for one's neighbors is what kept him in Wheeling. He remembers the story of a local physician who once bought $1,000 worth of restaurant gift coupons. When Tse replied that the man must have a lot of friends, the doctor stated that he did it for Tse in order to help him plant firm roots in Wheeling. And Tse has done just that. He bought Silver Chopsticks on National Road in 1998, which has kept him very busy. This is in keeping with the principle that his father, Sir Jim, taught him: hard work may or may not be noticed, but it will never be regretted. (BC; photograph courtesy Martin Tse.)

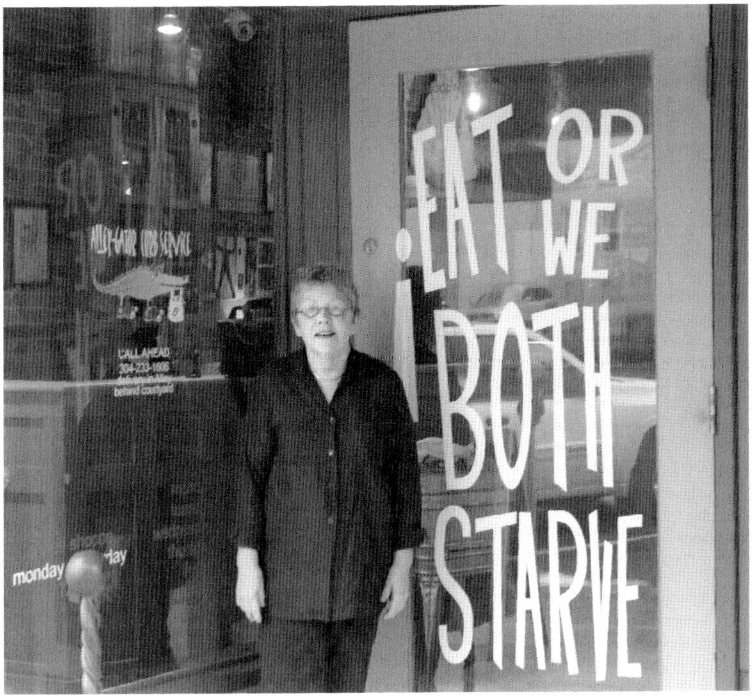

An Alligator in Wheeling

There was nothing conventional about how Susan Haddad came to be proprietor of the Later Alligator restaurant in Wheeling's historic Centre Market district. Believing Centre Market real estate to be a sound investment based on its proximity to the proposed Victorian Wheeling shopping mall, Haddad purchased some property. She planned to keep it a year or two, then sell it at a reasonable profit. But when the mall plans failed to materialize, Haddad found herself a landlord. Luckily, the building came with tenants: an antique shop on the ground floor and a second-floor resident. Their rent paid the bills, making everything relatively simple for two years.

Then things crumbled—literally. In the early morning of New Year's Eve 2002, Haddad was awakened by an urgent call from the antique shop proprietor: the ceiling had caved in under the pressure of water from broken pipes. Broken antiques were afloat. The disaster prompted Haddad to consider possibilities. "I was in a desk job that bored me to death," she recalls. "I now had an empty storefront and an opportunity to move on a few lofty ideas. The ceiling's collapse had the biggest impact. Above the waterlogged tiles was an original Wheeling Steel tin ceiling. I couldn't help wondering what other history this building might hide. So I quit my job and took on the project of gutting the ground floor."

The risky decision felt right. Haddad was motivated by each new discovery: Frank Lloyd Wright prism glass windows, a fireplace, and Wheeling Tile floors.

After a few years of hard work, the Later Alligator restaurant was born. When she opened it, Haddad could not have foreseen that numerous national chain restaurants would soon occupy the nearby Highlands development. Yet, even as most of Wheeling's downtown restaurants closed under the pressure, the Later Alligator persevered. But how? "Determination," Haddad answered. "Failure wasn't an option. It's been a labor of love from the beginning. Some of the best advice came from my banker. He told me to give my guests more than they'd expect. I try to keep this front and center."

Originally from Steubenville, Haddad has lived in Washington, DC, New York City, and Atlanta. She and her husband returned to Wheeling in the mid-1980s so that Susan could care for her ailing mother. "We realized that family brought us back to Wheeling, but Wheeling gave us the family, or community, that was lost in the metropolitan areas. I love the close-knit, quirky, everybody-knows-everybody vibe that Wheeling is all about." (SH.)

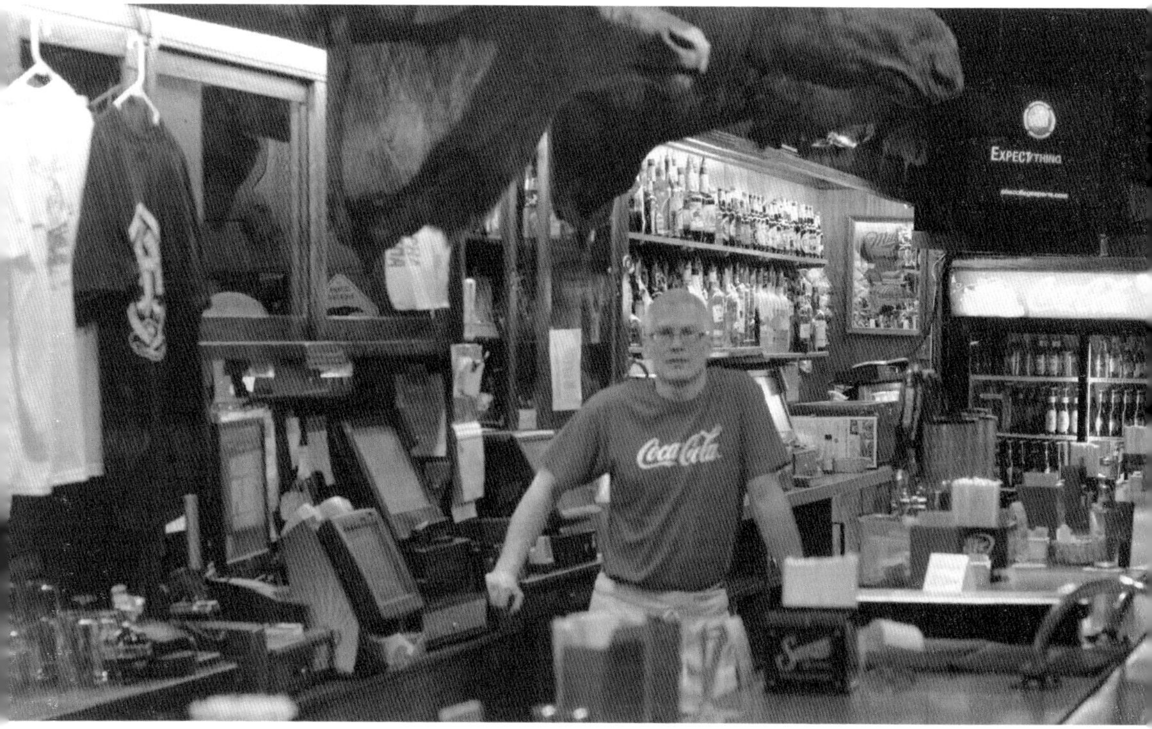

Charlie Schlegel

"Welcome home." That's what Dr. Thomas Ritz would say to Charlie Schlegel every time he visited Wheeling with his wife, Paula, Dr. Ritz's youngest daughter. It did not matter whether Charlie and Paula were living in Connecticut or New Hampshire; Dr. Ritz was a proud West Virginian who knew they belonged in Wheeling. That's the simplest explanation of how a Connecticut Yankee ended up in Wheeling.

Paula and Charlie moved to town to stay in August 2000 with their children, Killeen, Maggie, and Stephen. Five years later, Charlie purchased a venerable Wheeling institution, the Ye Olde Alpha restaurant, with business partner Mark Thomas. Owning "the Alpha" is a huge community responsibility. Generations of families have made it their home away from home, and the new owners needed to maintain that legacy and tradition while bringing the restaurant into the 21st century. "So we led a revolution through evolution," Charlie said, "slowly modernizing while focusing on improving the quality of the food."

The goal at Ye Olde Alpha is to be the best restaurant in the Ohio Valley. In order to achieve that standard, the new owners set out to accomplish five things: provide great food, service, and atmosphere; be a great place to work; and be profitable. "We ensure our future by hiring people committed to helping us achieve those goals and empowering them to make decisions that best serve our customers," Charlie said.

"We would never achieve success without our vendors and business partners. So every holiday season, we deliver complimentary luncheons to our accountants, produce market, fishmonger, bank, beer distributors, liquor store, and numerous others. We want to thank them."

Charlie and staff like to recognize the behavior they want to see. So, if someone is doing something good in the community, they support them. And they believe the best way for them to show support is with food. "Giving away our food is the best advertising we do. People eat our advertising dollars." The Alpha hosts a weekly radio program, and Charlie has an hour-long cooking program on West Liberty University's television station.

"I started as a dishwasher and loved the satisfaction of getting the job done at the end of a busy night. And that sense of immediate gratification has kept me going for over 30 years in this business. . . . Ye Olde Alpha has been around since 1932, but it will never get old." (CS.)

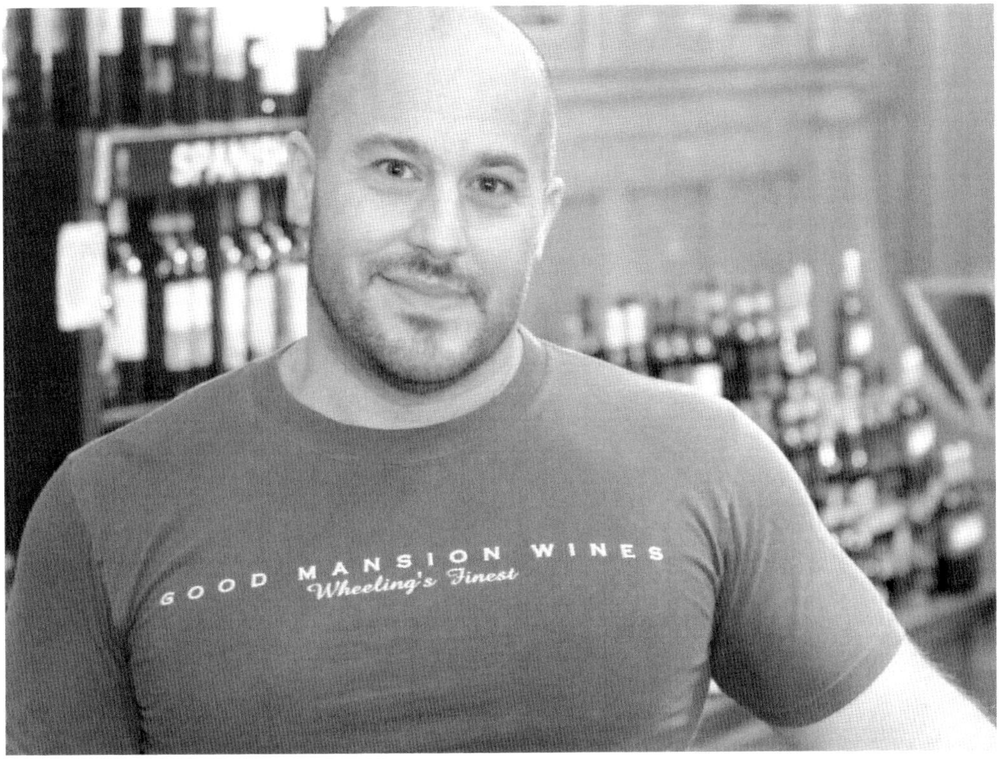

Good Mansion Wines

In 2006, Wheeling native Dominick Cerrone had an empty building and an idea. The building was the legendary L.S. Good Mansion, a Neoclassical townhome built in 1905 by Wheeling department store founder Lee Samuel Good (see page 76). Cerrone had the idea that Wheeling could use a wine shop, and he made this a reality when he opened Good Mansion Wines on Fourteenth Street in East Wheeling.

The business was based on the premise that if a large variety of wine was offered, people would come from all over. Combine that with the notoriety that the L.S. Good Mansion already had as one of Wheeling's premier homes, and a recipe for success is made.

Despite some locals seeing the enterprise as a doomed proposition, as no wine shop had survived the precipitous Wheeling economy, Cerrone saw it as an opportunity. "Here you have hundreds of professionals, thousands of wine drinkers, and millions of Pennsylvanians minutes across the border unhappy with their state stores," says Cerrone. "These were all a built-in customer base. It was a no-brainer."

When he first opened the shop, Cerrone had to plunge into the world of wine. That meant branching out from the comfortable confines of Sunday jug wine that he had drunk since his childhood as the son of Italian immigrants. "When customers ask us how we have become so knowledgeable about wine, we tell them we are very well drunk," jokes Cerrone. However, the knowledge of the staff is no joking matter, and, like good librarians, the staff is well versed in the thousands of items on the shelf.

Today, the store offers more than 2,000 varieties of domestic and imported wines from all over the world—West Virginia's largest variety of wine. It draws customers from both the Pittsburgh and Columbus markets, but local loyal customers with a passion for wine are the bread and butter of the shop.

The wine, however, is not the only selling point of the shop. People may come for the wine, but it is the stately home that holds them. The L.S. Good Mansion, with 26 stained-glass windows, bird's-eye maple, and quarter-sawn oak creates a shopping ambience that is unparalleled.

In seven years of business, the shop has served more than 25,000 customers. For Cerrone, that is just the beginning. "We look forward to having a contest one day for who will be our 100,000th customer!" (DC.)

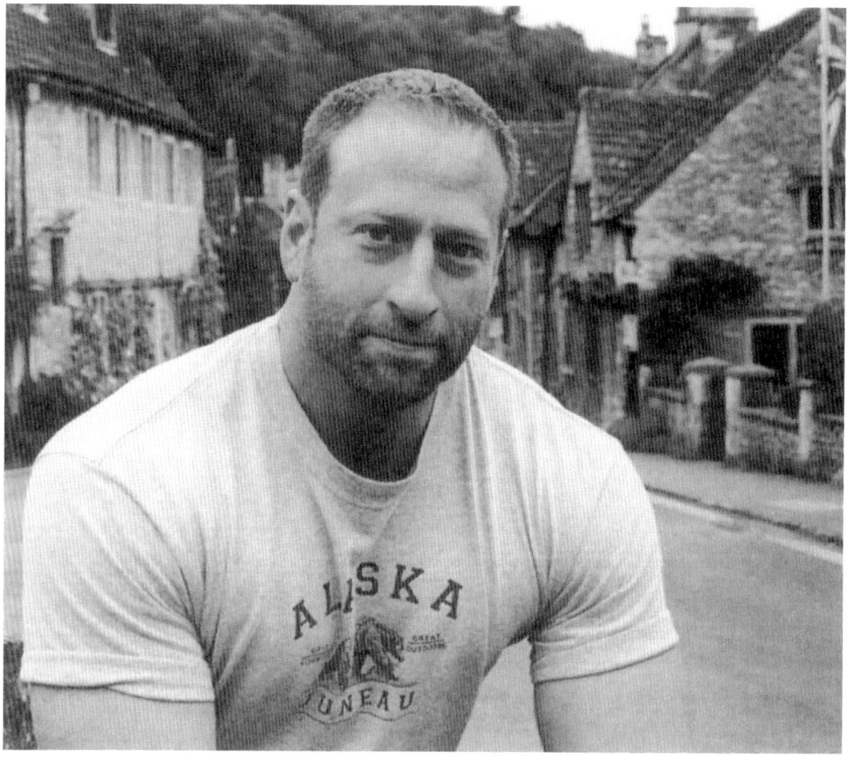

INWheeling Magazine

When David Allinder and Dominick Cerrone sat around a kitchen table one morning browsing Pittsburgh city magazines, a light went on in their heads. Allinder, a business consultant and native of Pittsburgh, had a firm sense that a city magazine could thrive in Wheeling. Cerrone, a business entrepreneur and native of Wheeling, had just the idea of how to do it.

The two quickly ran some numbers. "We realized that if we created a high quality, glossy quarterly that covered the city's boundless society and culture scene, the math would work out," explains Allinder (shown here). By doing some direct distributing to the southern and western Pittsburgh markets, the magazine would serve as an ambassador of Wheeling. Through the advertising inside, it would bring Wheeling businesses and culture to Pittsburgh residents and also offer Pittsburgh businesses access to Wheeling residents.

In the fall of 2007, the first issue of *INWheeling* was released. The glossy magazine, by all accounts, put a positive spin on a city hit hard by recent economic downturns. The magazine's optimistic and refreshing take on all that the city has to offer was for many a breath of fresh air. That perspective allowed Allinder and Cerrone to turn a profit by the second issue, a feat unheard of in the industry.

For the team of two, who had no previous publishing experience, marketing the Wheeling brand was beneficial for both them and the city. The magazine boasts a circulation of 8,000, which includes almost 1,000 subscribers and dozens of local and national retail locations. It features dozens of advertisers from the Pittsburgh market and has spanned the print media market "iron curtain" that had existed between Pittsburgh and Wheeling for years.

The magazine's edginess is offset by its well-articulated articles on the city's vibrant and rich history. Inside its pages are both catchy photo shoots as well as thought-provoking narratives of Wheeling's national historical significance. However, the winning ingredient in the magazine is the people. "Every issue has dozens if not hundreds of faces," says Allinder. This keeps the buzz of the magazine going strong all quarter long on radio talk shows, on social media, and at society events. (DC; photograph courtesy David Allinder.)

CHAPTER FIVE

Architecture, Science, and Medicine

Despite numerous unfortunate losses, a walking tour of Wheeling still reveals a strong architectural legacy featuring an impressive variety of styles and amazing structures. Many of the designers of Wheeling's most celebrated buildings and residences were homegrown, including Millard Filmore Giesey, who designed the L.S. Good Mansion, and Edward Bates Franzheim, who designed Vance Memorial Church and Altenheim, among numerous other structures. The late Wheeling architect Tracy R. Stephens created renderings of original decorative artwork that proved vital to the restoration of West Virginia Independence Hall. And a number of groups, including the Wheeling National Heritage Area Corporation, Friends of Wheeling, the Wheeling Convention and Visitor's Bureau, and the South Wheeling Preservation Alliance, work diligently, often in community partnerships, to preserve what remains of Wheeling's rich architectural heritage. Heroic individual preservationists like Beverly Fluty, Frances "Pinkie" Williams, Hydie Friend, Jeanne Finstein, Snookie Nutting, Hester Byrum, and Margaret Brennan have often led the way.

Even as land was cleared to make way for manmade structures, Wheeling managed to retain its natural beauty. Nestled between the Ohio River and Appalachian hills, the town's woodlands and abundance of waterways ensured diverse fauna and flora. This natural setting helped produce or attract a number of fine naturalists and biologists, including George Breiding, A.B. Brooks, Scott Shalaway, and photographer Bill Beatty. Ecologist Dr. Ben Stout has made a name for himself by studying local wetlands and aquatic ecosystems. As director, Penny Miller has helped make Oglebay Park's Good Zoo into a first-class attraction and nature education center. Robert and Libby Strong and Richard Pollack maintain Smart Centre Market, a wonderful, interactive science store with fossils and ice cream.

Wheeling has also produced its share of fine doctors and medical pioneers, including Simon Hullihen, the "father of oral surgery," and one of the founders of Wheeling Hospital. Born in Wheeling in 1866, Dr. Howard Lowrie Fisher was on his way to France in May 1915 to help establish a field hospital during World War I when the ship he was aboard, the RMS *Lusitania*, was sunk by a German U-boat. Fisher survived. His brother Walter had served as secretary of the interior under President Taft from 1911 to 1913. Now an internationally respected neurosurgeon and team neurosurgeon for the Pittsburgh Steelers, Dr. Joseph Maroon, born in Bridgeport, Ohio, calls Wheeling home and maintains a practice at Wheeling Hospital.

George Breiding

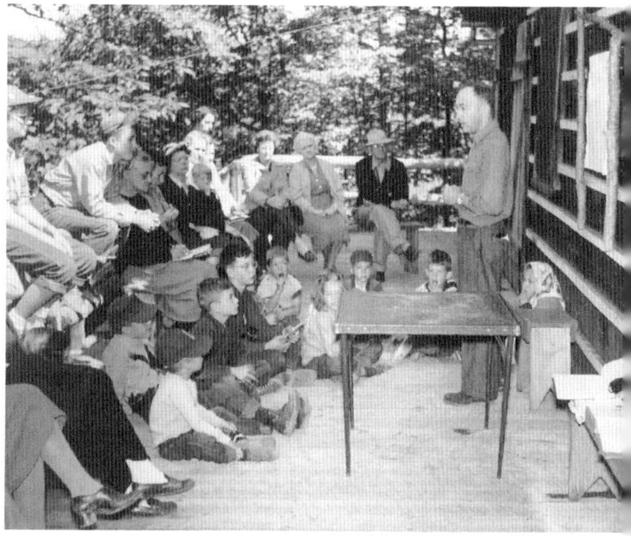

At an early age, George Breiding (1917–2007) developed a love for the outdoors. From 1950 to 1963, he served as naturalist for Oglebay Park. He also wrote a weekly newspaper column on nature and participated in radio shows promoting nature education. His lifelong teaching passion was evangelical in its scope, longevity, and importance, and he touched the lives of thousands of people while spreading the gospel of loving, understanding, and appreciating the world of nature. (KQ; photograph courtesy Mike Breiding.)

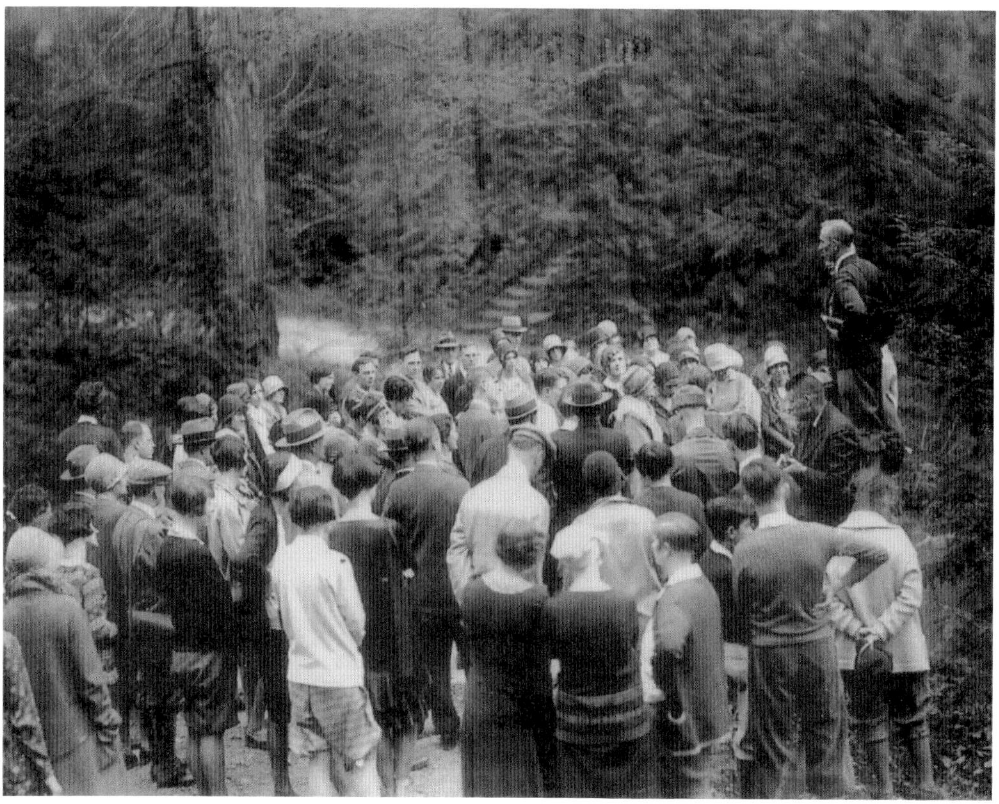

Alonso Beecher Brooks

"A.B." Brooks (1873–1944) was West Virginia's first game warden and was best known for promoting nature education while serving as naturalist for Oglebay Park. His popular, early-morning bird walks were an educational and social occasion. He founded the Brooks Bird Club, and in 1928, the Nature Leaders Training School, which became Senior Nature Camp. The Junior Nature Camp serves children ages 12 and up. (KQ; photograph courtesy Museums of Oglebay Institute.)

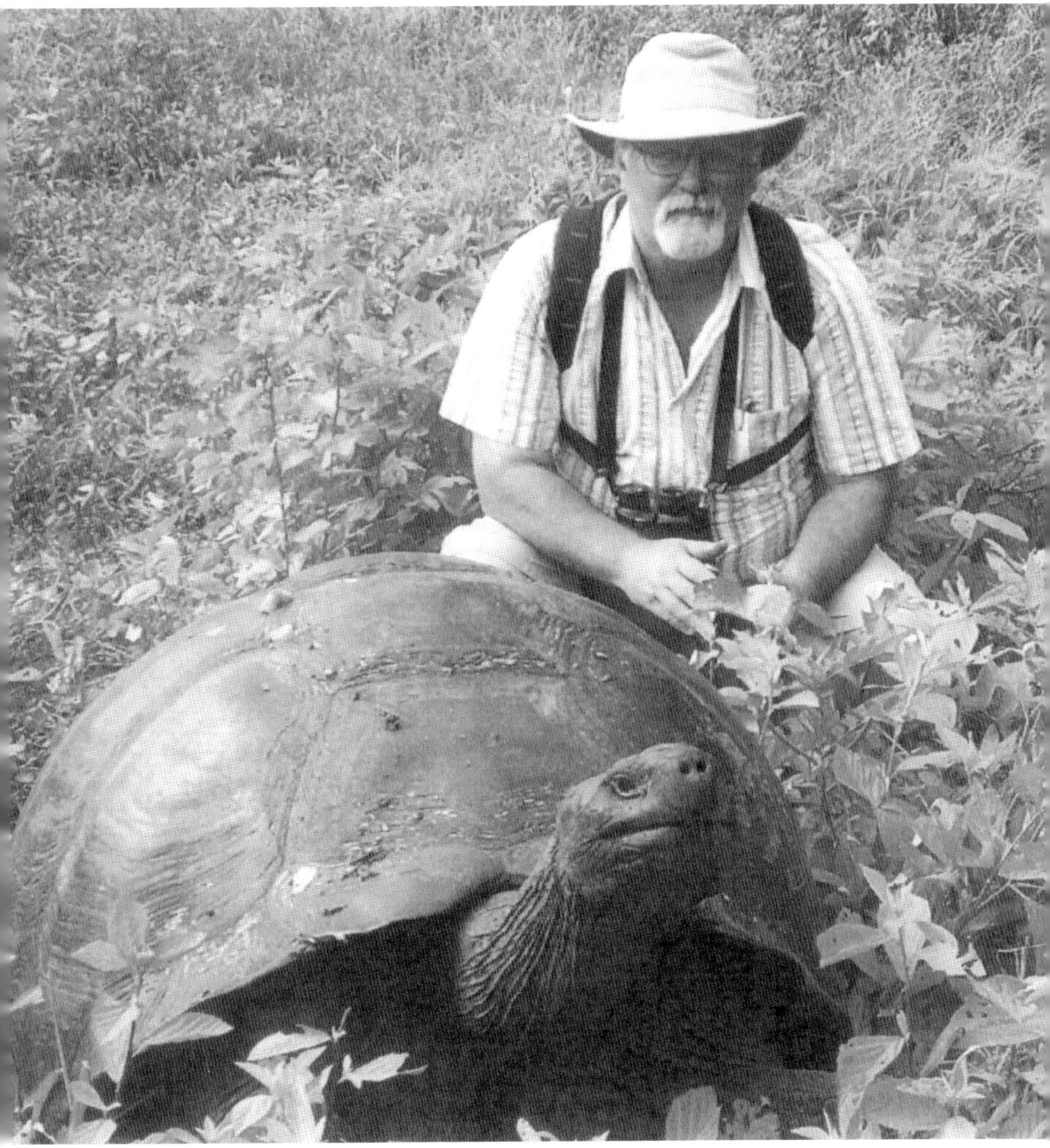

Dr. Scott Shalaway

Dr. Shalaway makes his living as a nature writer, naturalist, and ornithologist. After earning a doctorate in wildlife ecology at Michigan State University and teaching for eight years at Oklahoma State University and the University of Oklahoma Biological Station, Shalaway and his family moved to West Virginia, where he began a career as a nature writer. Since 1986, his weekly column has appeared in the *Sunday News-Register* and newspapers in West Virginia, Ohio, Pennsylvania, Michigan, and New York. In 1992, he began a weekly radio talk show, on WVLY in Wheeling, about birds and nature. His work also appears regularly in *Wild, Wonderful West Virginia* magazine. On a daily basis, Dr. Shalaway enjoys hiking and birding in his woods in southern Marshall County. (SS.)

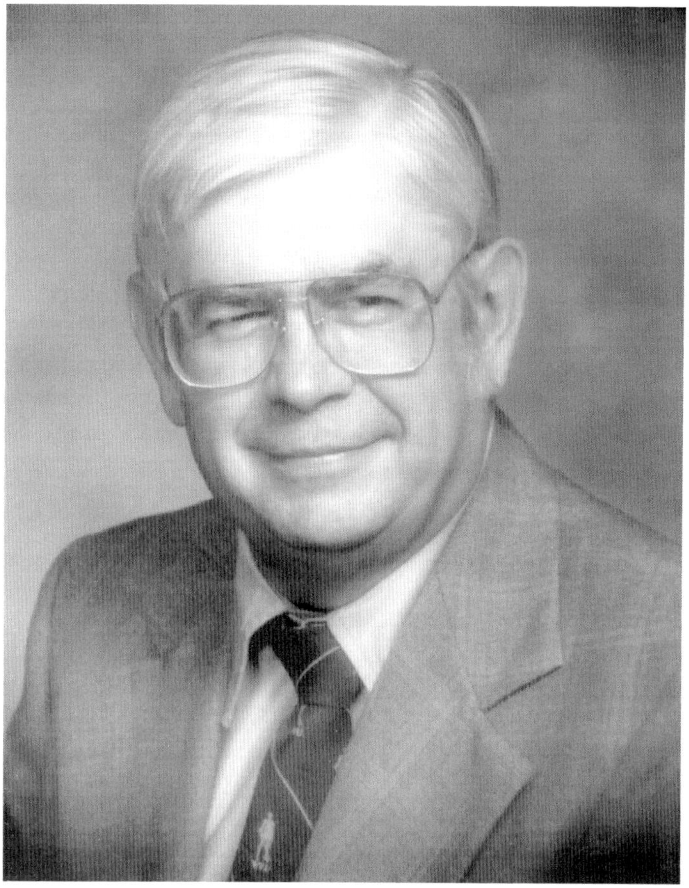

Carl Richard Huss

Huss (1925–1996) was a distinguished aeronautical engineer and a member of NASA's Space Task Force Group. He worked in the Mission Planning and Analysis Division for the Apollo lunar landing missions, Space Lab, Apollo-Soyuz, and the space shuttle program. He was awarded NASA's Outstanding Leadership Medal. (WHOF.)

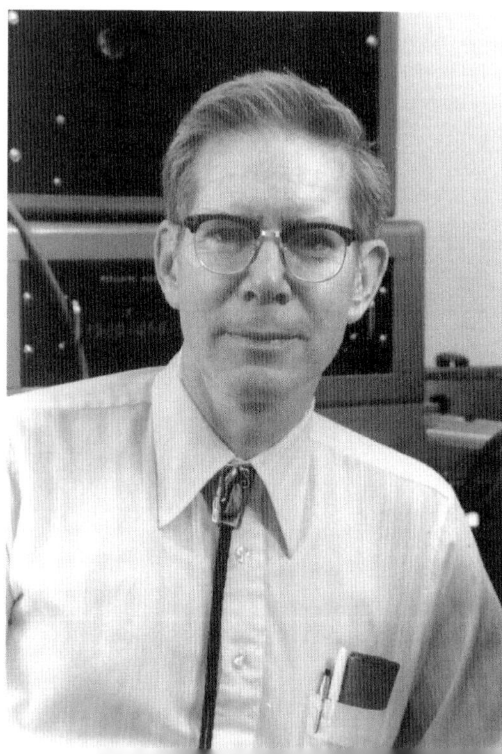

Harlan J. Smith

Smith (1924–1991), a leading American astronomer, was credited with discovering the optical variability of quasars as well as the existence of a class of dwarf variable stars. He was awarded NASA's highest award for civilians, the Distinguished Public Service Medal. The citation reads: "For a lifetime of service to the astronomy and space communities, students and public through teaching, research, public speaking and leadership of advisory and oversight groups." (WHOF.)

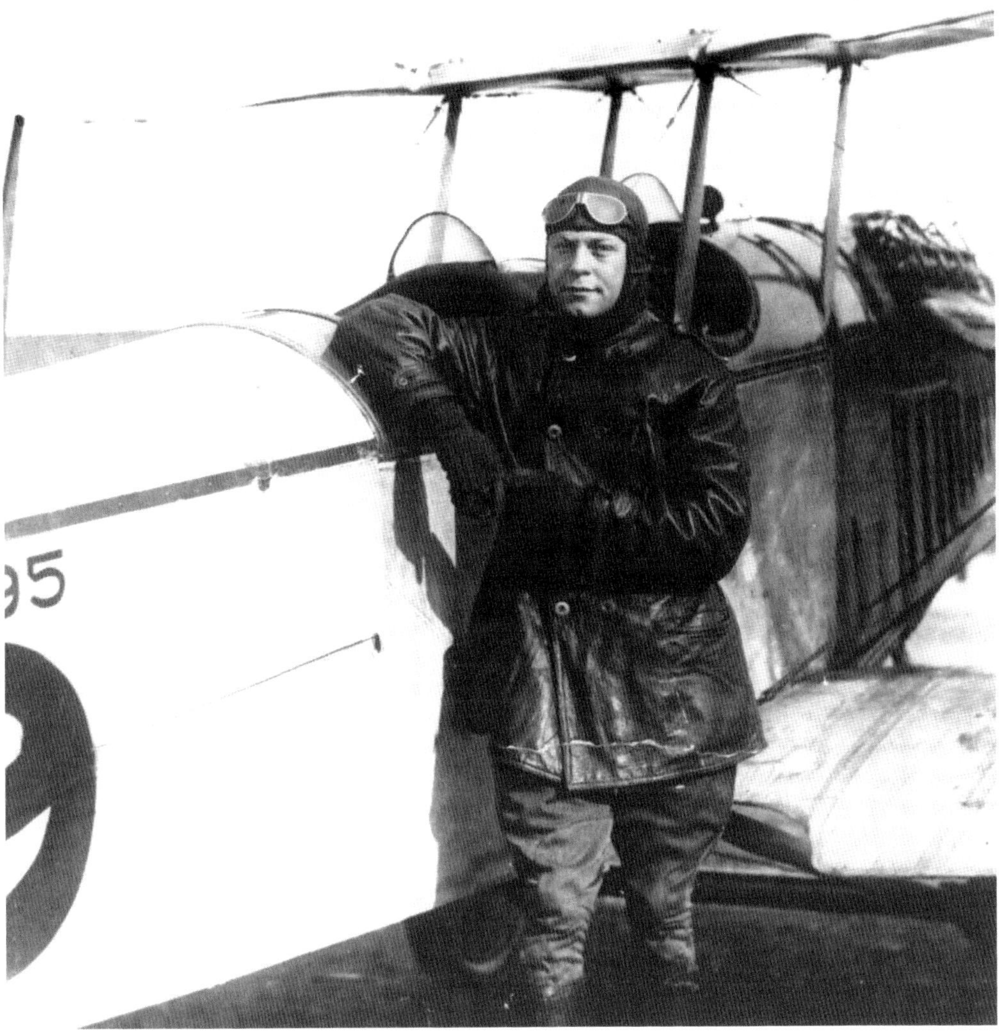

James Kindelberger

James Howard Kindelberger (1895–1962) was a World War I pilot, engineer, and designer of military and civilian aircraft and one of the most influential men in his field. He developed key mass-production techniques for airplanes during World War II and was a pioneer in the development of nuclear reactors and guided missiles and rockets. His contributions resulted in his induction into the Aviation Hall of Fame and the International Aerospace Hall of Fame. (WHOF; photograph courtesy San Diego Air & Space Museum.)

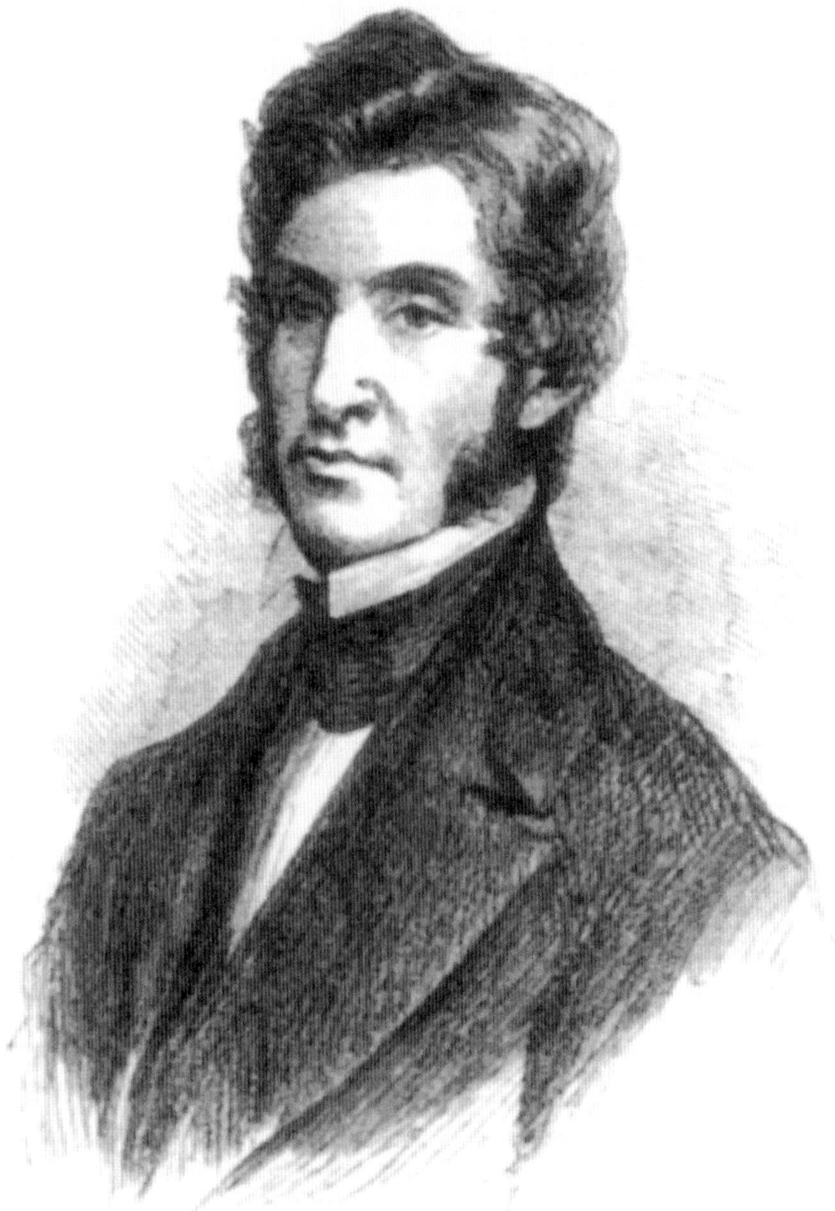

Charles Ellet Jr.

Civil engineer Charles Ellet Jr. (1810–1862) bridged the Ohio River at Wheeling, Virginia, with a suspended span of 1,010 feet, making it the longest single-span suspension bridge in the world at the time. The first official crossing of the Wheeling Suspension Bridge took place on October 20, 1849, when Ellet drove a carriage over its entire length. On May 17, 1854, the bridge collapsed in a windstorm. Soon rebuilt by Ellet, the bridge reopened later that year. Ellet convinced Secretary of War Edwin Stanton of the feasibility of a steamboat ram fleet as an "official weapon of war" for use on the Mississippi River. Col. Charles Ellet was in charge of the fleet on June 6, 1862, during the greatest naval battle of the Civil War. Ellet completely destroyed Commodore James E. Montgomery's Confederate navy, resulting in the capture of Memphis. Ellet, wounded in the battle, died on June 16, 1862. (JB.)

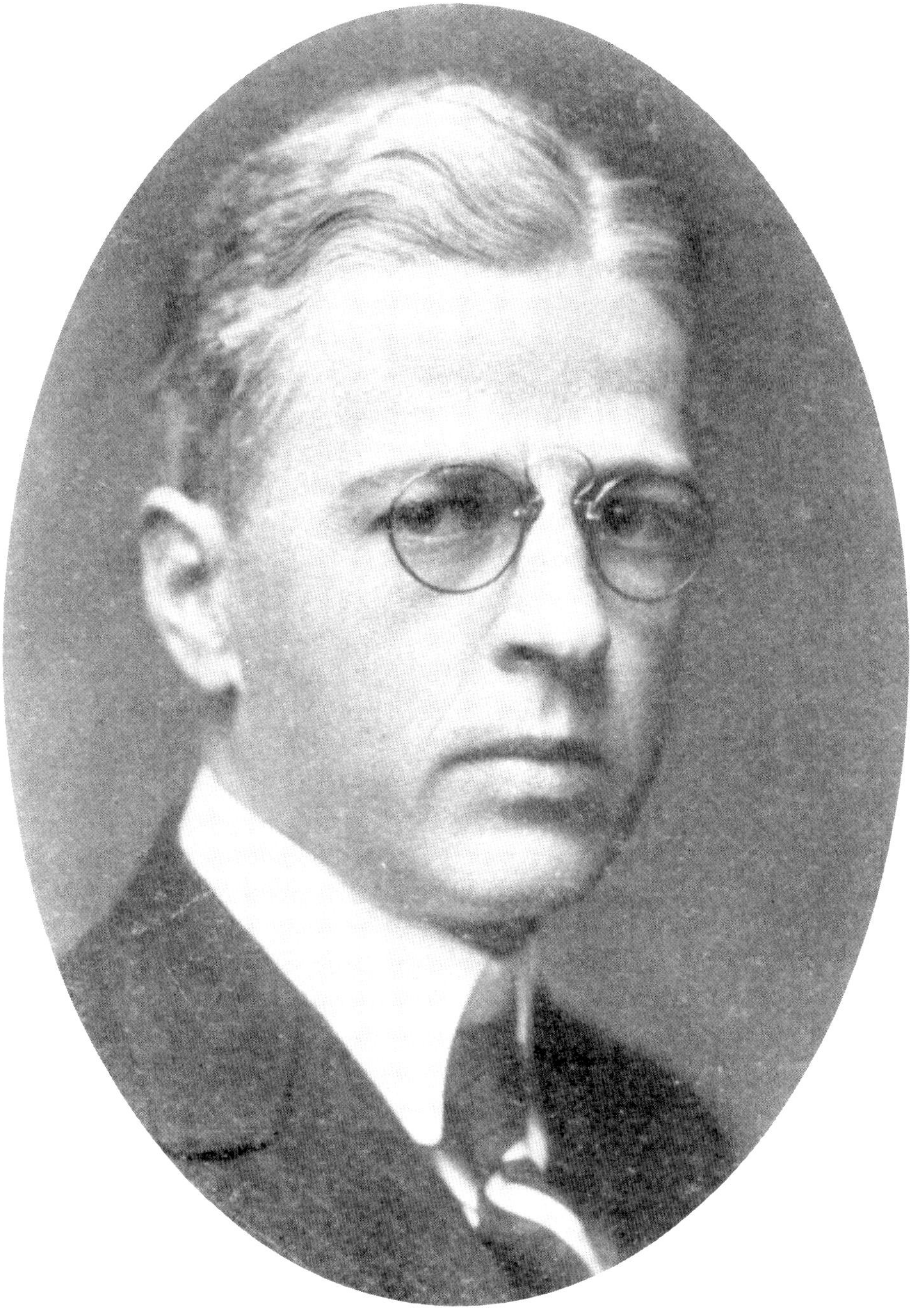

Charles Bates

Trained at the Art Institute in Chicago, Bates began his work as an architect in 1904 in Chicago and Pittsburgh and eventually came to Wheeling, where he designed the Capitol Music Hall, the Fort Henry Club, the Stifel Fine Arts Center, the old Ohio County Public Library, the Riley Law Building, Windsor Hotel, the Central Union Building, and many more significant edifices. He lived on Hawthorne Court in Woodsdale and had three sons. Bates died at the age of 51 from a cerebral hemorrhage in an ambulance on the way to the Cleveland Clinic. (KQ; photograph courtesy OCPL.)

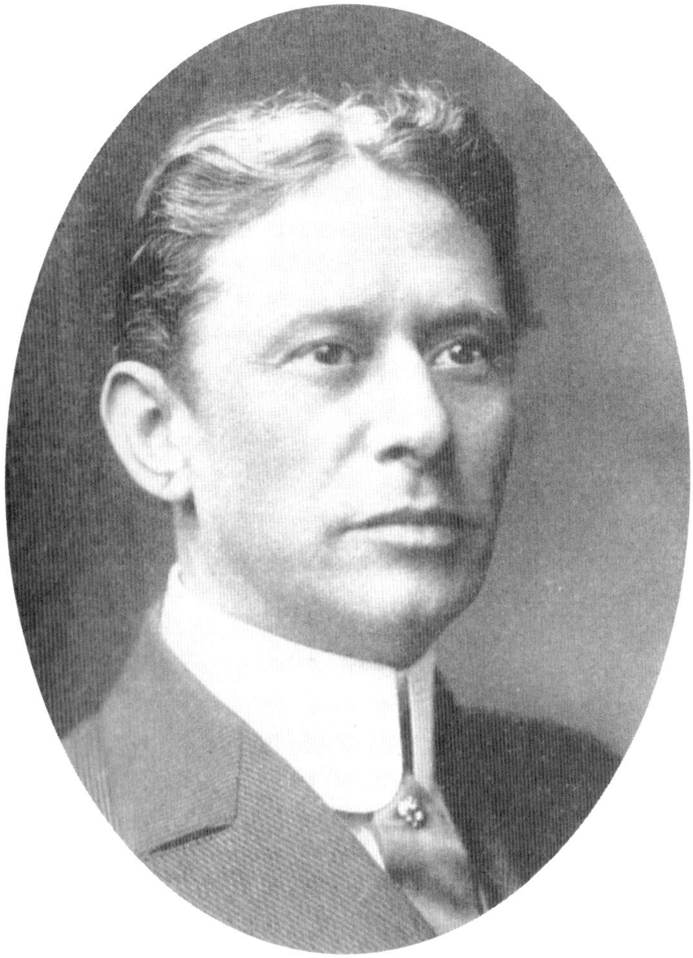

Frederick Faris

Born in St. Clairsville in 1870 to the noted artist J.A. Faris, Frederick attended public schools in Wheeling and had no formal training for his profession. After working in the office of Edward Wells, another Wheeling architect and builder, Faris formed a partnership with Joseph Leiner. After joining with Millard Giesey in 1902, historian Gibson Cranmer said that Faris, in six years, had been "personally interested in and designed . . . most of the prominent buildings and residences in the city." The 1915 issue of *Ohio Architect* magazine was devoted to his work.

Using many different architectural styles, Faris provided Wheeling with a plethora of beautiful buildings. Among his Wheeling edifices still standing are the Schmulbach Building, now the Severstal Building; the YWCA; Madison School; the Main Street Bank, formerly Wagner Wholesale Grocery; the Laconia Building, formerly the German Bank; Triadelphia Middle School; the Scottish Rite Cathedral; the Howard Mansion and Apartments; and the YMCA.

Buildings of his design that are no longer standing include Wheeling High School, North Wheeling Hospital, the Market Auditorium (West Virginia's longest building at the time), and the Gothic-style Children's Home in Woodsdale.

Probably the most unusual of Faris's work is the Mount Carmel Monastery, a Mission-style edifice built in 1917 and located on Carmel Road in the Woodsdale section of Wheeling. To honor the memory of St. Teresa, of Spain, Faris designed the monastery with a distinctive Spanish flavor. (KQ, photograph courtesy OCPL.)

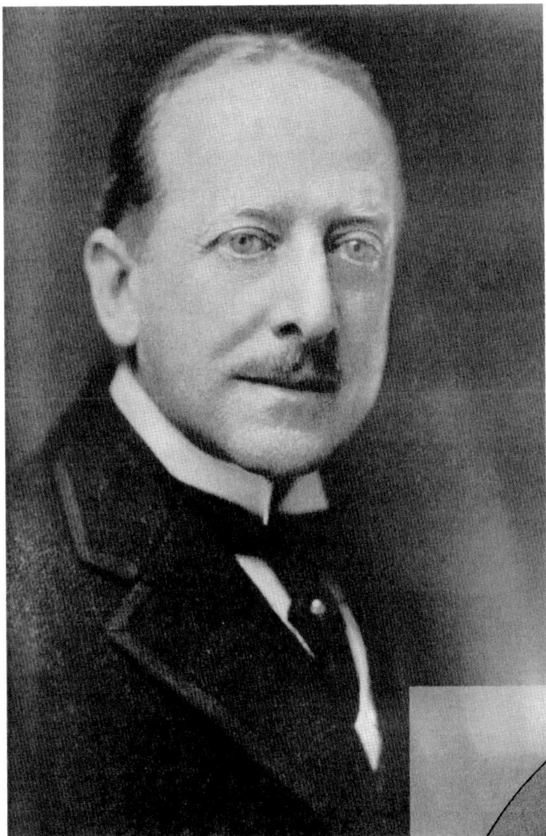

Edward Bates Franzheim
The son of a German immigrant, Franzheim was the architect behind several Wheeling structures, including the YWCA, Rogers Hotel, Vance Memorial Presbyterian Church, and the homes of Henry Stifel (Shadow Knoll) and John O. Schenk (Uplands, now known as Altenheim). Franzheim (1866–1942) was also responsible for the design work for major renovations of Earl Oglebay's country home, now called Oglebay Mansion. Other noted structures were designed in collaboration with Charles Bates, Frederick Faris, and Millard Giesey. (JF; photograph courtesy OCPL.)

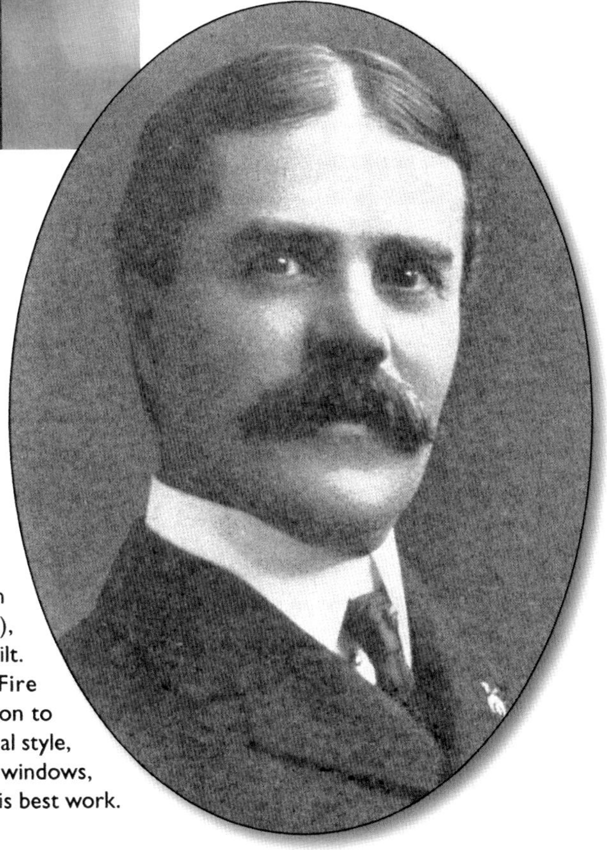

Millard F. Giesey
A self-taught architect, Millard Giesey had worked as a contractor before joining forces with Frederic Faris and E.B. Franzheim to collaborate on the Schmulbach Building (later the Wheeling Steel Building), the tallest structure in the state when built. Giesey also designed the Warwood Fire Station, St. John's Church, and the addition to the Moundsville Prison. With a Neoclassical style, an imposing facade, and 22 stained-glass windows, the L.S. Good Mansion is an example of his best work. (KQ; photograph courtesy OCPL.)

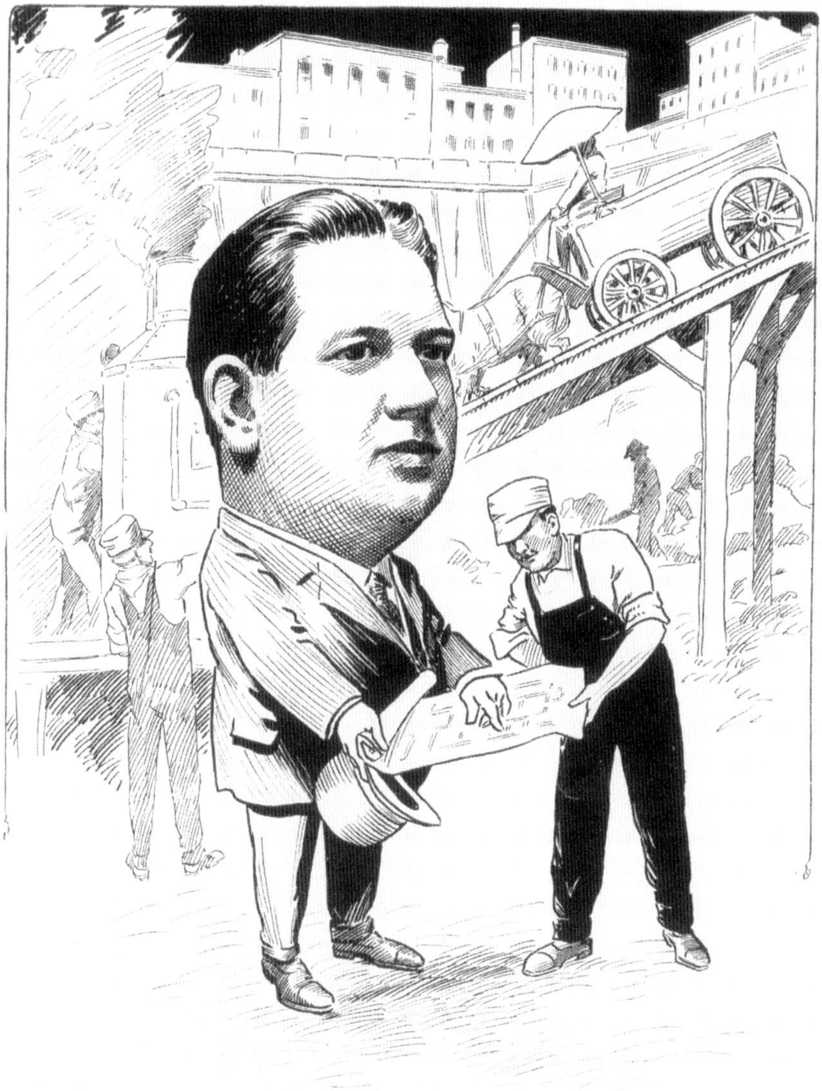

RALPH R. KITCHEN
General Contractor
Wheeling, W. Va.

Ralph R. Kitchen

Born in Bangor, Maine, Ralph Ross Kitchen (1881–1930) moved to Wheeling as a young man to supervise construction of a portion of Ohio Valley General Hospital. After starting his own local business, the R.R. Kitchen Contracting Company, in 1913, he began a career building some of the most substantial buildings in town. Through his efforts, Wheeling has been left a legacy of public and private structures that have stood the test of time. They include the White Palace at Wheeling Park, Central Union Building, Stifel Fine Arts Center, Scottish Rite Cathedral, St. Joseph's Cathedral, and the Capitol Theatre. (JF; image courtesy OCPL.)

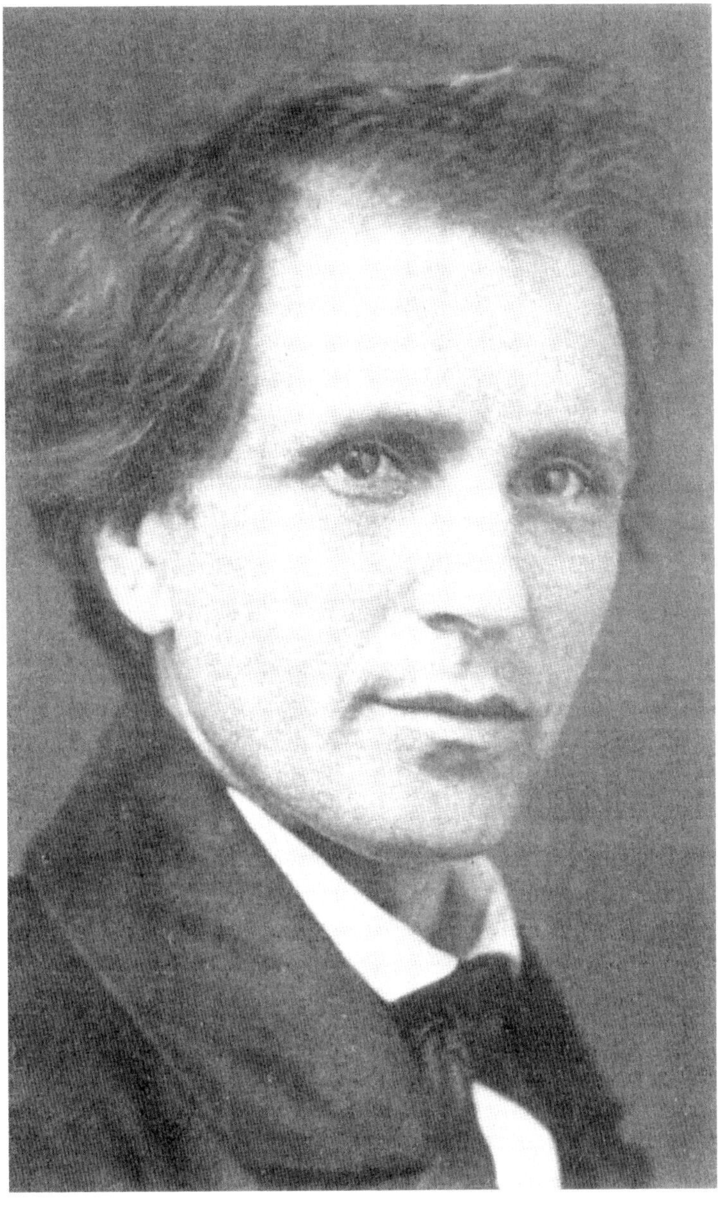

Dr. Simon Hullihen

Simon P. Hullihen, MD, DOS (1810–1857) is considered the father of oral surgery and founding doctor of Wheeling Hospital. Born in Northumberland, Pennsylvania, he received his medical degree from Washington Medical College in Baltimore and arrived in Wheeling in 1835. Before there was a dental school in the country, he specialized in the surgical treatment of the mouth and head. When instruments were not available, Dr. Hullihen invented his own, and variations of six are still in use. Dr. Hullihen became an influential author, noted lecturer, and humanitarian, known for his acts of charity.

In 1845, he opened a private infirmary and then worked with the Catholic bishop to establish a hospital. Dr. Hullihen died at age 46, and the newspaper proclaimed his demise "a public calamity." He is buried in Mt. Wood Cemetery, where the citizens of Wheeling erected a 30-foot marble monument to his memory. (MBr.)

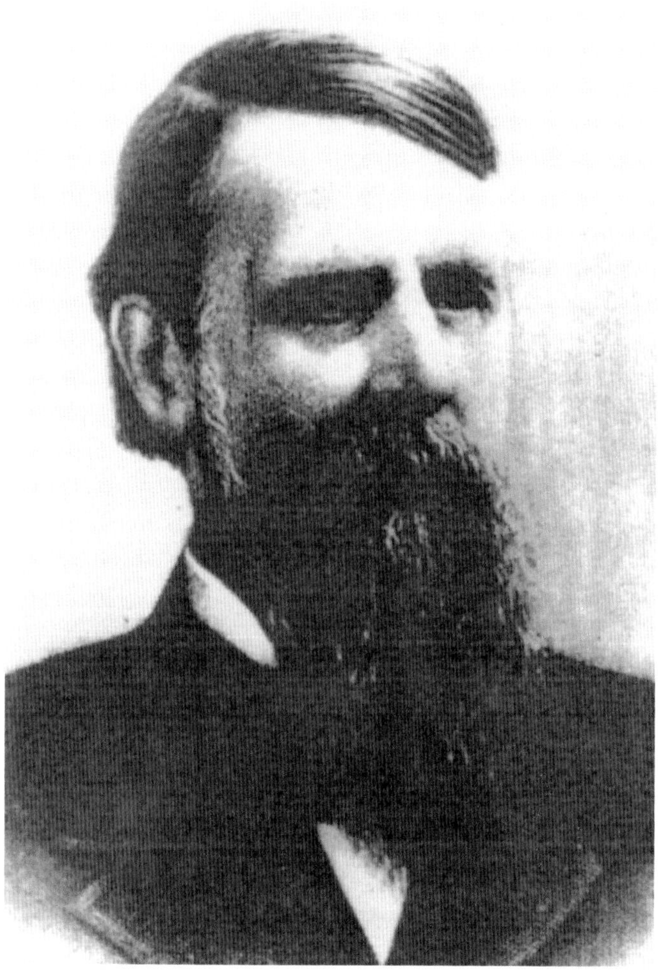

Dr. James E. Reeves

Though not born in Wheeling, James Edmund Reeves, MD, gave his all to the city, serving as the first public health officer, writing the state health laws, and founding the first West Virginia Medical Society and the American Association of Public Health. He wrote several papers cataloging the various industries of the city and warning owners of the health dangers to their workers.

He organized the first International Medical Congress, which was attended by renowned and famous figures of the medical world of 1876. For his service in teaching sanitation to her soldiers, Queen Victoria presented Dr. Reeves with a medal at a reception in his honor. When he diagnosed himself with terminal liver cancer, eight doctors from Wheeling rushed to his side in Chattanooga, Tennessee, but were unable to help. He is buried at Greenwood Cemetery. (KQ; photograph courtesy WHOF.)

Dr. Thomas Haskins

Born on a farm in Wetzel County, Haskins became superintendent of schools before enrolling in the College of Physicians and Surgeons of Baltimore. Eventually, he moved to Benwood and treated mill workers from his tiny apartment. In 1891, he began building a grand mansion and hospital at Thirty-third and Eoff Streets. The private hospital soon proved too small, and an annex was added. The Haskins hospital served mostly very rich clients; their luxurious rooms cost from $10 to $25 per week. All patients were required to have a Turkish bath before surgery. A nursing school and pharmacy were also on the premises.

In 1902, Haskins purchased a glass factory in Martins Ferry and began producing a large variety of cut and pressed glass for illumination. His Haskins's Natural Eye Auto Lens for automobiles proved so popular that the plant could hardly keep up with demand. When Haskins moved to Oklahoma in 1918, he sold the hospital to the Salvation Army, to be used for transients and storage. (KQ; image courtesy OCPL.)

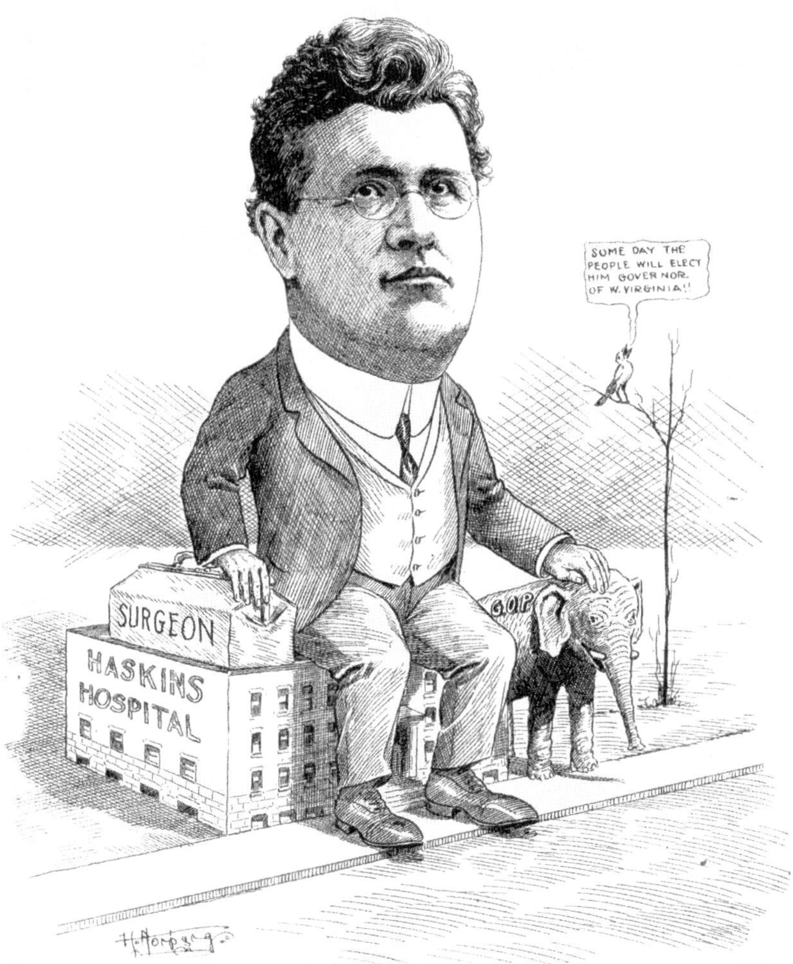

DR. THOMAS M. HASKINS
Board of Control
Wheeling, W. Va.

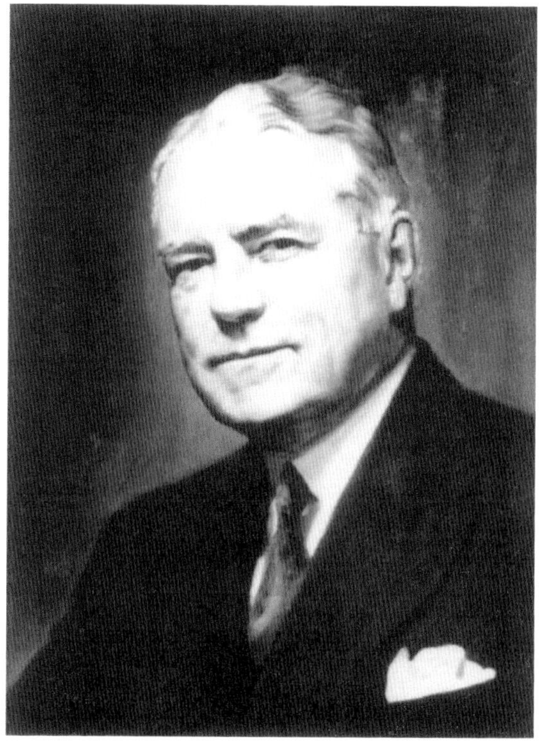

Dr. William S. Fulton

Dr. William Stuart Fulton (1873–1938) was a distinguished physician and surgeon best known for establishing the Wheeling Clinic. Dr. Fulton brought in trained specialists and gave them a free hand to practice their professions, developing a medical center rare for a city the size of Wheeling. Since there were relatively few surgeons in the smaller towns in the surrounding area who did major surgery, clinic surgeons were constantly called to operate in hospitals all over the region. (WHOF.)

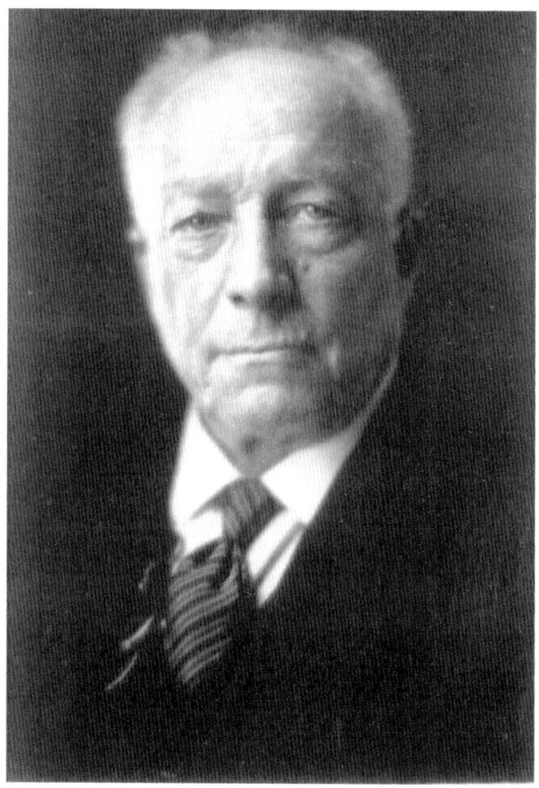

Dr. Jacob Schwinn

Swiss-born Jacob Schwinn (1854–1941) established himself as a surgeon of brilliant skill, often performing operations in his own home in the early days. Dr. Schwinn was considered the dean of the staff of Ohio Valley General Hospital and was head of the research department. In 1938, at the age of 83, using only a local anesthetic, Dr. Schwinn supervised his own operation for a strangulated hernia—an event so unusual that it made national news. (WHOF.)

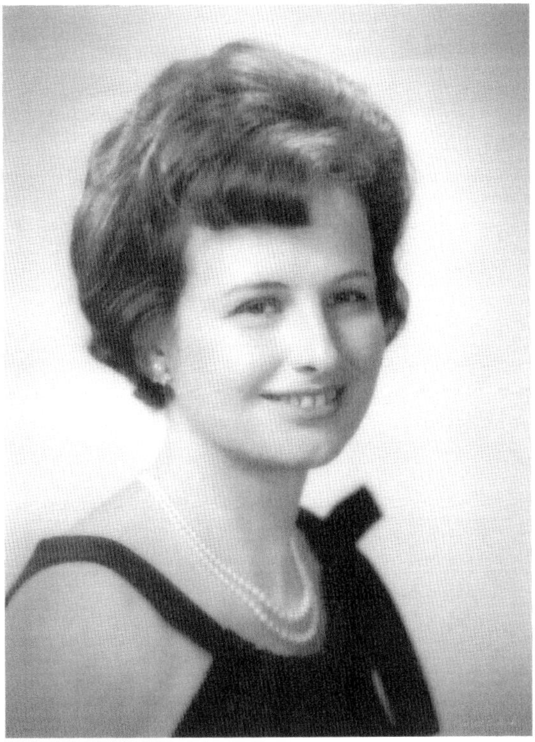

Mary Louis Snyder Efron

Efron (1926–1967) was a leading researcher in the field of mental retardation and children's diseases. She and her associates developed programs for mass screening of newborn infants to detect amino acid deficiencies and phenylketonuria, which results in mental retardation unless detected and treated. The screening is now required throughout the United States and the world. (WHOF.)

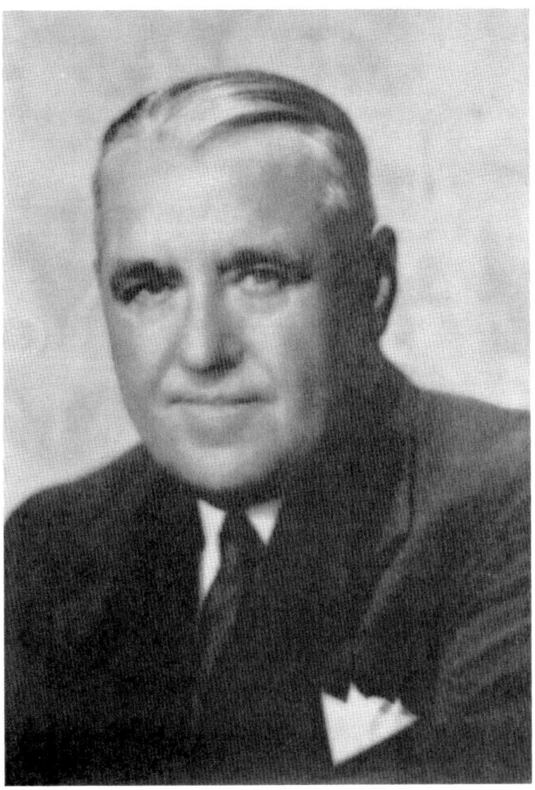

William E. Weiss

In 1900, William Weiss (1979–1942), a 21-year-old graduate of the Philadelphia College of Pharmacy, owned a formula for a patent medicine called Neuralgine, which he peddled door-to-door within horse-and-buggy range of Wheeling. From those humble beginnings, Weiss grew the Sterling Drug Company to one of the world's largest manufacturers of proprietary remedies. (WHOF.)

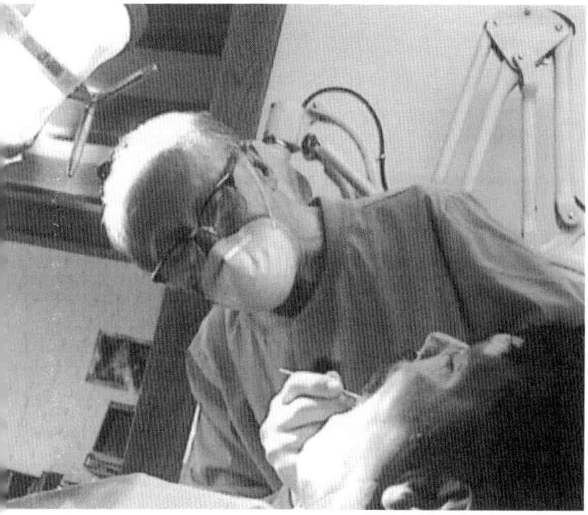

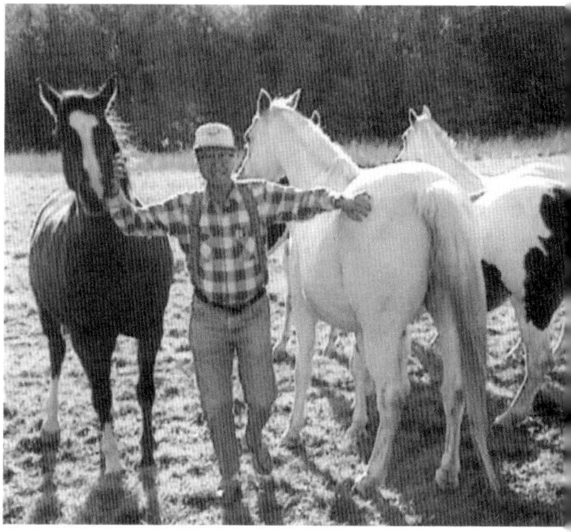

S. Arthur Rybeck Jr.

Dentist, organic farmer, and civic leader, Dr. S. Arthur "Art" Rybeck Jr. was born in Wheeling on August 8, 1923, the son of Samuel "Ry" and Rosalind "Buddie" Rybeck.

After graduating from Triadelphia High School, he attended West Virginia University before serving in World War II. After leaving the Army, he earned his doctor of dental surgery degree from the University of Pennsylvania through the GI Bill.

He declined big-city opportunities so he could go back to his hometown and work on preventive dental care and nutrition. He said every tooth he pulled made him feel like a mortician. So he became a West Virginia "Johnny Appleseed" for flossing and other home-care techniques that did not cost much but depended on public health education. Dr. Art did not hesitate to break out into song to liven things up as he taught flossing and better brushing at his office or around campfires when he trekked out each summer with his wife, Sivia Brody Rybeck, and their five children.

Dr. Art practiced dentistry in downtown Wheeling and then with his partner, Dr. Donald Lough, as part of Gentle Dental Care on Washington Avenue. Eventually, Dr. Art built the Viewpoint Free Dental Clinic at his organic farm on Dallas Pike. He funded the effort through proceeds from dental inventions that he came up with alongside gifted engineer L.D. "Curt" Curtis, whom he hired into his regular practice. The inventions were manufactured in a converted section of the goat barn next to the chicken coop. A conventional distributor then sold the inventions around the world while Dr. Art hand-delivered organic eggs and vegetables across the county.

Along with his younger brother Walter, Dr. Art spent his youth learning from Oglebay Park's first naturalist, A.B. Brooks. The experience gave Dr. Art and his family a lifelong love for the Oglebay Institute and Oglebay Park, where he helped build the nature programs and the Schrader Environmental Center. He and Sivia, his wife of 57 years, were also strong supporters of Oglebay Institute's folk dancing, theater, opera, and music programs. He also had a lifelong role in Temple Shalom and worked to make the state's tax system fairer with his group, Mountaineers United for Sane Taxation (MUST).

Active to the end, Dr. Art was treating patients at Viewpoint until the day before he died on January 18, 2008. (TR and The Rybeck family.)

CHAPTER SIX

Public Service

Wheeling's stature can perhaps best be measured by the inexhaustible generosity of so many of its citizens. From religious leaders, educators, and philanthropists to labor leaders, military veterans, public servants, and tireless preservationists, Wheeling has been blessed with an array of good citizens willing to give of themselves. These community builders have made Wheeling a consistently great place to live, helping to establish its reputation as "the Friendly City."

Wheeling has long benefited from strong leadership by mayors, from Andrew Sweeney and Charles Ihlenfeld to Jack Fahey and current mayor Andy McKenzie. At the state level, Col. Thomas O'Brien (great-grandfather of musicians Mollie and Tim) served as state treasurer, and Chester R. Hubbard served four terms in the West Virginia House of Delegates and three in the state senate. US Congressman David McKinley, a seventh-generation resident of Wheeling and West Virginia, has dedicated his life to public service. Attorneys like Henry Stifel Schrader, Robert Fitzsimmons, and Pat Cassidy have fought for justice while providing community leadership. Alfred A. "Happy" Cooper was one of Wheeling's first African American firefighters, and William Turner was the city's first African American police officer.

Clergy have served a vital role in Wheeling's history. Bishop Richard Whelan was an admired leader for Catholics in Wheeling. The Sisters of the Visitation founded Mt. de Chantal Visitation Academy, a school for girls of all faiths, in 1848. Meanwhile, the Sisters of St. Joseph arrived in 1853 to help grow Wheeling Hospital into a premiere medical center. Bishop Joseph Hodges wrote and promulgated "This Land is Home to Me," a pastoral letter addressing poverty in Appalachia.

Wheeling has also benefited from an abundance of dedicated educators, such as Pat Temple (Clay School), Sister Anne Regina O'Leary, and Joseph "Doc" Viglietta, who served as principals of Wheeling Central Catholic High School. It was there that Lou Volpe fostered a love for literature and community volunteerism in his students. Wheeling Jesuit University's Fr. Jim O'Brien taught his students the importance of peace and justice in Appalachia, and Levering C. Bonar started teaching in a one-room school on Fish Creek in 1914 and worked his way up to superintendent of Ohio County Schools. Wheeling native Dr. Robert E. Lee Strider served as president of Colby College in Maine, and Dr. Forrest H. Kirkpatrick was a professor and dean whose expertise was sought by educational and business organizations all over the world.

Finally, Wheeling can boast a long line of philanthropists whose generosity has helped keep the city's cultural life vibrant. Department store owner George Stifel, for example, established an endowment fund to provide annual awards for Wheeling's best students, while James "Doc" White did something similar for African American students. South Wheeling's Irene Doretta Meagel left a trust that now benefits 16 local organizations, and Margaret McCluskey Schiffler advanced from office clerk to secretary-treasurer of Centre Foundry, amassing a personal fortune that allowed her to contribute generously to Wheeling Hospital and other organizations. And Elizabeth Stifel Kline's foundation supports programs like the summer entertainment series at Oglebay Park, annual concerts of the Wheeling Symphony, and much more.

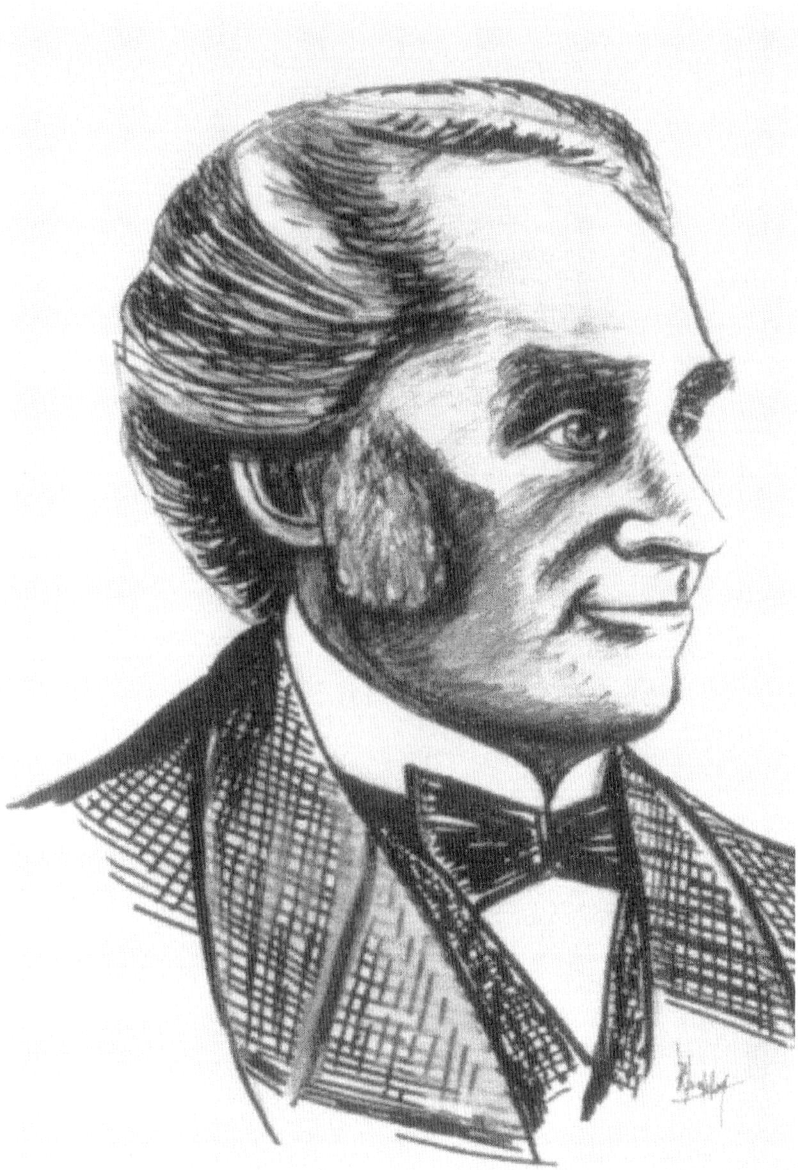

Noah Linsly

Linsly (1774–1814), a teacher and lawyer, arrived in Wheeling in 1799 as a 25-year-old stranger. Described as a man of fine presence, extremely particular in his dress, and dignified in his manner, Linsly strove to be scrupulous in all his dealings, preferring the life of an honest lawyer rather than one who obtained riches by questionable means. He became a leading Wheeling citizen, serving as councilman, prosecuting attorney, and the city's fourth mayor (1807–1809). At age 41, Linsly died from hemorrhage of the lungs. He was later dubbed "the Friend of Youth and Benefactor of Mankind." The majority of his estate was willed "for the use, benefit and advantage of a Lancastrian School" in Wheeling, which was incorporated on November 29, 1814, by the assembly of Virginia as the Lancasterian Academy (now Linsly School). (CJu; image courtesy WHOF.)

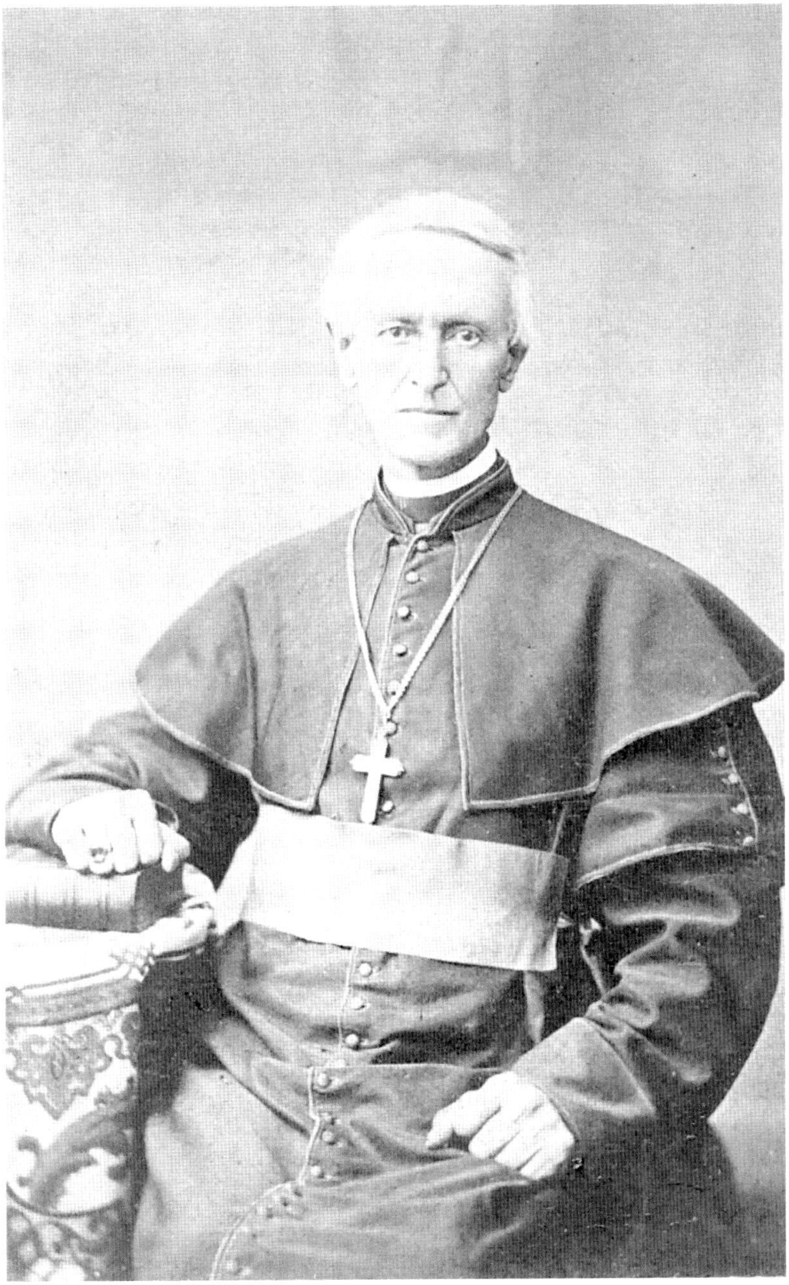

Bishop Richard Whelan

Richard Vincent Whelan (1809–1874) was the first bishop of the Diocese of Wheeling-Charleston. At age 10, he entered Mount Saint Mary College, graduating in 1826 and being ordained in 1831. While serving in Harpers Ferry, Whelan was named the first bishop of the Diocese of Richmond. The expansive geographic area of this diocese caused it to be split, east and west, in 1849 with centers at Richmond and Wheeling. Whelan went west to become the first bishop of the Diocese of Wheeling, established on July 19, 1850. He was instrumental in the propagation of the Catholic faith in Western Virginia until his death on July 7, 1874. (JG; photograph courtesy Archives, Diocese of Wheeling-Charleston.)

The Sisters of St Joseph

Wheeling Hospital, the oldest medical institution in West Virginia, was incorporated on March 12, 1850, by Bishop Richard V. Whelan, working with Drs. Simon Hullihen, John Frissell, and Matthew Houston. The hospital grew when six Sisters of St. Joseph arrived from Missouri in April 1853. By 1856, a larger building opened in North Wheeling (middle). The Civil War exploded five years later, and soon, Wheeling Hospital was drawn into the conflict. In March 1864, the hospital received 47 ill soldiers from the Athenaeum, the Union prison. The sick were, as superior Mother de Chantal (pictured at top) observed, "all prostrated with disease." In April 1864, part of the building was rented for a post hospital, with Dr. John Kirker as surgeon in charge. Dr. John Frissell, appointed by Governor Pierpont as medical supervisor of prisoners and soldiers, also served there.

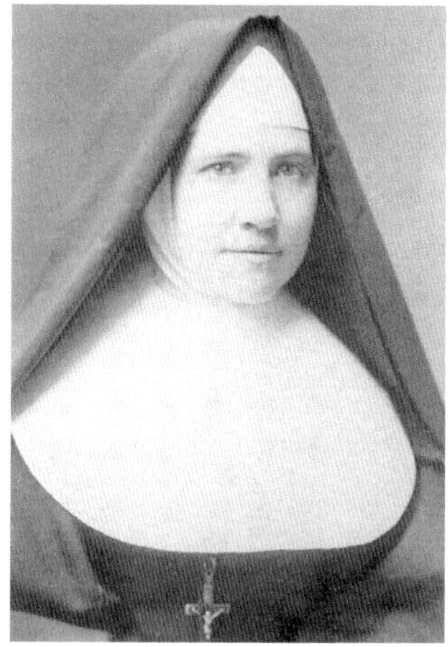

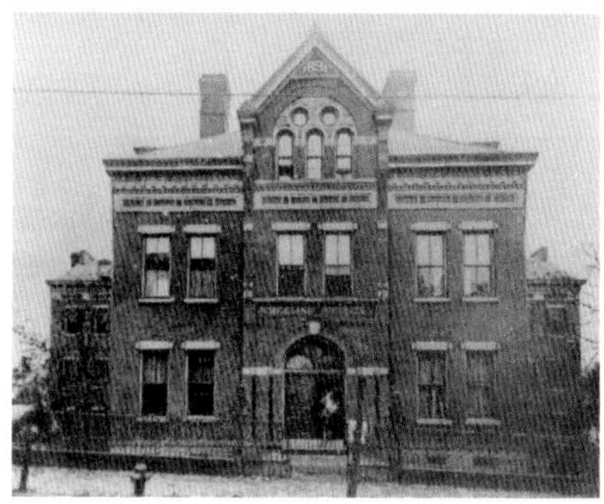

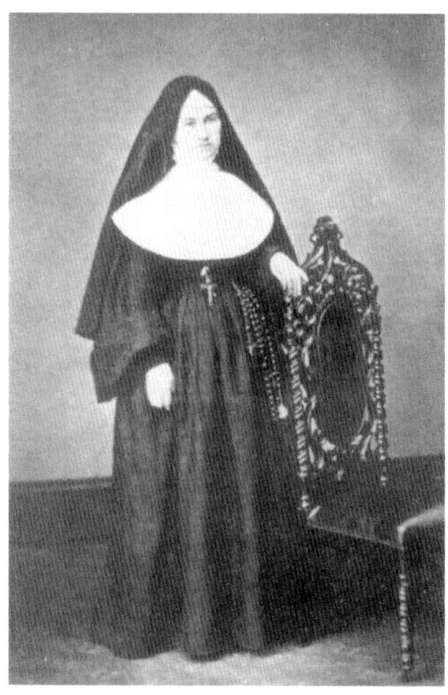

During the bloody year of 1864, Union and Confederate wounded had to be sent farther from the front for care, and Wheeling, on the Baltimore & Ohio Railroad, began receiving hundreds of soldiers. On July 26, 1864, some 200 invalids arrived unexpectedly, and the entire building was commandeered. Mother de Chantal wrote: "We laid them on the floor in rows of blankets . . . some of them are great sufferers." Tents were eventually erected on the grounds. The six Sisters became enrolled as army nurses: Sisters Mary de Chantal, Vincent, Ignatius, Agnes, Stanislaus, and Aloysius. Sr. Ignatius Farley (pictured at bottom) later recalled: "There were so few of us that it was necessary to work almost without stopping . . . they were from both armies and no difference was made in the manner of their care." One evening, Sister Ignatius returned to the chapel dormitory, as the Sisters had given their beds to the wounded. She found "seven professed sisters, worn out by severe hospital duty, lying fast asleep on the floor," with a pillow stuffed with leaves from the grounds.

Soon, Wheeling Hospital was designated a US Army General Hospital. There, several survivors of Andersonville Prison were treated. One soldier was described as "a complete skeleton, and his legs were frozen up to his knees." He did not survive. A neighborhood child remembered there were no screens on the doors, and the flies were thick and aggravating. She would brush them off the wounded soldiers. In February 1865, the army had not paid its bills, so Mother de Chantal traveled to Washington to demand accountability. The arrears were quickly settled. By July 1865, the hospital began returning to normal, and the sisters invited local patients and doctors to return. (MBr; photographs courtesy Archives, Diocese of Wheeling-Charleston.)

Rev. Clifford M. Lewis, SJ

Lewis (1911–1983) was a founding father of Wheeling College, where he served in development, alumni, and public relations. He also took an active interest in the history of the Wheeling area. In 1968, he launched the first issue of the *Upper Ohio Valley Historical Review* (still in print), and he played a central role in acquiring federal funds for the restoration of the West Virginia Independence Hall in Wheeling. For his efforts, he was known as "the Dean of Wheeling Historians." (JG; photograph courtesy Archives, Diocese of Wheeling-Charleston.)

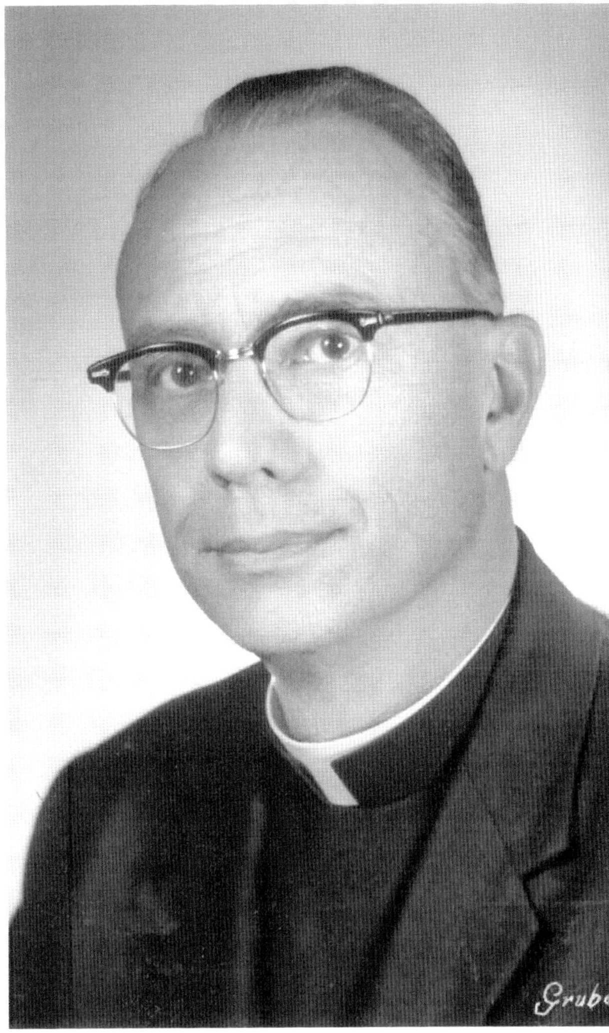

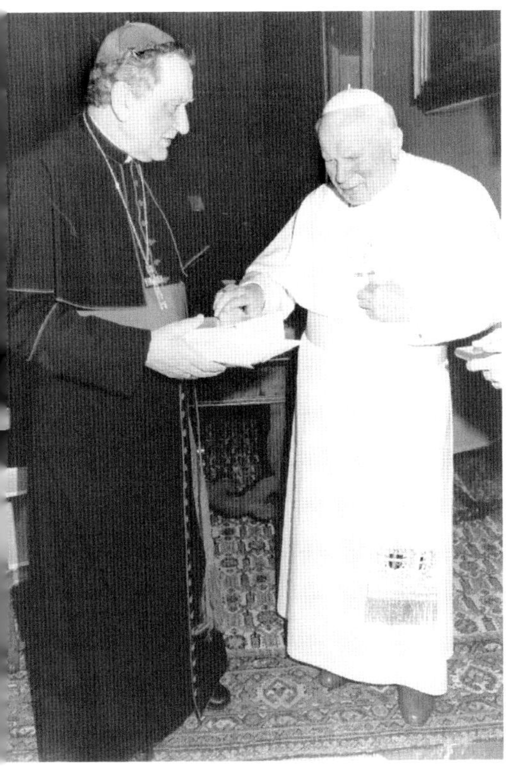

Bishop Bernard W. Schmitt

Bernard Schmitt (1928–2011), seventh bishop of the Diocese of Wheeling-Charleston, holds the distinction of being the only American bishop born in Wheeling. He was appointed auxiliary bishop in May 1988 and was named ordinary in March 1989 on the departure of Bishop Francis B. Schulte. Schmitt (pictured with Pope John Paul II) consolidated and strengthened the Catholic Church in West Virginia and oversaw pastoral planning, stewardship, and spiritual development. Schmitt also oversaw a renovation of St. Joseph Cathedral. (JG; photograph courtesy Archives, Diocese of Wheeling-Charleston.)

Clara Welty

Welty (1879–1960) received a strong Catholic education at St. Alphonsus School and Mount de Chantal Academy. Her concern for the needy prompted her in 1950 to donate the family home for use as a home for the aged population of Wheeling. She established a charitable trust that continues to operate three Welty facilities in Wheeling. For her efforts, Pope Pius XII awarded Welty a papal medal, the highest recognition for the laity. (JG; image courtesy Good Shepherd Nursing Home.)

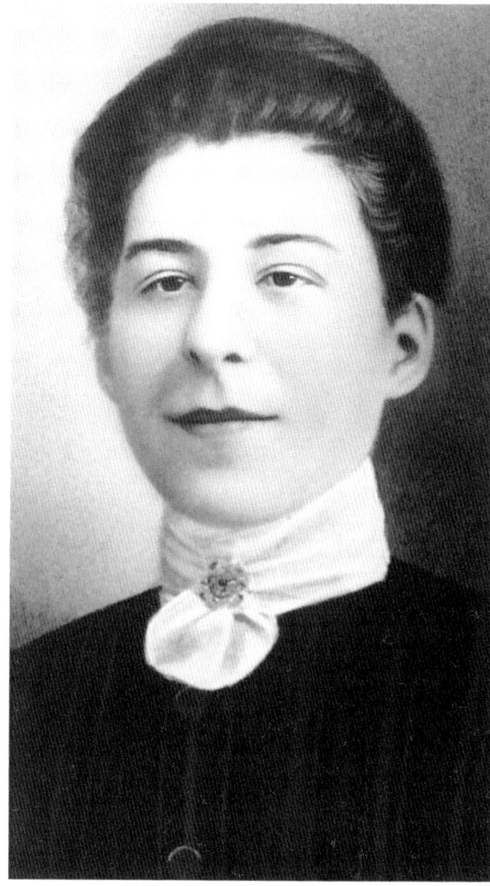

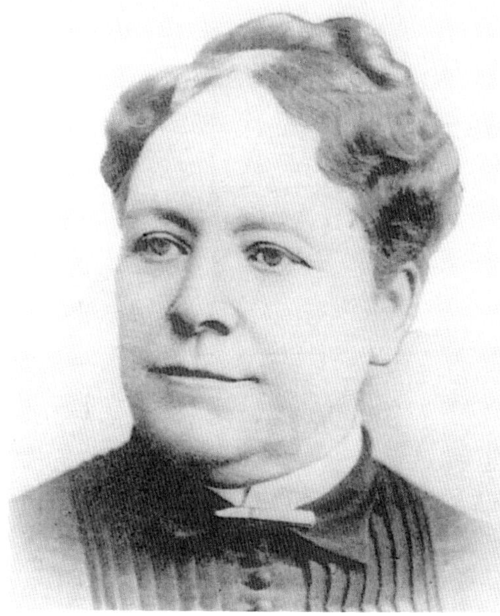

Annie Sinclair Cunningham

Cunningham (1832–1897) was a powerful force for good whose life's work in religious and charitable matters benefited many at home and abroad. The wife of the Reverend David Cunningham, pastor of Wheeling's First Presbyterian Church, she was the originator of the Home for the Aged and Friendless Women, now Elmhurst, the House of Friendship. She also was elected president of the International Union of Women for Foreign Mission Work. (WHOF.)

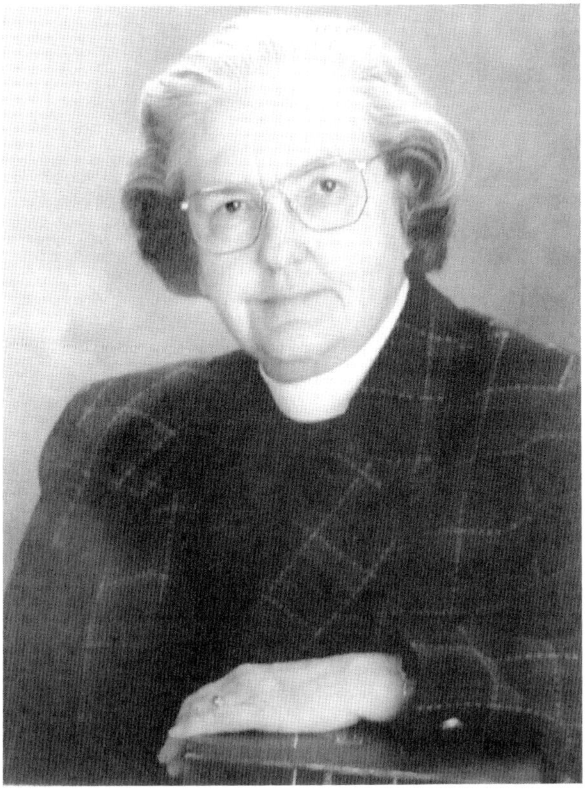

Rev. Margaret Bird Caldwell Phillimore
One of the first women ordained a priest in the Episcopal Diocese of West Virginia, Rev. Margaret B.C. Phillimore (1915–2004) served as interim vicar or rector in churches in six diocesan deaneries and was on eight diocesan boards and commissions. In England, she was the first woman ever to preach at the cathedrals of Canterbury, Carlisle, and Rochester. (WHOF; photograph courtesy St. Matthews's Episcopal Church.)

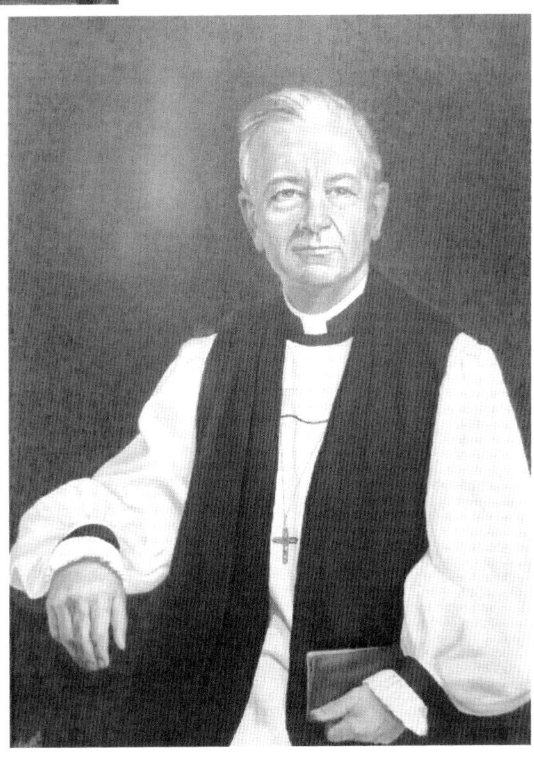

Rt. Rev. Robert E. Lee Strider
Robert Edward Lee Strider (1887–1969) became rector of St. Matthew's Church of Wheeling in 1915. His immense popularity was demonstrated when he was called, in 1937, to become the dean of the Virginia Seminary at Alexandria. So many people came forward to ask him to stay, that he declined the post. Named third bishop of the Episcopal Diocese of West Virginia, Strider became diocesan head in 1939. He moved the headquarters from Charleston to Wheeling. (WHOF; image courtesy St. Matthews's Episcopal Church.)

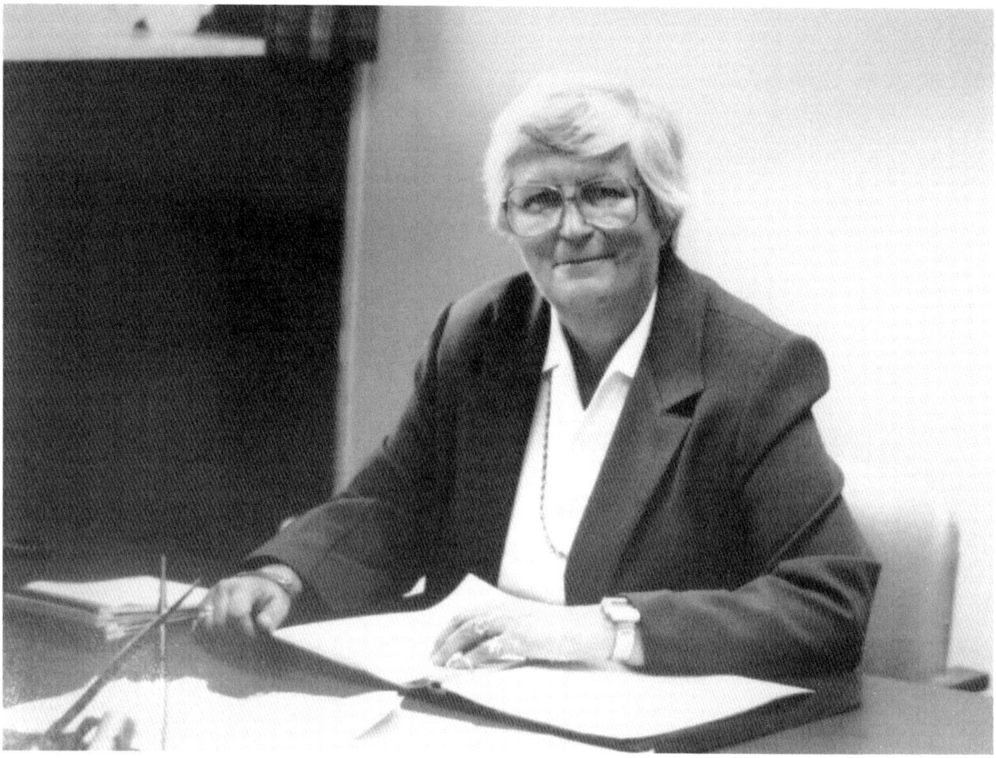

Phyllis Beneke

After graduating from Triadelphia High School, Phyllis A. Beneke (1929–1988) returned as dean of women from 1956 to 1966. She became the last principal of Wheeling High School (1973–1976). When Wheeling Park High School opened, she became its assistant principal and, eventually, principal in 1983. Beneke's estate left several million dollars for a scholarship fund for Park High students. A member of Vance Church, she donated three stained-glass windows, and her collection of Royal Doulton and Hummel figures was given to the Oglebay Mansion Museum. (KQ; photograph courtesy Wheeling Park High School.)

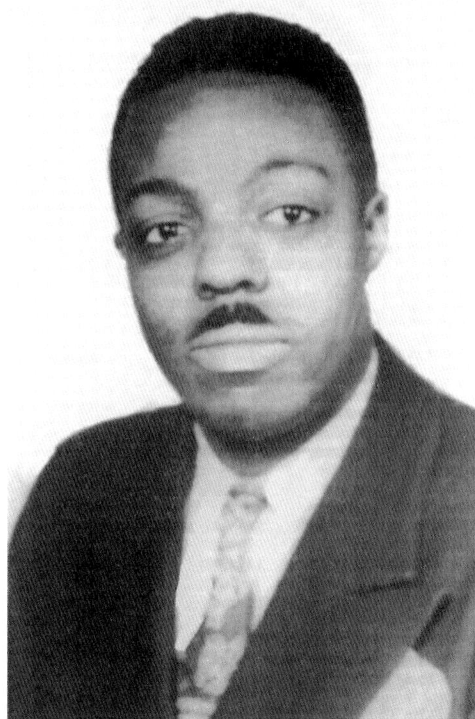

Phillip Nathaniel Reed

Reed (1914–1975) served as principal at segregated Lincoln School and helped steer Ohio County Public schools through integration. The first director of guidance for Ohio County Schools, Reed headed the committee tasked with developing a drug education policy for the school board. He also served on the Northern Panhandle Employment of the Handicapped Committee. (WHOF.)

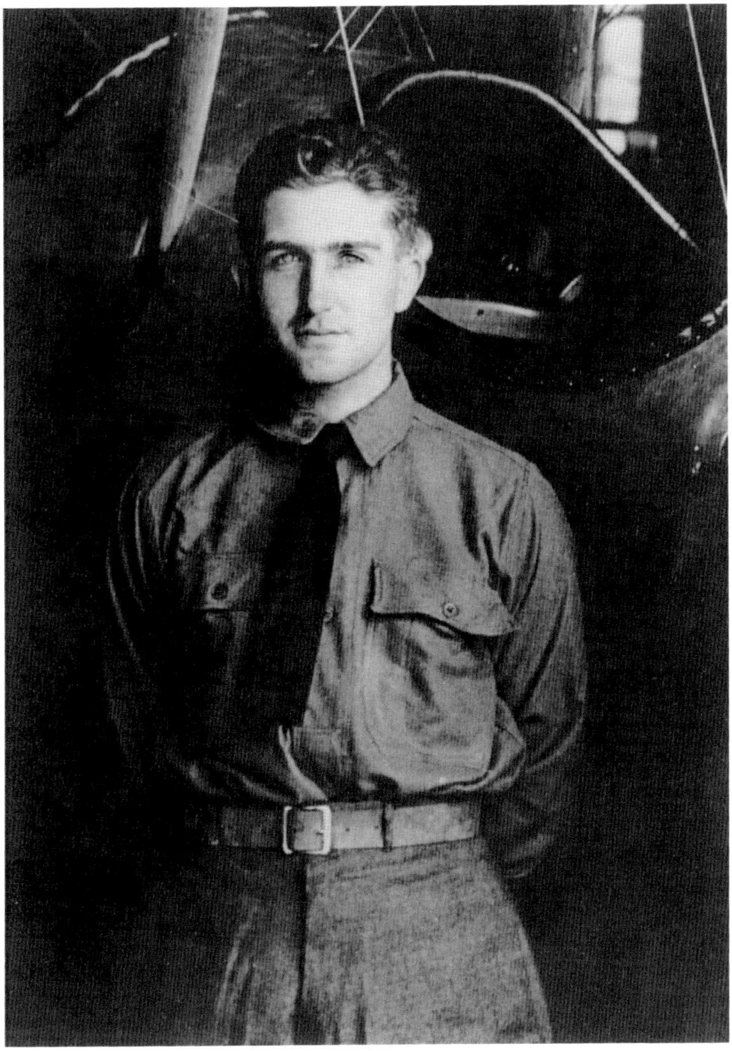

Louis Bennett Jr.

Lt. Louis Bennett Jr. (1894–1918), an avid supporter of preparedness and aviation, became West Virginia's only World War I flying ace. In founding the West Virginia Flying Corps, Bennett sought to train a cohesive combat unit "ready to serve" West Virginia and the nation. He founded the West Virginia Aircraft Company (with a plant on Hess Avenue in Warwood), flew from an airfield in Beech Bottom, and maintained an office in Wheeling's Schmulbach Building. To stimulate local interest, the West Virginia Flying Corps offered a free flight around the Ohio Valley. The number of people who came to fly was so numerous and the crowd so large that, as darkness neared, lots were drawn to determine who would go aloft. Bennett died in battle over France on August 24, 1918, serving as a member of the British Royal Air Force. Bennett's mother honored her son and the Royal Flying Corps with a stained-glass window for London's Westminster Abbey. She also commissioned a memorial bronze statue, *The Aviator*, in 1925. It still stands on the campus of Linsly School. The Bennett Memorial Museum, featuring Bennett's war trophies, antique firearms, curios, and relics, opened on the second floor of the old Wheeling Public Library on Market Street in 1920. "With the exception of the Museum of Natural History in New York City," the *Wheeling News-Register* bragged, "it is doubtful if there is another such collection of world relics." (CJu; image courtesy West Virginia and Regional History Collection.)

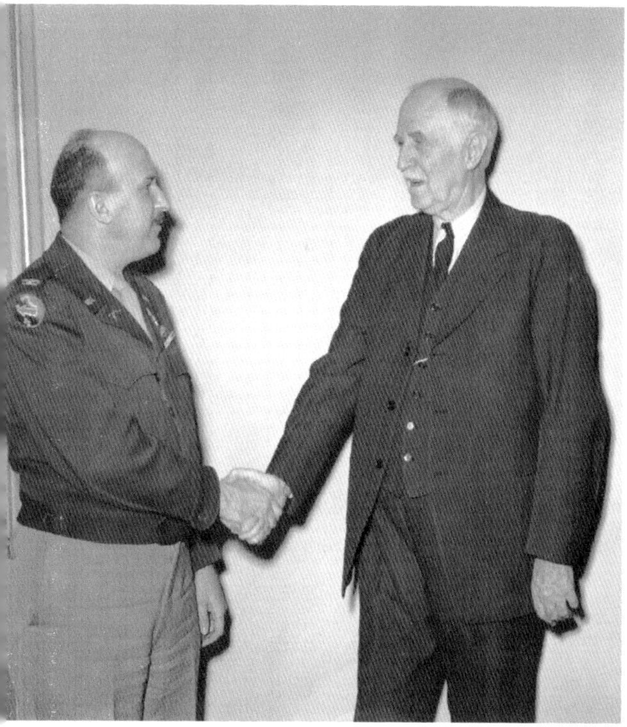

Col. Julian G. Hearne

Julian Hearne (pictured at left in 1947) was an attorney who helped write legislation that created Wheeling's nonpartisan council–city manager form of government, enacted in 1935. Hearne (1904–1995) joined the Army in 1941 and was assigned to the 24th US Infantry Regiment, an African American unit. As the regiment's leading officer, he attended to the surrender of a Japanese army garrison on Aka Island on August 22, 1945, and later donated the sword he received from the Japanese commander to the Smithsonian Museum. During the war, Hearne began writing musical compositions. His most noted work was "West Virginia, My Home Sweet Home" (1947), which was declared the first of West Virginia's three official state songs. Following his retirement from the Army, Hearne wrote *Some Unknown Facts of American History: The Saga of Governor Pierpont* (1987). (JL; photograph courtesy West Virginia and Regional History Collection at West Virginia University.)

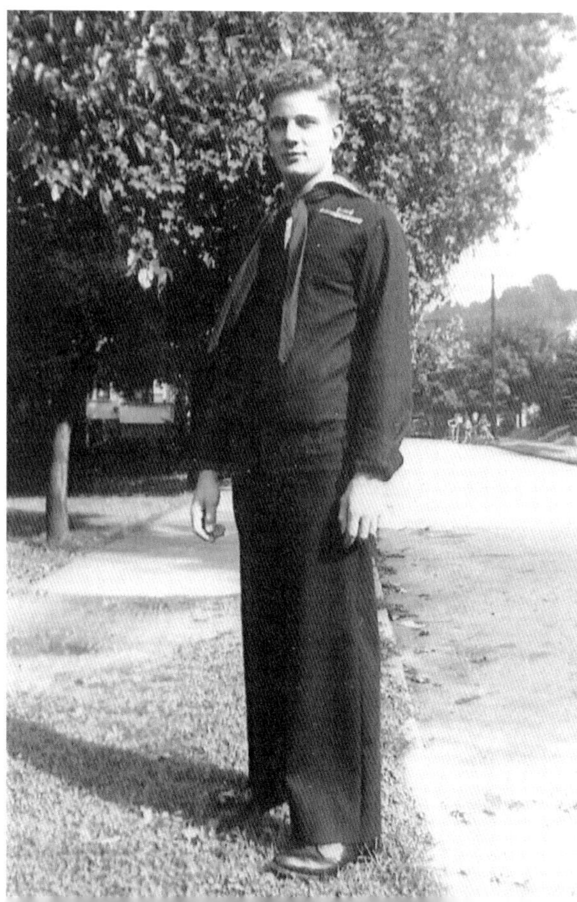

Paul W. McGinnis

Signalman McGinnis, 19, was aboard the US Navy cruiser *Indianapolis* in July 1945 when it was sunk by Japanese torpedoes. The survivors spent five days adrift—thirsty, exhausted, and relentlessly harassed by sharks. Of the 1,196 crew members, only 317 survived, including McGinnis, who remembers waking up on the wing of a PBY plane. The incident is famously recounted by the character "Quint" in the movie *Jaws*. (SD: photograph courtesy Paul McGinnis.)

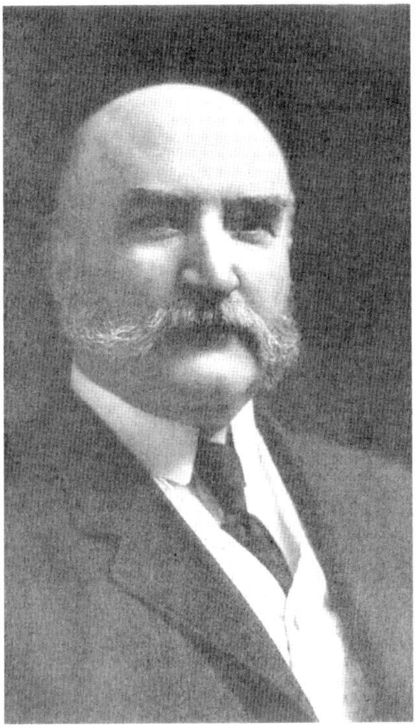

George Lutz
George Washington Lutz (1855–1940) was owner of one of the largest industrial supply companies in the tri-state region. He was responsible for much of the urban beautification of Wheeling Island. Lutz chaired the Landscape Commission of the W.E. Stone Fund, which continues to this day to provide for the floral ornamentation along National Road. Lutz, known as "the Father of the Market Auditorium," was partly responsible for placement of the Mingo Indian statue at the top of Wheeling Hill. (WHOF.)

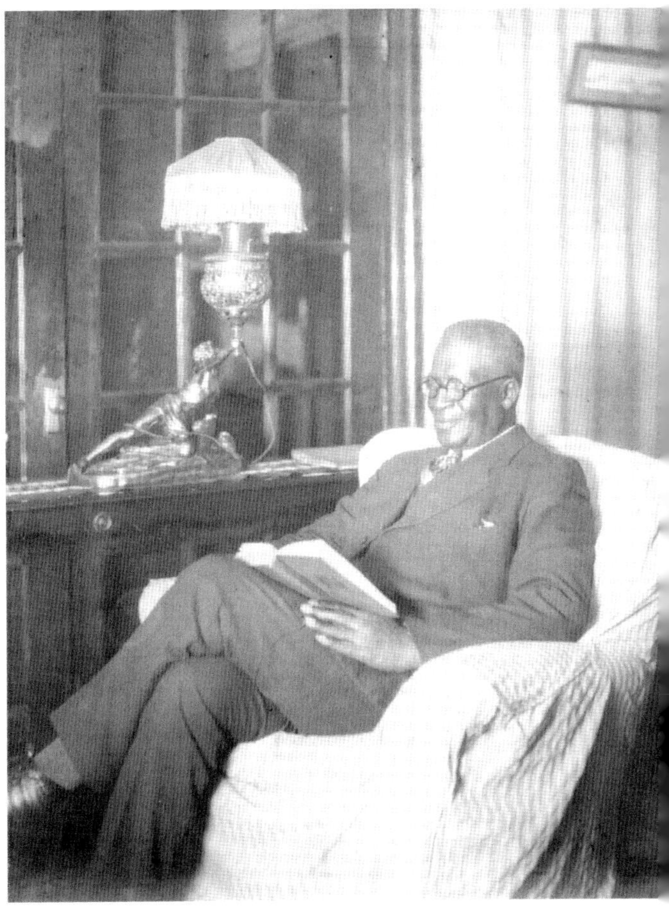

William Alexander Turner
Wheeling's first African American police officer was a man named William "Bill" Turner (1865–1928). An officer for 35 years, he helped capture the notorious Mabel Felway (Lizzie Ford) in 1926. In this photograph, Turner is enjoying his retirement at home. (SD, BC; photograph courtesy Katherine Snead/OCPL.)

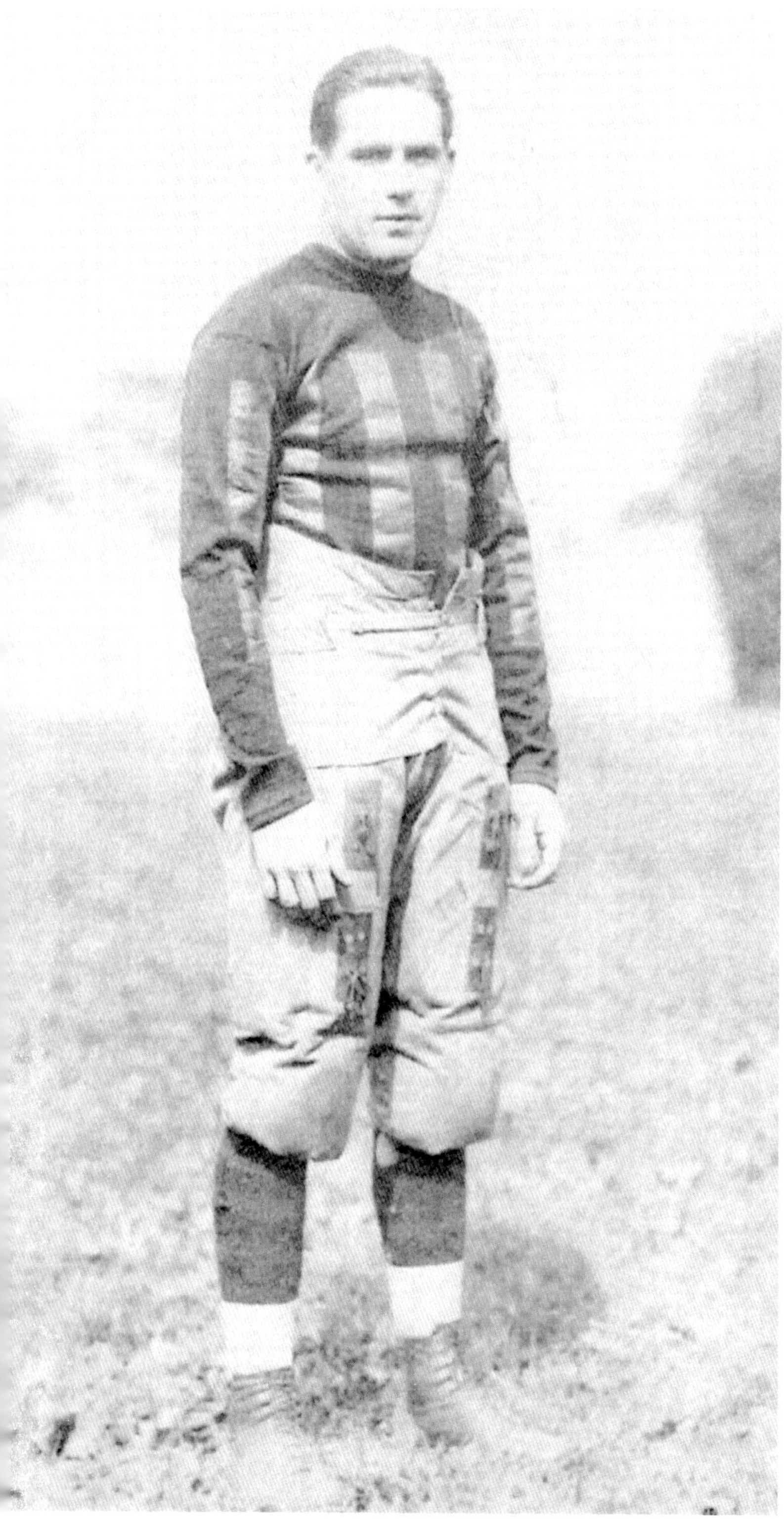

C. Lee Spillers

Spillers devoted his life to the service to others. After serving in the Marines in World War I, he returned to Wheeling and won a full scholarship to Linsly Military Institute because of his ability to drill the cadets. He went on to Washington and Jefferson College, where he was a member of the undefeated football team of 1922 that competed in the Rose Bowl.

After Harvard Law School, Spillers returned to Wheeling and served as sheriff, prosecuting attorney, judge of the Intermediate Court, and state senator. He was a Navy captain during World War II and afterward became a member of the law firm Goodwin, Spillers, and Mead.

His motto was "Not how much I can get, but how much I can give." He enjoyed playing catch in the yard with his sons or competing in a game of dominoes with his law partner Russell Goodwin while listening to a radio broadcast of a football game. In a tribute from the Ohio County Bar Association, it was said that Spillers "will be remembered not for his accomplishments, but for what he was." (KQ; photograph courtesy George Spillers.)

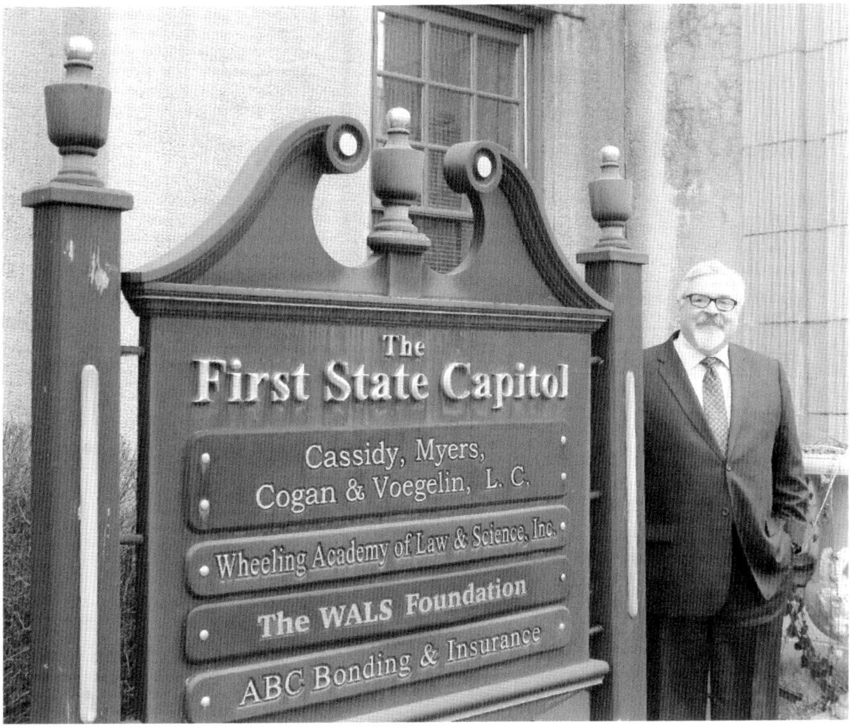

Patrick S. Cassidy

The son of a steelworker and union organizer, Cassidy graduated from Weirton Madonna High School in 1966, obtained a degree in philosophy from Wheeling College in 1970, and earned the degree of juris doctor in 1973 from the Catholic University of America.

A trial lawyer, Cassidy has represented employees, union members, and other individuals in employment and civil rights matters and in other issues related to the workplace and professional careers since 1973. Active in community affairs, he served as cochairman of the Wheeling National Heritage Area Commission and was the first chairman of the board of directors of the Wheeling National Heritage Area Corporation (WNHAC), serving in both capacities for a total of 10 years. During this time, WNHAC designed and developed the Wheeling Artisan Center, the Robert C. Byrd Intermodal Transportation Center, and the Wheeling Heritage Port. Cassidy's love of Wheeling's heritage inspired he and his wife to purchase the First State Capitol of West Virginia in 1993, which they have lovingly restored over the last 20 years. They hope to have it completed in 2013, the 150th anniversary of the founding of the State of West Virginia.

Cassidy and his wife, the former Mary Ellen Arthur of Wheeling, are cofounders, and he is president, of the Wheeling Academy of Law and Science (WALS), and the WALS Foundation, both of Wheeling. WALS serves as an educational and networking "free space" for the promotion of local economic opportunity, jobs, and career-enhancing educational programming. The WALS Foundation maintains the Reuther-Wheeling Library in the First State Capitol, and it has created and developed a "mock trial" program for elementary and high school educators in West Virginia that allows students to learn about the American legal system while acting out scripts that teach, indirectly, of the dangers of illegal drug abuse. More than 10,000 students statewide have participated in the program, which is now being made available to the state for its continuing use.

Cassidy wrote, produced, and directed an original musical drama (with music by collaborator Dr. Geoffrey Schoolar) titled *The Good European*, which had its world premiere at Wheeling's historic Capitol Music Hall on August 25, 2000, the centenary of the death of the German philosopher Friedrich Nietzsche. The play is based on the last day of life of the German philosopher. (PC.)

Justice Thomas B. Miller

Justice Miller (1929–2008) was one of the finest jurists in the history of the state. Elected to the West Virginia Supreme Court in 1977, Miller's most prominent opinions include *LaRue* v. *LaRue* (fairness to women in the distribution of marital assets upon divorce) and *Orr* v. *Crowder* (free speech rights for government employees). In 1994, Gov. Gaston Caperton selected Miller as the recipient of the Distinguished West Virginian Award. (WHOF.)

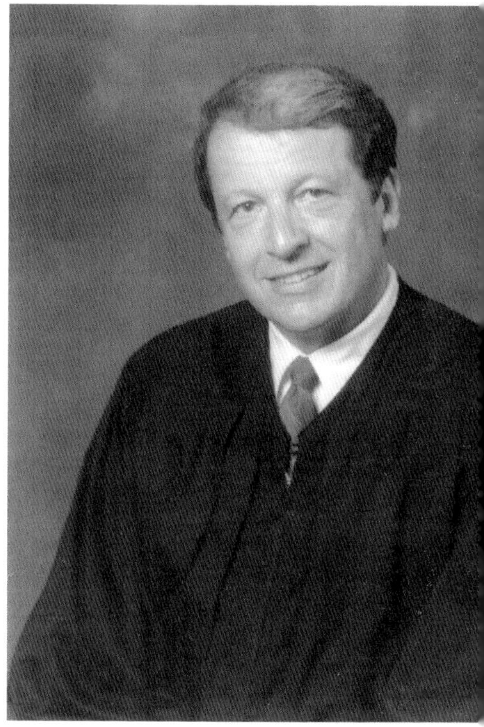

Jack Fahey

In his distinguished career, John Edward "Jack" Fahey (1928–) has served Wheeling on the city council, as mayor, as Ohio County commissioner, and as a West Virginia delegate. He has always been a tireless ambassador for Wheeling, and his accomplishments include completion of the Wheeling Creek Watershed project and establishment of the Wheeling Hall of Fame. Fahey (second from left in the second row) worked for many years for the Baltimore & Ohio Railroad, and he is proud of his family and his Irish heritage. (WHOF.)

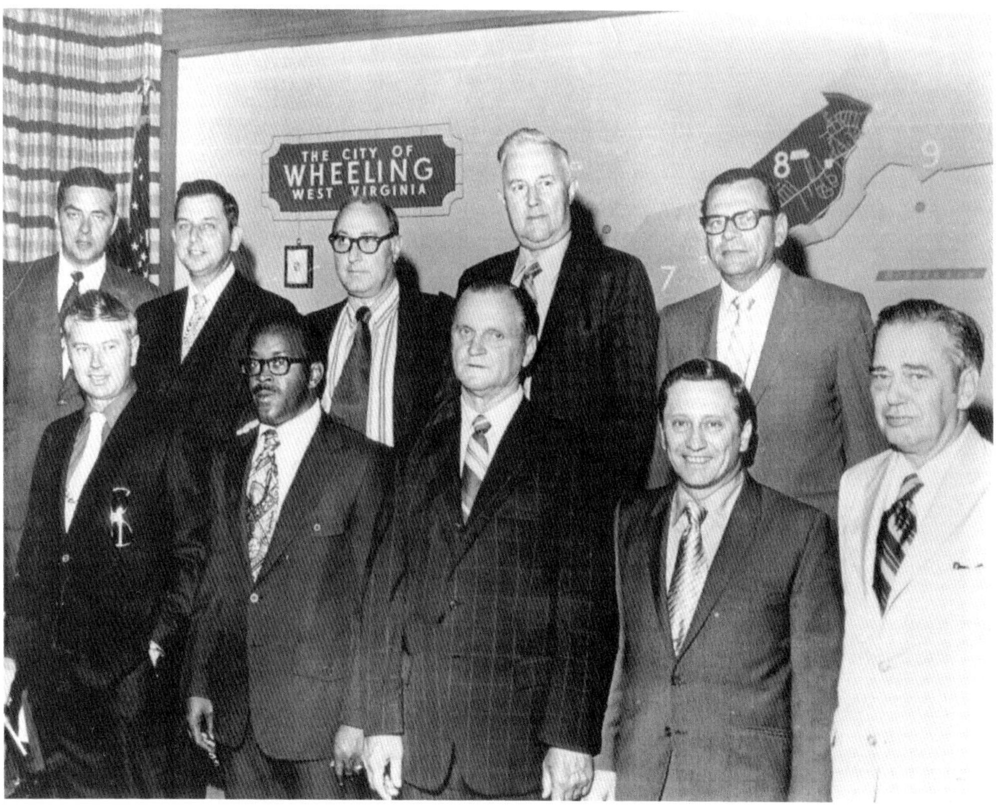

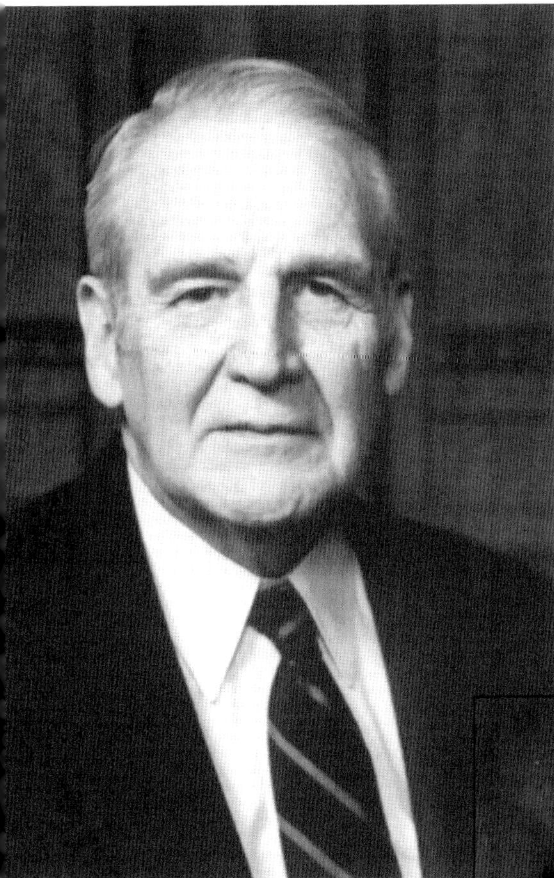

George Seibert
George H. "Bud" Seibert Jr. (1913–1986) served as minority leader in the West Virginia House of Delegates for 18 years, an all-time record in the Mountain State. Seibert's popularity with the voters of Ohio County was unwavering. First elected to the state legislature in 1952, he usually led the ticket every two years until he declined to run in 1976. Seibert received the West Virginia Distinguished Service Award from Gov. Arch Moore. (WHOF.)

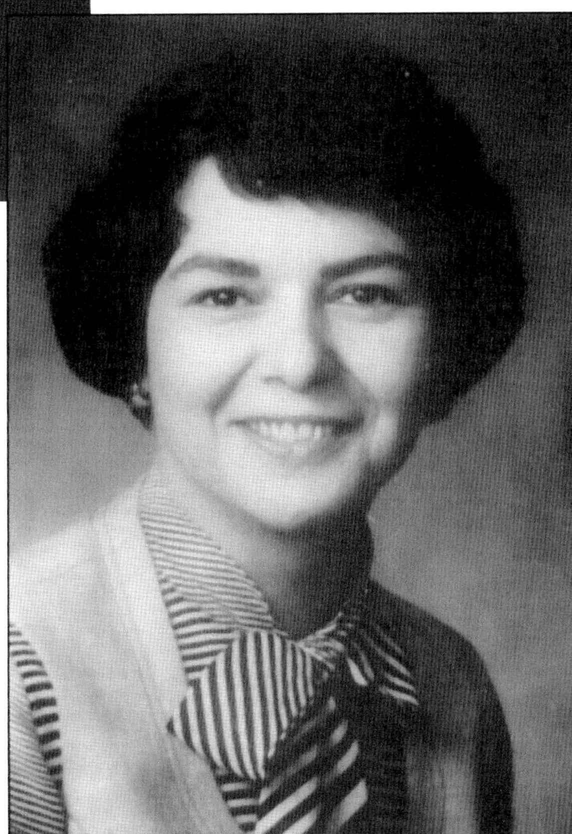

Judith Herndon
Judith Herndon (1941–1980) distinguished herself in a career that was ended too soon by her death at the age of 39. As a member of the House of Delegates and State Senate, she was a leader for tax reform, sunset legislation, and sexual assault legislation. About his colleague, state senator Odell H. Huffman wrote, "Had she lived, she might have been West Virginia's first woman governor. . . . But her destiny of service was not higher office. It was to inspire, by her example of courageous integrity, the lives of many." (WHOF.)

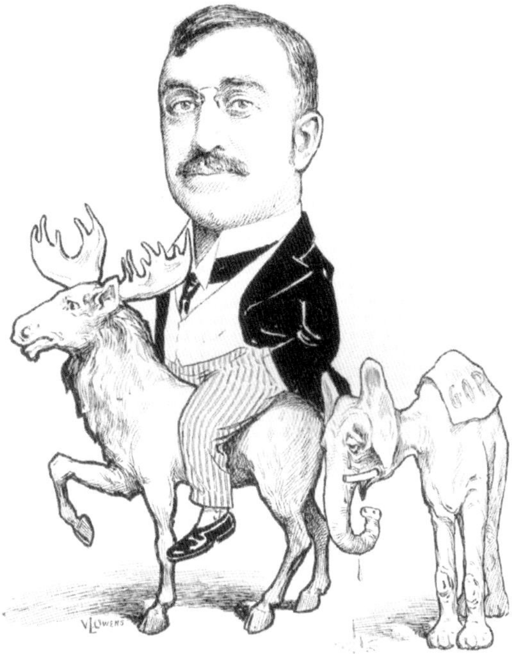

HON. GEO. A. LAUGHLIN
Manufacturer
Wheeling, W. Va.

George Laughlin

George A. Laughlin (1862–1936) made a career in the iron and tin-plate business. He founded the Wheeling Board of Trade and served as president of the *Wheeling Intelligencer* until its purchase by H.C. Ogden. Laughlin donated the Eighteenth Street Chapel of the First Presbyterian Church to the community; it is now known as Laughlin Memorial Chapel. He was the driving force behind the development of Warwood, and he established the Laughlin Plan for interest-free loans to aid people in purchasing homes. (WHOF.)

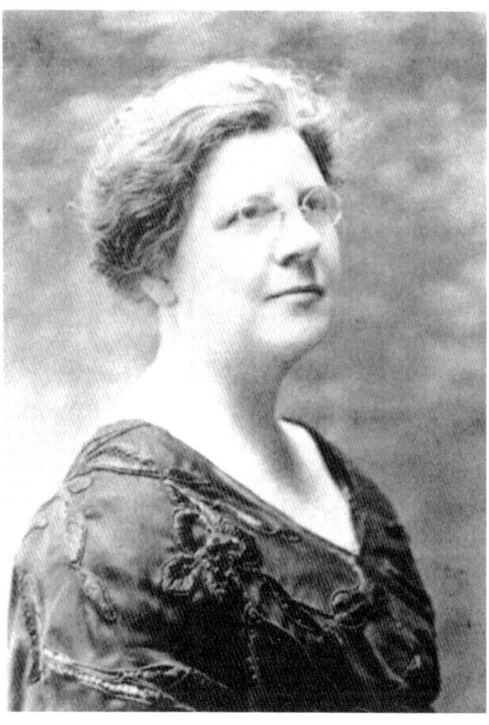

Mary Louise Butler Reed

When Reed headed the International Order of King's Daughters and Sons (1919–1924), she was known as "the great missionary president." Her devotion to child welfare resulted in the establishment of the King's Daughters Nursery in Wheeling. Reed (1861–1939) was a leading spirit in the founding of the Wheeling YWCA, and she served as its president for 10 years. (WHOF.)

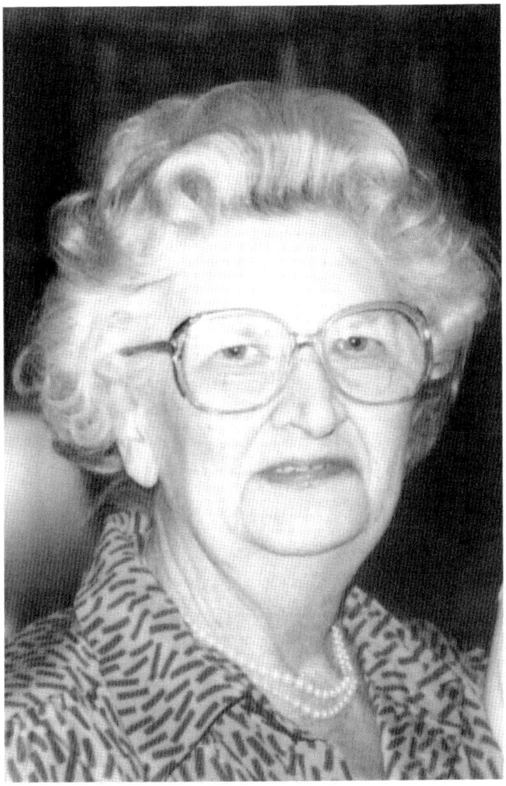

Helen Gaither
An only child who never married, Gaither (1900–1996) will be remembered by her friends and neighbors as a kind, shy woman who adored her Gaidoune Scottish terriers. Her house was filled with the cups, ribbons, and medals the show dogs won. Neighborhood children believed that the dogs had their own bedroom. On her death, she left half her vast wealth to the Stifel Fine Arts Center and the remainder to the Ohio County Public Library, Ohio Valley Medical Center, and St. Matthews Episcopal Church. (KQ; photograph courtesy WHOF.)

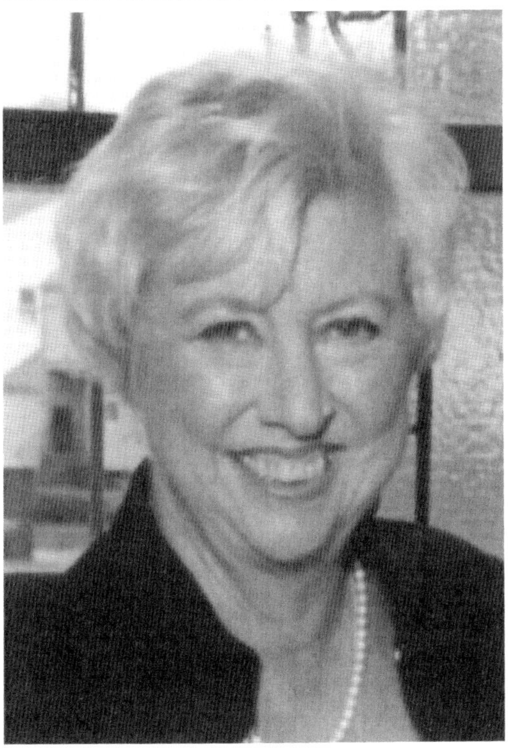

Elizabeth Stifel Kline
Elizabeth Stifel Kline (1925–2000) will be remembered for a lifetime of public service and philanthropy. She was a lifelong member of St. Matthew's Episcopal Church, where she was an organizer and volunteer for the food pantry. She demonstrated her love of the arts by supporting Oglebay Institute's Stifel Fine Arts Center. In 2000, she was honored with the NAACP Community Service Award. Numerous local institutions have benefited from her philanthropic spirit. She created the foundation that bears her name to support nonprofit organizations that make a difference in the community. (WHOF.)

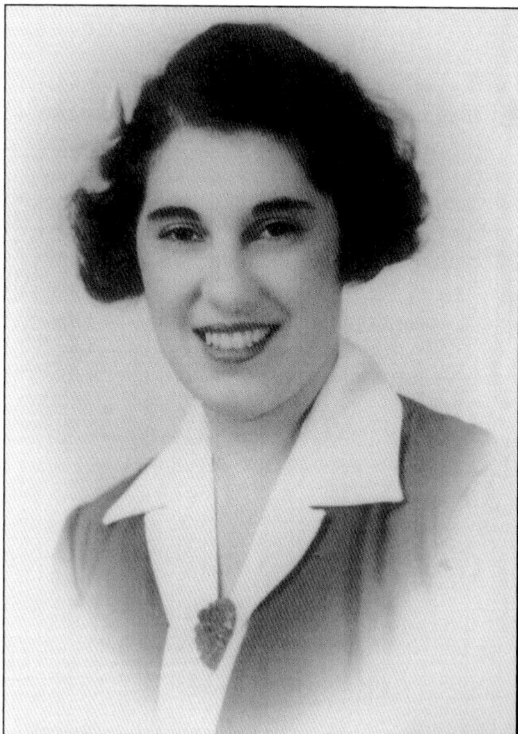

Ethel Clare Elikan

Elikan (1911–1998) worked with the visually handicapped for more than half a century and founded the Seeing Hand Association of Wheeling. She opened the Seeing Hand Workshop and organized activities for the visually impaired. (WHOF.)

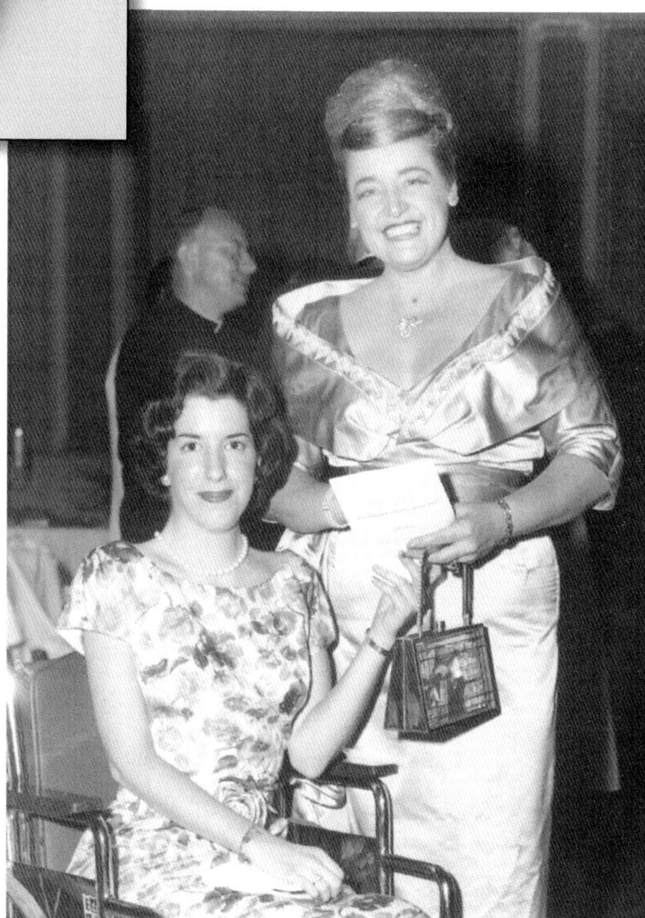

Rosemary Front

Afflicted by polio at a young age, Rosemary Front (1940–2009) continued her schooling in a wheelchair. After obtaining a master's degree as a speech pathologist, she worked for the Society for Crippled Children from 1966 to 1998 and eventually became executive director of the West Virginia Easter Seals Society. The organization built a day care and treatment center on the National Road. Front was influential in advocating for curb alterations for wheelchairs, disabled parking, and other means of access for the disabled around the city. Front (left) is pictured in 1960 with opera star Eleanor Steber (see page 32) in a photograph by George Kossuth (see page 43) from a collection donated to the Ohio County Public Library. (KQ; photograph courtesy OCPL.)

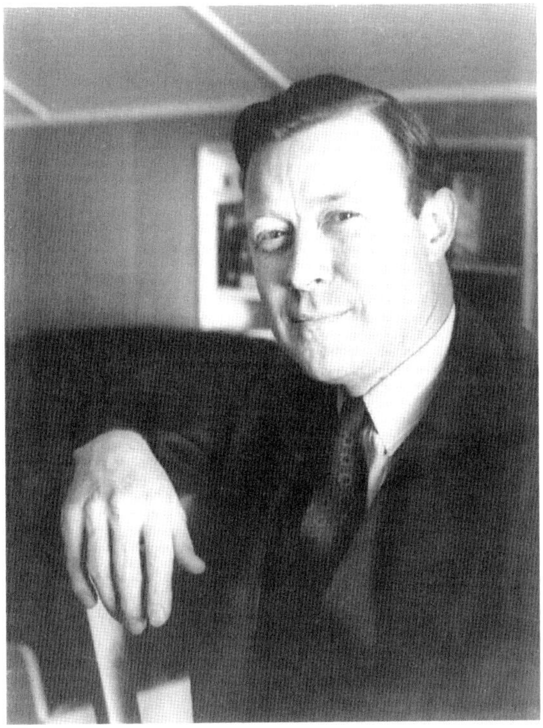

Walter Reuther
Born in Wheeling on September 1, 1907, fittingly just one day before Labor Day, Walter P. Reuther (1907–1970) became one of the most innovative, influential, and charismatic labor leaders of the 20th century. His father, Valentine Reuther, was influential in developing a sense of social justice, leadership, and activism in his four sons and daughter. While other children were sent outside to play, the Reuther children were sent to the library to do research for an upcoming kitchen table debate on the issues of the day, including women's suffrage, child labor laws, capital punishment, partisan politics, and, most important, labor rights.

On May 26, 1937, Reuther and his union colleagues were peacefully handing out leaflets at the Ford Motor Company's River Rouge Plant in Michigan when they were brutally attacked by company thugs. Photographs of the bloodied but not beaten Reuther and his friends were seen around the country, resulting in a public relations victory for the tough labor leader from Wheeling. In 1946, Reuther became the president of the United Auto Workers (UAW), and in 1952, he became the president of the Congress of Industrial Organizations (CIO). As president of the UAW from 1946 to 1970, Reuther achieved a great deal for his fellow workers. Under his leadership, autoworkers' standard of living doubled. In 1963, Reuther was one of the few non–African American speakers at the historic March on Washington. He marched with Dr. Martin Luther King Jr. in Selma and was referred to as "the White Martin Luther King." Reuther had weekly meetings with Pres. Lyndon Johnson to discuss ways to help less-fortunate Americans. Beginning in May 1965, Reuther began pressing Johnson to accept new technologies, such as prefabricated housing, to redesign much of urban America. Reuther hoped to provide safe, affordable, and desegregated housing to the poorest Americans.

Supporting a lifetime of achievements was Walter Reuther's personal philosophy that "There is no greater calling than to serve your fellow man. There is no greater contribution than to help the weak. There is no greater satisfaction than to have done it well."

Through collaborative effort among the United Auto Workers, the City of Wheeling, and the Wheeling National Heritage Area Corporation, a monument honoring Walter Reuther stands at Heritage Port. (BC; photograph courtesy Walter P. Reuther Library at Wayne State University.)

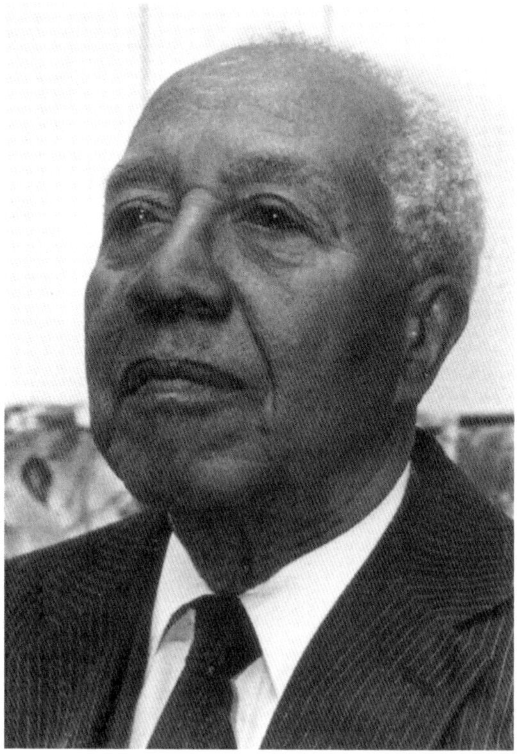

James "Doc" White

White (1901–1988) was a true servant of the people, regardless of race or creed. A man of sincerity, courage, and keen insight into the human condition, he devoted his life to the betterment of his community. He was born in Roanoke, Virginia, and his family moved to Pittsburgh in 1903. White graduated cum laude from the University of Pittsburgh College of Pharmacy in 1922.

White migrated to Wheeling and eventually operated Northside Pharmacy. His building eventually became a social center for the African American community. The store had a soda fountain in the back, while the front was more of a general store. In the basement of the drugstore were a jukebox and old wire tables and chairs; on weekends, it was the place to be. Doc White often arranged for black entertainers, like James Brown, to perform at Wheeling Park at the White Palace. People came from afar to see the shows Doc brought to town.

A registered pharmacist in Ohio, Pennsylvania, and West Virginia, White was a member of the Simpson Methodist Church for more than 50 years. Some of his most significant work was done as a member of the Wheeling Housing Authority. During his 22 years of service, he helped to secure for his community hundreds of units of public housing and millions of federal dollars.

Doc White's efforts certainly contributed to the betterment of race relations in the city where he was held in such esteem. Back in the days when Lincoln High School and Blessed Martin High School were in operation, prior to the integration of the local schools in 1955, White presented cash awards to African American students and encouraged them to pursue higher education.

In 1970, Doc White was cited by the *Charleston Gazette* for a "Black Honor Roll" in West Virginia. He also received commendations from the City of Wheeling, Lincoln High School, the Black Student Council at Wheeling College, the Ohio-Marshall Pharmaceutical Association, Clay School, Horizons Unlimited, the US Department of Housing and Urban Development, and the Wheeling Housing Authority.

Doc and his beloved wife, Geneva, who shared in his hopes and aspirations and in his devotion to people, had no children of their own; however, many children of several generations owe a debt of gratitude to White for making their path in life a bit smoother and more pleasant. (WHOF.)

Ann and Clyde Thomas

Ann Prince Thomas (1938–) is a pioneer and witness to history. She was just six months old when her mother moved to Wheeling from a North Carolina tobacco farm to help Ann's aunt and uncle run the New Dixie Restaurant on Chapline Street in the middle of what was, at the time, an established African American neighborhood. Ann grew up during the turbulent transition from segregated Wheeling to desegregated Wheeling. From first grade, she attended Lincoln School. But, thanks to the landmark Supreme Court decision in *Brown* vs. *Board of Education* (1954), she graduated from Wheeling High School in 1956.

After graduation, Thomas enrolled in the Ohio Valley General Hospital's school of nursing. Despite many obstacles, in 1959, she became the first African American to graduate. She passed her boards and worked at Ohio Valley General Hospital for 12 years, then as an Ohio County school nurse for 30 more.

The roller-skating rink in the market auditorium (now Market Plaza) was open to African American teens on Monday nights. That's where Ann met her future husband, Clyde Thomas (1940–2006). They were married in Wayman A.M.E. Church in 1960.

An all-state athlete in basketball and football at Bellaire High School, Clyde started at running back for Ohio in the 1958 OVAC All-Star Football Game, alongside quarterback John Havlicek, the future Boston Celtics legend. Clyde Thomas played college football for Ohio University and starred on the undefeated Mid-American Conference Championship team as a senior in 1960. An All-American, Clyde was mentioned in *Sports Illustrated*.

He went on to a successful career as a hard-running halfback for the Wheeling Ironmen, the local semiprofessional football team. Clyde later played for a little over a year with the Philadelphia Eagles before a broken foot ended his NFL career. He returned to Wheeling, continued playing for the Ironmen, and finished his college degree at West Liberty. When he retired from the Ironmen, he was the franchise's all-time rushing leader. In 1964, he led the United Football League with an impressive 6.6 yards per rush. He was inducted into the American Football Association's Minor Football Hall of Fame in 2000.

After retiring from football, Clyde ran for city council, won by a landslide, and served four terms. Also serving as vice mayor, he helped get the Wheeling Civic Center built and led the proposal for a downtown Wheeling shopping mall. He was the first and, to date, the only African American elected to Wheeling's City Council.

Since her husband died in 2006, Ann Thomas has continued to organize reunions of players from the Wheeling Ironmen. (SD; photographs courtesy Ann Thomas.)

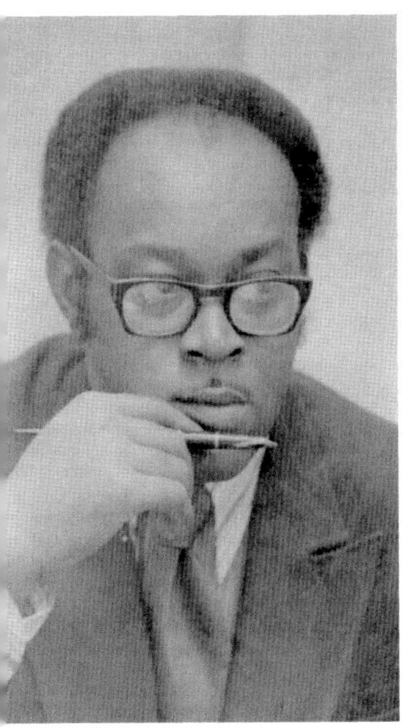

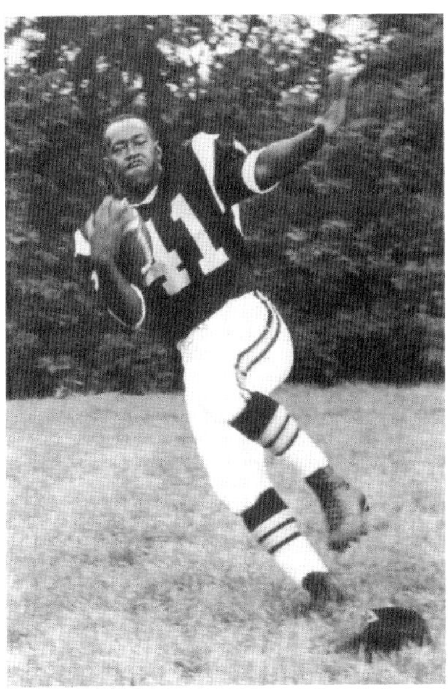

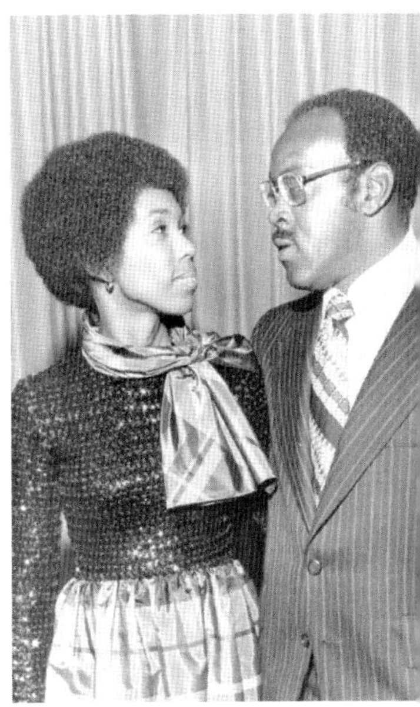

Harry Hamm

Harry C. Hamm was a newspaperman for 50 years. As *Wheeling News-Register* editor, Hamm championed causes such as quality education and health care, crime control, bridge construction, urban renewal, and good government. Hamm (1923–1991) also helped secure millions of dollars in funding for local parks, colleges, hospitals, cultural institutions, and public improvements. Hamm authored the WHEELING 2000 revitalization plan. He is pictured here (left) with Randy Worls. (WHOF; photograph courtesy OCPL/Harry Hamm Collection.)

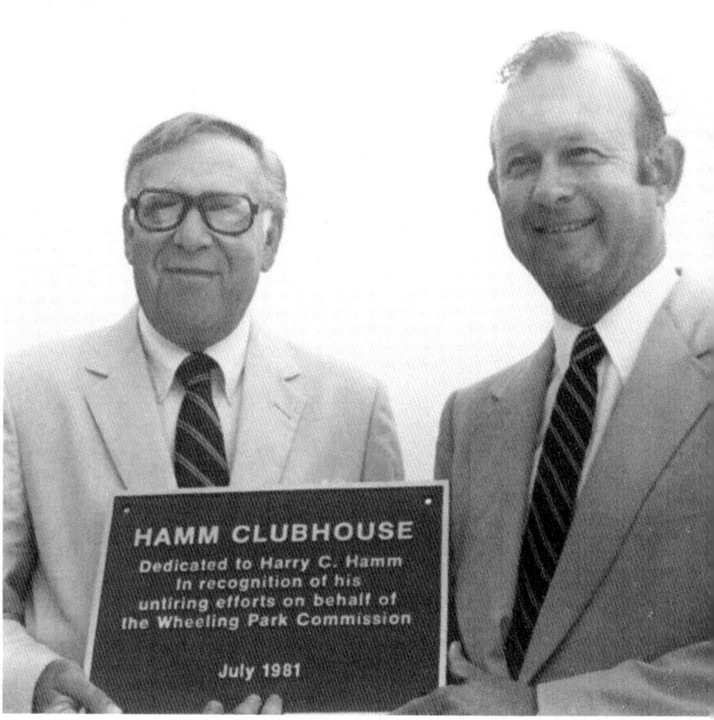

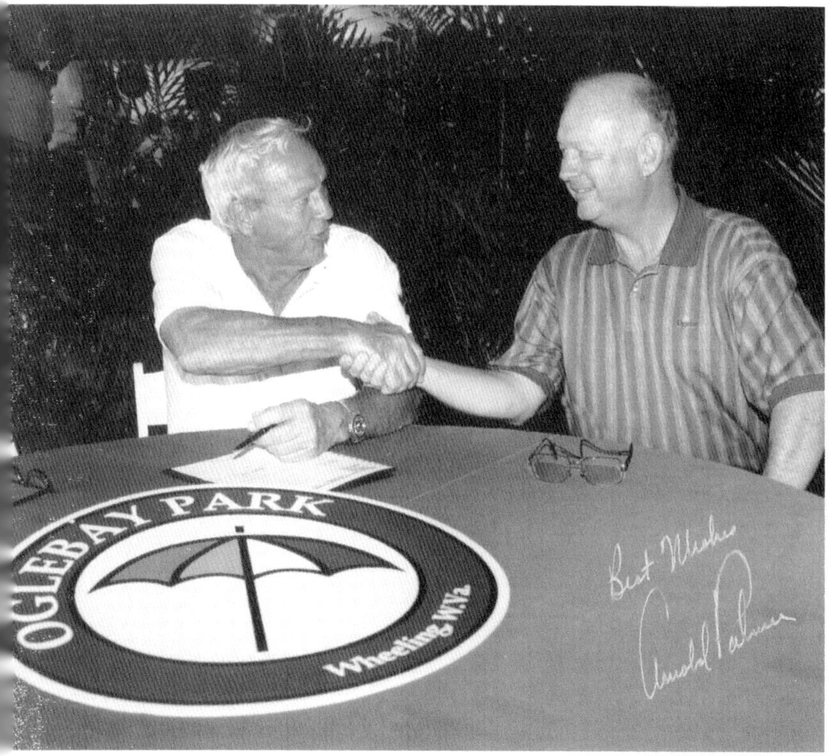

Randy Worls

Starting out as a lifeguard at the pool, Randy Worls, as chief executive officer of the Wheeling Park Commission, helped make Oglebay Resort the only totally self-sufficient city park in the country. Overseeing the Festival of Lights and Oglebayfest and now as chief executive officer of the Parks System Trust Fund, Worls has brought delight to millions. For nearly 60 years, he has stood as a guardian to the parks for the people of Wheeling. Worls is pictured here with golf legend Arnold Palmer. (KQ; photograph courtesy Randy Worls.)

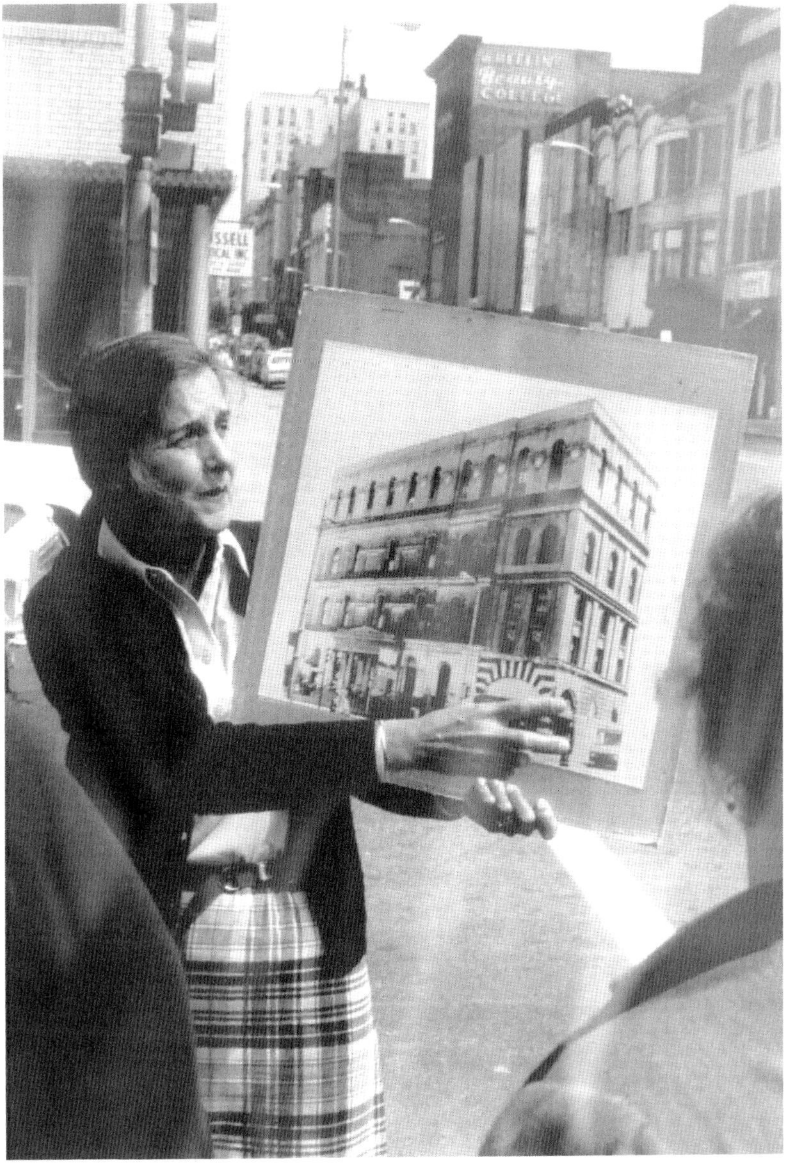

Beverly Fluty

Fluty (1931–2009) and her family moved to Wheeling in 1968, and she was astounded at the city's rich history and culture. She awakened her new community, galvanizing local citizens and fellow preservationists to appreciate, preserve, and enhance the city's architectural heritage. Fluty's roles in saving the Wheeling Suspension Bridge, which was seriously deteriorating, and in the restoration of West Virginia Independence Hall, cannot be overstated. Both have been designated as National Historic Landmarks, underscoring their national significance and the city's contribution to the heritage of the United States.

But it was also schoolchildren that Fluty so cared about. She led classes through downtown, pointing out architectural details and telling stories of the history and people behind the buildings. A great love of hers was throwing a birthday party for the suspension bridge, complete with cake and balloons! Fluty's leadership and unstoppable enthusiasm touched many lives and left a community proud of its achievements, history, and place in the nation's story. (HF; photograph courtesy West Virginia Independence Hall.)

Margaret Brennan

Margaret Brennan knows that so much can happen in a single moment—that brief flash of time that we all take for granted that quickly passes without thought and certainly no historical record. She does her best to capture these many "moments," both past and present. At any event, whether mundane or important, one will find Brennan taking notes, diligently writing her observations onto paper. Pausing only to take out her camera and snap a few photographs, she returns to writing and documenting what is happening before her.

A public historian of remarkable talents, Margaret, or "Peg," was born in South Wheeling, in a house located at Thirty-seventh and Wood Streets.

Though hard to imagine, she was not at first drawn toward the academic study of history until a teacher at Wheeling College suggested she consider the academic major when she showed a strong interest. She graduated with an undergraduate degree in history in 1967 and went on to earn a master's and to study public history at WVU with some of the state's finest historians in the 1980s.

Brennan taught many of the area's youth while a member of the Sisters of Saint Joseph and working at Wheeling Central Catholic High School. Later, she worked in archival administration for the Diocese of Wheeling-Charleston. Since then, she has served as a contract historian for Mt. de Chantal, the Wheeling Symphony, Wheeling Hospital, and Wheeling National Heritage Area Corporation, to name only a few.

Brennan has been a staunch ally and protector of Wheeling's history for many years. She was president of the Wheeling Area Historical Society for more than 20 years until it disbanded in 2010, and she was the major force behind both the organization's events and the publishing of the *Upper Ohio Valley Historical Review.* Active in the Wheeling community, she has served on numerous boards and committees and was appointed to the West Virginia Archives and History Commission.

Though her accomplishments are many, the dearest to her heart is her work with slavery and the Underground Railroad, as well as local Irish history. Because, she jokes, she is 99 percent Irish, she was the driving force behind the installation of the Celtic cross monument honoring the area's early Irish immigrants, located at Heritage Port and pictured here. (RK.)

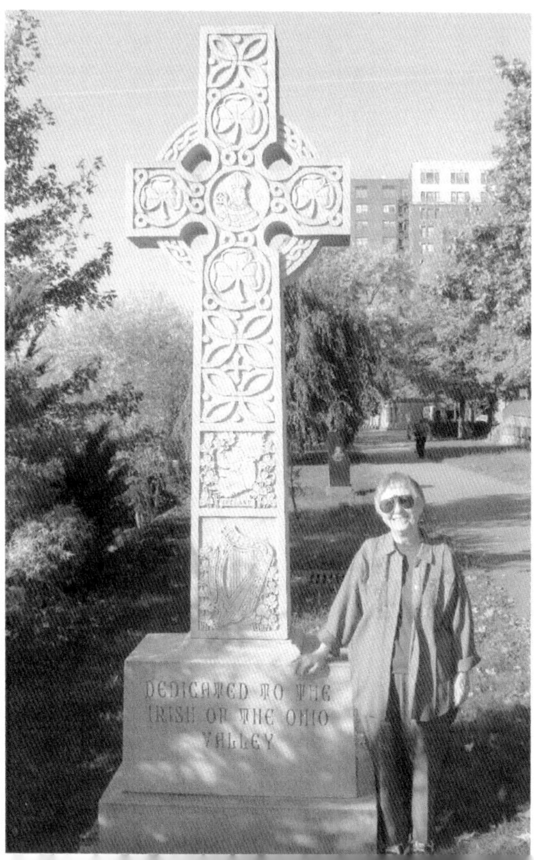

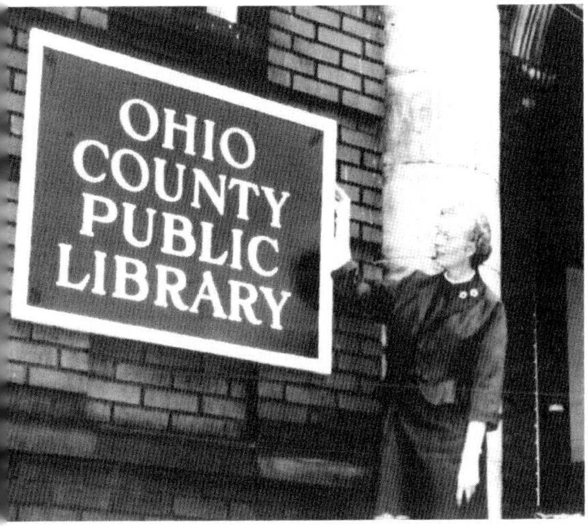

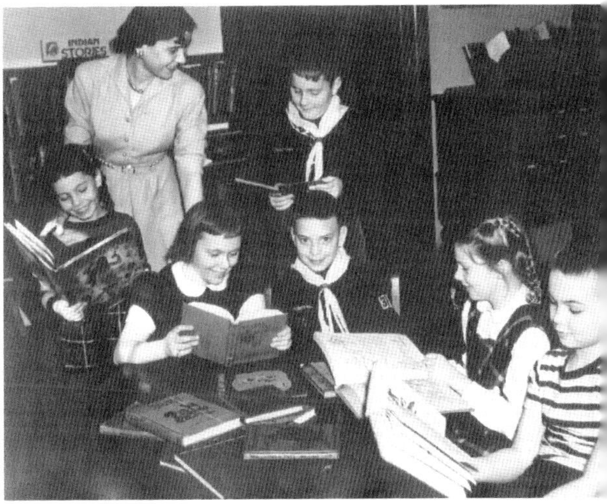

Librarians!

There is perhaps no less-heralded community leader than the local librarian. Yet, many residents will cite library visits as among the most cherished of childhood memories and librarians as some of the most admired, quiet heroes.

The library was and is a sanctuary for people from all walks of life, and particularly for writers. "The library was the key institution in my early life," author George Fetherling (see page 27) reported, "far more so than school. . . . My brother and I pretty much read our way through the collection day by day and week by week." Author Keith Maillard (see page 28) called the library "a place of refuge for me all during my high school years."

Wheeling's Ohio County Public Library is West Virginia's oldest public library. Several subscription libraries operated in Wheeling from as early as 1807, but the current library was established by the city's board of education on October 12, 1882, and was first housed over R.J. Smyth's grocery at the corner of Fourteenth and Market Streets (later the Hub building). The first librarian was Henry Pendleton, who was followed by Anna B. Wilson.

Wheeling is one of the few major cities in the region without a Carnegie library as, in 1904, Wheeling voters, influenced by local labor organizations, rejected an offer from Andrew Carnegie to fund a new library building. Instead, the board of education assumed the expense of a new facility, designed by Charles W. Bates (see page 91). The library opened in 1911 at 2100 Market Street, with Etta Roberts as librarian. Most Wheeling residents of a certain age fondly remember Virginia Ebeling (top left), the beloved librarian who served as director from 1950 to 1966 at the Market Street location. Ebeling, along with Fr. Clifford Lewis (see page 105), also helped save and revitalize the Upper Ohio Valley Historical Society in 1962.

The library's children's department opened in March 1912, and thousands of local children have benefited from story time programs in the ensuing decades. In the early 1920s, the library was recognized as one of the largest collections in the state, and it continued to lead the state by providing innovative services, such as the first bookmobile (1935), music libraries, branch libraries, and audiovisual materials.

The library has had many champions over the years, including Archie Paull, who floated a loan of $300 to keep the library solvent in 1933 when bills "smote with dismay an impecunious though honest [library] board."

On May 31, 1933, the West Virginia Legislature passed special legislation creating the Ohio County Public Library, housed since 1973 at 52 Sixteenth Street. And the library continues to serve a vital role in the community. (SD; photographs courtesy OCPL.)

INDEX

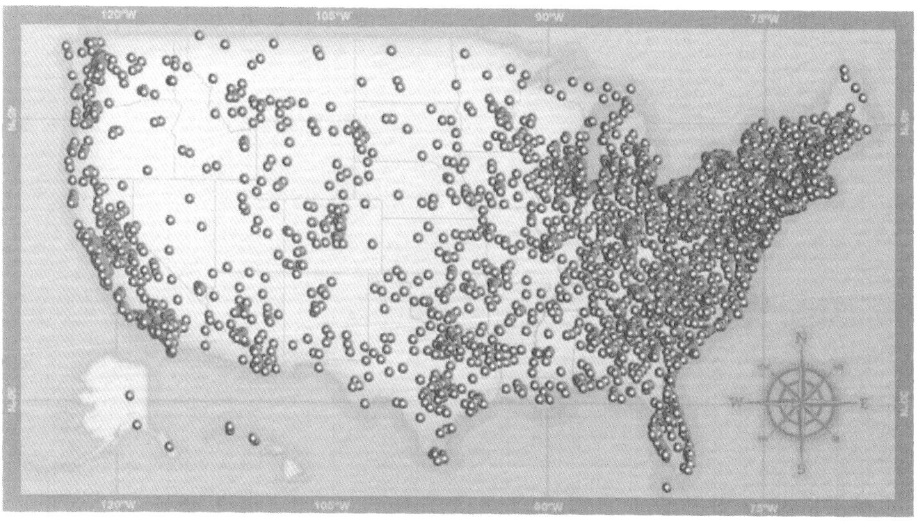